Shattered Consensus

First American edition published in 2015 by Encounter Books,
an activity of Encounter for Culture and Education, Inc.,
a nonprofit, tax exempt corporation.
Encounter Books website address: www.encounterbooks.com

Manufactured in the United States and printed on
acid-free paper. The paper used in this publication meets
the minimum requirements of ANSI/NISO Z39.48—1992
(R 1997) (*Permanence of Paper*).

FIRST AMERICAN EDITION

LIBRARY OF CONGRESS CATALOGING-IN-PUBLICATION DATA

Piereson, James.
Shattered consensus : the rise and decline of America's postwar political order /
by James Piereson.
pages   cm
Includes bibliographical references and index.
ISBN 978-1-59403-671-2 (hardcover : alk. paper)
ISBN 978-1-59403-672-9 (ebook)
1. United States—Politics and government—1945–1989.
2. Political culture—United States—History—20th century.
3. Liberalism—United States—History—20th century. 4. Consensus
(Social sciences)—United States—History—20th century.
5. Kennedy, John F. (John Fitzgerald), 1917–1963. I. Title.
E839.5.P55 2015
973.91—dc23

2 0 1 4 0 4 4 6 2 0

Shattered Consensus

THE RISE AND DECLINE OF AMERICA'S
POSTWAR POLITICAL ORDER

James Piereson

Encounter Books New York · London

Contents

PART IV. THE POLITICS OF HIGHER EDUCATION

America's Shattered Consensus

In the excited aftermath of the 2008 election, many pundits saw Barack Obama as a liberal messiah who would inaugurate a new era of liberal reform and cement a Democratic majority for decades to come. He was predicted to become a Franklin Delano Roosevelt or perhaps even an Abraham Lincoln for our time. The pundits were not alone in saying this: Obama himself said much the same thing.

These forecasts sounded grandiose at the time, and today, more than six years into the Obama presidency, they seem more than a little foolish. In contrast to 2008, Obama now looks less like a transformational president than like a typically embattled politician trying to keep his head above water against a mounting wave of opposition. Extravagant hopes have given way to a struggle for survival. Few still believe that Obama will lay the foundations for a new era of liberal governance. Some observers are pointing toward a more surprising outcome: that Obama, far from bringing about a renewal of liberalism, is actually presiding over its disintegration.

Whether or not that turns out to be so, it is clear in retrospect that President Obama and his supporters were kidding themselves in thinking that his election marked the start of a new era in American life. In fact, the reverse is true: Obama came to power near the end of an era, at a time when America's postwar system was beginning to come apart under the weight of slowing economic growth, mounting debt, the rising costs of entitlement programs, and a widening polarization between the two main political parties. The consensus that sustained that system had been fraying for decades. A new president taking office in the midst of the most serious financial crisis since the Great Depression might have tried to repair that consensus by seeking compromises to address the challenges of growth, debt, and entitlements. President Obama instead did something very nearly the opposite. Believing that he was elected to bring about "change," he exploited a temporary partisan supermajority to push through an expensive new health-care program while doing little about the long-term problems that have the potential to bring down the nation's tottering system of governance. He placed more burdens on the system when the urgent task at hand was to shore up its foundations.

One consequence of Obama's tenure has been to fray the postwar consensus beyond the possibility of repair. There is no longer enough agreement in the American polity to address any of the nation's systemic problems before they escalate to the point of crisis. When it comes, the next crisis—whether in the form of a recession, a stock market collapse, a terrorist attack, or some combination of the above—will force Americans across the board to adjust to a lower standard of living and the various levels of government to renegotiate the promises made to seniors, students, government employees, and the various individuals and groups that rely on public subsidies. Americans will then be compelled to organize a new system of governance on the remnants of the postwar order, one that can generate the kind of growth and dynamism to support the way of life to which they have become accustomed. Failing that, they will watch their country cease to be a high-functioning nation-state and world superpower.

* * *

The aim of this book is to make sense of the rise and decline of America's postwar political order. To a great degree, it is a tale of the rise and decline of the consensus that evolved in the 1940s and 1950s around the role of the federal government in maintaining full employment at home and containing communism and promoting freedom abroad. That consensus seemed so strong and durable during the 1950s that many historians and political analysts thought it was a permanent feature of American life. It came under heavy attack during the 1960s from student protest movements on the left and from the new conservative movement on the right. It held together, barely, during the Reagan and Clinton years in the 1980s and 1990s, but since then it has come apart altogether. This is evident in various arenas of American life, from politics to higher education and even the world of philanthropy. Parts II and III of this book examine the rise of the postwar dispensation and the centrifugal forces that developed against it in the 1960s, including the Kennedy "legend" that formed a counternarrative to the consensus view of American society.

A major theme of this book is that unsettled transitional periods of the kind we are now living through have happened before in American history—in the 1850s and 1860s, for example, and later in the 1930s and 1940s. In each period, an old order collapsed and a new one emerged out of an unprecedented crisis; and in each case, the resolution of the crisis opened up new possibilities for growth and reform. No particular consensus or set of political arrangements can be regarded as permanent in a dynamic country like the United States.

The political economy of American capitalism has evolved in distinct chapters, not in cycles or in an orderly sequence as Marxists or developmental theorists would have it. Part I elaborates on this theme, especially in "America's Fourth Revolution." The United States has had three such chapters in its history: (1) the Jefferson-

Jackson era stretching from 1800 to 1860, when slavery and related territorial issues broke the prevailing consensus apart; (2) the capitalist-industrial era running from the end of the Civil War to 1930, when the regime collapsed in the midst of the Great Depression; and (3) the postwar welfare state that took shape in the 1930s and 1940s and extends to the present, but is now in the process of breaking up. Each of these regimes accomplished something important for the United States; each period lasted roughly a lifetime; and each was organized by a dominant political party: the Democrats in the antebellum era, the Republicans in the industrial era, and the Democrats again in the postwar era. The first two regimes fell under vastly different circumstances: the sectional conflict was a crisis of America's constitutional system, while the Great Depression was a crisis of capitalism.

The postwar order emerged out of the twin crises of the Great Depression and World War II, and it represented something new in the unfolding history of American democracy. In terms of prosperity and world influence, this era was probably the most successful period in America's national history. The postwar consensus took some time and political effort to construct. In 1932 there was no consensus in the United States around the programs and ideas that would eventually shape the New Deal, and in 1940 the nation was sharply divided between interventionists who wanted to assist Great Britain in the European war and isolationists who wanted no part of any such entanglement. Yet by 1950 a bipartisan consensus had been hammered into shape, one that assigned the national government responsibility for maintaining full employment and for policing the world in the interests of democracy, trade, and national security. It was a signal political achievement in view of the resistance that had been built up through the nineteenth century against large government establishments and American involvement in foreign disputes. Moreover, there have been continuous efforts coming from both left and right to alter, redefine, or undermine the consensus.

John Maynard Keynes was the theoretical architect of America's postwar political economy, as elaborated in Part I. Keynes argued in several important works published in the 1920s and 1930s that the old order of nineteenth-century capitalism had been destroyed both by the Great War of 1914–1918 and by the evolution of capitalism from a system organized around small producers and local markets to one increasingly dominated by large corporations and labor unions. In *The Economic Consequences of the Peace*, his controversial attack on the Treaty of Versailles, he first broached the idea that the capitalist order needed to be placed on new political and intellectual foundations. Later, during the Great Depression, he worked out the theoretical argument for government to take a leading role in stabilizing the market economy with the aims of full employment and maximum output. His *General Theory of Employment, Interest, and Money*, with its policy prescriptions for a managed economy, is probably the most influential work of economics published in the twentieth century, at least in the Anglo-American world.

The Keynesian system involved a significant revision in the relationship between the state and the market, as the state assumed a steering function over the economy never envisioned by the eighteenth-century founders of the liberal order. A state that commands sufficient resources to stabilize consumer demand and investor behavior stands in sharp contrast to the classical liberal state that preceded it. This new kind of state is an elemental part of the postwar regime, a point whose implications are examined in the chapter titled "The Keynesian Revolution in Political Economy," which also argues that the Keynesian era itself is now approaching an end.

The unfolding of the postwar era has entailed various surprises, perhaps chief among them the revival of nineteenth-century free-market ideas in the 1980s and beyond as a challenge to the Keynesian order. It would be wrong to suggest that the "age of Keynes" ended in the 1980s. The consensus surrounding the Keynesian regime has been badly weakened but not broken, and the financial crisis of 2008 provided a new occasion for the application of Keynesian policies.

Thomas Piketty's recent work, *Capital in the Twenty-First Century*, has called attention to the surprising return of inequality in European and North American countries. While Piketty argues that inequality is somehow intrinsic to the capitalist order, the chapter titled "American Capitalism and the Inequality Crisis" suggests that it is linked more closely to specific elements of the postwar regime, especially in the expansion of global markets and the explosion of asset prices. From 1980 to 2012, the value of world stock markets increased from $2 trillion to more than $50 trillion, an unprecedented development that was bound to produce more inequality as one of its side effects. Even if one thinks inequality is a bad thing, the stock market boom has had beneficial consequences in the areas of innovation and productivity that far outweigh this particular downside. When the stock market contracts again, as it inevitably will, the inequality "crisis" is likely to deflate along with it.

* * *

The evolution of the postwar regime has found expression in various aspects of national life—for example, in assumptions about capitalism, the American economy, and the role of government in the marketplace; in the development of the major political parties; in the changing definitions of liberalism and conservatism; in the interpretation of pivotal events and the assessment of influential personalities; and in the life and operation of important professions and institutions, such as law, philanthropy, book and magazine publishing, and higher education.

After nearly every national election, there is a new debate as to whether one of the dominant ideologies in American life is expiring. During the 1980s and 1990s, some conservative pundits asserted that "liberalism is dead!" Following the election of 2008, several loud voices on the left proclaimed the "death of conservatism." These were mostly ill-informed forecasts, as argued in Part II, primarily because liberalism and conservatism are woven into the postwar regime as two sides of the contest over the role of the state in the marketplace. Each side has built up a vast infrastructure of supporting institutions, interest groups, think tanks, television networks, newspapers and magazines. Meanwhile, the nation has divided into more and more polarized doctrinal groups—into a conservative nation and a liberal nation. It is true that one or both of these doctrines could disappear, but only as part of a process that involves the collapse of the postwar regime itself, in much the same way that the secession movement disappeared with the Civil War, and laissez-faire capitalism with the Great Depression.

This polarization is also apparent in other institutions of American life—for example, in philanthropy, a field that is usually thought to be purely charitable in nature and thus nonpolitical. The chapter "Investing in Conservative Ideas" describes how liberal philanthropy first evolved in the United States in the 1960s under the leadership of the Ford Foundation and several other large New York institutions. These foundations invented the concept of "advocacy" philanthropy, through which they funded groups in different fields that lobbied, filed lawsuits, and staged protests in behalf of liberal policies. This strategy proved so effective that several conservative foundations followed suit in the 1970s to fund their own mix of advocacy groups, magazines, and university programs. Though the liberal foundations have had far more money at their disposal, the conservative philanthropies have fought them to a draw in promoting their particular philosophy of government and economics.

A somewhat different iteration of this process has played out in higher education, where the liberal-left has seized nearly total control, to the point that conservatives are hard to find on major college faculties. As I argue in "The Left University," the American university evolved roughly in tandem with American liberalism. In the early decades of the twentieth century, Progressives invented a public or political purpose for higher education when they argued that professors and university-trained researchers could staff government bureaus and regulatory bodies as neutral experts to act in the public interest. The university, it was argued, would stand above and outside politics, in contrast to economic groups like corporations and labor unions. Liberals in this way gradually took control of higher education under the conceit that their research agenda was neutral or objective in matters of politics and policy. Later, in response to the activism of the 1960s, university faculties embraced the new doctrines of feminism, environmentalism, group rights, diversity, and cultural change, at exactly the same moment as liberals outside the academy began to embrace them. It was not long thereafter when liberals came to dominate the Democratic Party. By the late 1970s, the politics of the American university looked very much like those of the national Democratic Party.

Naturally, conservatives and Republicans are about as welcome in that academic setting as they would be at a Democratic national convention. In response, they set up their own intellectual institutions to provide an outlet for their views and to counter the influence of the academy. Here, as in other areas of national life, the opposing sides in the national debate have retreated into their respective subcultures.

* * *

Shattered Consensus outlines the lineaments of the postwar consensus and the gradual process by which it has come apart. It does not endeavor to specify when or how the current regime will fall or what will replace it. Rather, it only suggests that a certain degree of consensus is required in order for a polity to meet its major challenges and argues that such a consensus no longer exists in the United States. That being so, the problems will mount to a point of crisis where either they will be addressed through a "fourth revolution" or the polity will begin to disintegrate for lack of fundamental agreement.

This forecast of a "fourth revolution" in the years ahead does not mean that Americans should be hoarding gold or stockpiling canned food. The end of the postwar regime need not bring about the end of America. On the contrary, it could open a dynamic new chapter in the American story. The journey is likely to be difficult, but Americans are obliged to remain optimistic even as they contemplate impending upheavals. The United States has survived such upheavals in the past, and a case could be made that the nation has grown and prospered as a result. It could do so again.

PART ONE

The Political Economy of the Postwar Order

CHAPTER ONE

John Maynard Keynes and the Collapse of the Old Order

John Maynard Keynes was a liberal revolutionary who aimed to place the capitalist order on new economic, political, and cultural foundations. Not solely an economic theorist, he was a *political* economist in the tradition of Adam Smith, John Stuart Mill, Schumpeter, and Hayek. His theories pointed toward a far-reaching revision in the relationship between the state and the economy in capitalist systems. While the institutions of government inherited from the eighteenth and nineteenth centuries had been designed to check the power of the state for the purpose of protecting liberty, Keynes assigned new power to the state in order to promote stable economic growth and full employment.

The Keynesian revolution in economics thus implied a second revolution in politics, to circumvent both the constitutional and the cultural barriers to state action that had been erected in the era of classical liberalism. The "Keynesian state" is larger and far more interventionist than the forms of government anticipated by Adam Smith, the authors of the U.S. Constitution, and nearly all of the influential statesmen and theorists of the nineteenth century. Many of the core conflicts of our time grow out of the friction between

Keynes's vision of a managed economy and the constitutional order crafted to achieve quite different and far more limited goals.

Keynes was sensitive to the historical nature of the capitalist system as it evolved through different phases, created new institutional forms, and adapted to crises and new challenges. He questioned whether it was still appropriate to use theories formulated in 1800 or 1850 to account for the economic realities of the 1920s and 1930s. The "age of laissez-faire," he wrote in the 1920s, had been brought to an end first by the development of large corporations and labor unions, and then by the destructive effects of the world war. If the old order was dead, then a new one must be built on a different intellectual basis. This was the campaign that Keynes engaged in during his stints in public service and in the books and articles that he wrote between 1919 and his death in 1946.

* * *

A thinker of the widest interests, Keynes wrote on subjects ranging from Isaac Newton to modern art, and interspersed his treatises on economics with sage references to history, politics, and psychology. His biographer Robert Skidelsky asserts that he was as much a moralist as an economist.[1] Keynes, he wrote, searched for a vision of capitalism that promoted both efficiency and justice in equal parts. In an essay on Alfred Marshall, his mentor at the University of Cambridge, Keynes wrote that the "master economist" must possess many gifts: "He must be a mathematician, historian, statesman, and philosopher, in some degree. No part of man's nature or his institutions can be outside his regard."[2] Nor was Keynes an "armchair" or merely academic theorist; he participated actively in every important political debate that took place in Great Britain during the tumultuous years from the outbreak of World War I through the close of World War II. Progress in economics, he maintained, must arise from the interplay between theory and urgent practical problems.

Keynes thus began working out his theories on the necessity of refashioning the capitalist order while he served as a member of the British delegation to the Paris Peace Conference in 1919. For Keynes and his generation, the Great War of 1914–1918 demolished the foundations of European civilization. The old order in Europe had been built upon a network of interlocking principles and ideals: Protestantism and Victorian morals in culture; nationalism, empire, and monarchy in politics; laissez-faire, free trade, and the gold standard in economics. The big question after the war was whether those principles and institutions could survive in a new era of sovereign debt, despair and dashed hopes, debauched currencies, and a permanently changed balance of world power.

Keynes set forth his reflections on the war and the damage it did to the social order in *The Economic Consequences of the Peace*, the no-holds-barred attack on the Treaty of Versailles that he wrote in a few months in 1919 after the peace conference had concluded.[3] He predicted that unless the treaty was revised, it would lead to financial ruin across Europe and possibly to another, more destructive war. The book was an immediate bestseller, turning Keynes into an international celebrity. It ran through five editions and was translated into eleven languages within a few years. Today it is regarded as one of the more important and controversial books published in the twentieth century, for in it Keynes not only criticized the treaty but declared the obsolescence of the prewar order in Europe along with its associated institutions, ideals, and cultural assumptions.

He began the book with an insightful chapter titled "Europe before the War," a melancholic reflection on a golden age blasted away on the battlefields of France and Belgium. "What an extraordinary episode in the economic progress of man that age was that came to an end in August, 1914," he wrote.[4] Keynes marveled at the progress made across the continent after Germany began to emerge as a world economic power following its unification in 1871. Before then, most states except for Great Britain were largely agricultural and self-sufficient. Trade was carried on mainly within local markets. After that time, industry and population grew steadily as trade quickened across Europe, widening the sphere of prosperity and the reach of modern comforts. The gold standard maintained stable currency values and facilitated trade and capital flows. By 1914, Keynes wrote, "the inhabitant of London could order by telephone, sipping his morning tea in bed, the various products of the whole earth, in such quantity as he might see fit, and reasonably expect their early delivery upon his doorstep."[5] The generation that grew up before the First World War saw the world remade by the explosion in capitalist enterprise. It was the first era of globalization. Europe, led by Great Britain, France, and Germany, was the center of the world's economic order.

Germany played a leading role in this surge in trade and wealth. Its population increased from 40 million to nearly 70 million between 1870 and 1914, much faster than the populations of France and Great Britain. (In 1914, Britain had a population of 46 million, and France, 40 million.) German industrial output expanded at an even greater pace, spurred on by the speedy and efficient introduction of the factory system. By 1900, Germany was a main European supplier of pharmaceuticals, electrical equipment, steel, and coal. Germany quickly became an important trading partner for every other European nation, including Great Britain.

Keynes identified a cause of this rapid growth in a moral and psychological disposition among all classes to save and invest new wealth rather than to exhaust it in consumption. The wealthy, in particular, were responsible for the accumulation of capital because "they were not brought up to large expenditures, and preferred the power which investment gave to them to the pleasures of immediate consumption."[6] They had "the cake," so to speak, but on the condition that they abstained from eating it, or at least from eating all of it. (After all, the wealthy of that era lived in lavish homes, usually several of them.)

One of the reasons the prewar economy worked as well as it did was that the wealthy classes were at once the "savers" and the "investors." The founding entrepreneurs still owned and managed their enterprises. The laboring classes accepted this arrangement because the proceeds from their labor were continuously plowed back into the building of more factories and railroads. Much of this surplus was invested in the United States, which in turn sent back surplus foodstuffs to support Europe's growing population. Yet rapid population growth both in Europe and in America put pressure on agricultural prices. Keynes saw this trend as a destabilizing factor in the economic affairs of Europe, since some nations (Germany in particular) began to think of conquest as an alternative to trade for guaranteeing food supplies.[7]

The war permanently disrupted the delicate balance among the various factors of trade, psychology, population, and investment upon which the prewar order was constructed, leaving millions on the continent starving and destitute when the war ended. Nearly 20 million people were killed during the war and many millions more wounded or displaced; factories and transportation grids were destroyed across large swaths of the continent; food and medicine were in short supply; all countries were in debt from heavy borrowing to pay for armaments; national currencies were of uncertain value in relation to one another due to wartime inflation; and the accumulated wealth of the continent was consumed in a few years of war. The suffering was magnified by comparison with the comfortable lives that Europeans had enjoyed before 1914 and with the optimism for the future that nearly everyone had entertained just a few years earlier.

* * *

It was against this backdrop that European and American leaders gathered in Paris early in 1919 to hammer out a peace treaty. Many observers expected the French, British, and American leaders who controlled the Paris Peace Conference to craft a treaty that incorporated President Wilson's Fourteen Points and his general principle that there should be "peace without victory." In the months following the armistice, Wilson was by far the most popular political figure in the Western world—a leader who seemed to be carrying the hopes of the world on his shoulders. His program was one basis upon which Germany had agreed to lay down arms. Prior to the conference, Allied leaders made public declarations suggesting that the terms of the peace should be in accordance with Wilson's various addresses on the subject.

Keynes avoided taking sides on the question of which country was to blame for starting the war. In *Economic Consequences of the Peace*, he stressed the various elements of Wilson's program that pointed away from a punitive settlement. For example: "The removal so far as possible of all economic barriers and the establishment of an equality of trade conditions among all the nations consenting to the peace and associating themselves for its maintenance" (from the Fourteen Points); and, "There shall be no annexations, no contributions, and no punitive damages" (from an address before Congress), although Great Britain and France successfully demanded, as a rider to the president's statements, compensation for damage done to *civilians* and their property by land, sea, and air during the war. There was also, of course, the League of Nations that, in Wilson's mind, would treat all nations equally, arbitrate international differences, and enforce the peace.

Keynes viewed Wilson's program as a solemn contract binding upon the parties to the Paris Peace Conference—as did Wilson himself, at least prior to the conference. It is far from clear that the other parties, especially the French and British representatives, saw the complex situation in the same light. In fact, despite some rhetorical declarations, they did not.

Like many who pinned their hopes on Wilson's vision, Keynes

was dismayed when, after six months of negotiations running from January to June (1919), the conference adopted a regime of reparations and territorial concessions designed to punish Germany by making her bear most of the costs of the war—including military losses that went well beyond compensation for civilian damages. By this time, Wilson had adjusted his position somewhat, declaring that Germany had to be punished for the crime of aggression.

The Treaty of Versailles assigned to Germany the major blame for the war, and forced her to disarm and to cede territories and raw materials to France. Article 231, the so-called "war guilt" clause, stated: "The Allied and Associated Governments affirm and Germany accepts the responsibility of Germany and her allies for causing all the loss and damage to which the Allied and Associated Governments and their nationals have been subjected as a consequence of the war imposed upon them by the aggression of Germany and her allies." The Allied powers assessed $5 billion (22 billion gold marks at 1914 values) to be paid immediately in gold and raw materials, and "punted" calculations of the rest of the reparations to a commission of Allied representatives to be set up later. On the basis of Article 231, Keynes calculated that Germany might be assessed as much as $40 billion (170 billion gold marks) in reparations, which was about three times Germany's prewar GDP and four times the amount he estimated that Germany could afford to pay from remaining resources and proceeds from future exports. He argued that the sum needed to be cut back substantially to avoid out-of-control inflation and some form of revolutionary backlash in Germany.

For understandable reasons, the French feared a revival of German power and a renewed military campaign to reverse the decision of the war. One of the goals of the conference (insisted upon by France) was to establish as far as possible a rough equality between Germany and France in military and economic power. Due to the rapid growth in German population and industry over the previous decades, such a goal could not be accomplished without extreme measures either to shrink Germany or to stretch France. This, according to Keynes, was a wrongheaded approach:

> My purpose in this book is to show that the Carthaginian Peace is not practically right or possible. The clock cannot be set back. You cannot restore Central Europe to 1870 without setting up such strains in the European structure and letting loose such human and spiritual forces as will overwhelm not only you and your 'guarantees,' but your institutions and the existing order of your society.[8]

Here was Keynes's central point: the old order in Europe could not be restored. Germany would henceforth be a major power on the continent. The treaty could not reverse that evolution, and any attempt to do so would end in failure—and possibly in a future attempt by Germany to reverse the decision of the war.

Keynes reserved his sharpest words for Wilson, the American president who might have used his prestige and popularity to craft a treaty more in keeping with the ideals of fairness, self-determination, free trade, and collective security that he enunciated during the course of the war. Wilson's primary goal at the conference was to win European support for his League of Nations, an institution that he believed would secure the peace for future generations. European leaders dismissed this view as a delusion and had little difficulty in giving Wilson his League in return for his support for those elements of the treaty that they considered far more important: reparations and territorial concessions. Keynes portrayed Wilson as an American naïf, a "blind and deaf Don Quixote," in the company of seasoned European negotiators. "There can seldom have been a statesman of the first rank," Keynes wrote, "more incompetent than the President in the agilities of the council chamber."[9] According to

Keynes, Wilson was so thoroughly "bamboozled" by the French and British leaders—Clemenceau and Lloyd-George—that he headed back to America comfortable in the illusion that the Treaty of Versailles established the foundations for true peace. Those hopes were formally dashed at home when the U.S. Senate rejected the treaty after Wilson refused to accept a compromise that would have limited the power of the League of Nations to take the United States into war without the consent of Congress.

* * *

In pinning the blame for the treaty's flaws on Wilson, Keynes realized that any solution to the European crisis would have to come about through the intervention of the United States. The war had shifted the balance of world power westward, as the United States emerged from the conflict with reserves of wealth that Europe would not be able to match for years or decades to come. Great Britain and France sought heavy reparations from Germany partly to pay for the war and to punish Germany, but also to use the proceeds to repay American banks for loans taken out to underwrite the war. The amount of these loans, some $4 billion owed by France and nearly $5 billion by Great Britain, represented nearly half of France's prewar GDP and a third of Britain's. The principal and interest (5 percent per year) due on the loans imposed a burden on their economies that would prove difficult to bear under conditions of postwar austerity. Keynes maintained that President Wilson could have marshaled the financial power of the United States to impose upon the European allies a treaty more in keeping with the requirements of postwar peace.

He reasoned, probably correctly, that Great Britain would be better off by renouncing reparations and gaining cancellation of the debts than by winning phantom reparations (that might not be paid) and paying real debts. If the United States would cancel inter-ally war debts in an "act of statesmanship and generosity,"

he argued, then reparations imposed upon Germany might likewise be scaled back to a level that the Germans could afford to pay
without bankrupting themselves. Keynes and several other aides
floated this proposal behind the scenes at the peace conference.[10]
It went nowhere, for a host of very good reasons. The French were
more worried about the military threat from Germany than about
war debts. The Americans saw no reason why they should bear the
costs of the war when they had played no role in starting it.

Keynes feared that the twin burdens of German reparations and
inter-ally war debts would weigh heavily upon the international financial system for years to come. The transfer of vast amounts of
gold to the United States in payment of debts would foster a boom
in the creditor country at the expense of debtor economies. In the
decades before the war, the automatic adjustment mechanisms of
the gold standard prevented nations from running up large international debts. Now, after the war, the world was awash in debt, much
of it owed to the United States, a nation with little experience as
an international creditor and world economic power—and, to make
matters worse, a country used to protecting its domestic markets
from foreign competitors. Keynes understood (though he did not
press the point in his book) that Great Britain stood to lose its financial preeminence due to its debt position with the United States.
Thus, in pressing for a solution to the debt issue at the conference,
he acted more as a representative of British interests than as a disinterested analyst of the treaty. In any case, he was right to worry that
accumulated debts from the war might destabilize the international
economy in the postwar period. In confirmation of these fears, the
Allied powers—led by the United States—made continuous efforts
during the 1920s to reduce or restructure war debts and reparations,
with limited success. After the stock market crash in 1929, the issues
of debt and reparations gave way to new and bigger problems.

In the broader message of the book, Keynes argued that the

ideals and institutions of the prewar era could no longer serve as the foundations for progress. "The forces of the nineteenth century have run their course and are exhausted," he wrote. "The economic motives and ideals of that generation no longer satisfy us. We must find a new way and must suffer again the malaise, and finally the pangs of a new industrial birth."[11] From his point of view, the fundamental assumptions of Europe's liberal civilization had been badly shaken. Faith in automatic progress via saving and self-discipline was crushed. National currencies and terms of trade were distorted by wartime inflation. Workers would henceforth demand a larger share of the fruits of capitalism than they were willing to accept prior to 1914. Governments would have to take the lead in feeding their populations, establishing stable currencies, and re-starting commercial activity. Keynes concluded that all this pointed toward new roles for the state, labor unions, and corporations in the evolution of capitalism.

This was something that (according to Keynes) the statesmen at the time did not grasp as they negotiated over borders, reparations, and the League of Nations while the populations of Europe starved and established states were overturned in revolutions. They did not see "that the most serious of the problems that claimed their attention were not political or territorial but financial and economic, and that the perils of the future lay not in frontiers or sovereignties but in food, coal, and transport."[12]

The Economic Consequences of the Peace was an early intervention of the academic expert into the practical world of international politics and finance. As some have written, it may be read as an extended lecture on the errors of politicians from the standpoint of the professional economist and intellectual. Keynes wrote in 1922, "The economist is not king; quite true. But he ought to be. He is a better governor than the general or the diplomatist or the oratorical lawyer."[13] This appears to be one of the lessons he took from the Paris

Peace Conference: that it would be up to economists, experts, and intellectuals to step in where the politicians had failed to chart a path out of the European crisis.

*   *   *

Keynes's indictment of the Versailles Treaty, though widely popular in intellectual circles, was not so enthusiastically received in diplomatic quarters in Washington, Paris, or London. There, *The Economic Consequences of the Peace* was condemned as too pessimistic about the future course of world affairs, too sympathetic toward Germany, too negative about President Wilson's role at the peace conference, and too heavily focused on the economic aspects of the treaty. One prominent reviewer branded it "an angry book," which was undoubtedly true. Some later blamed Keynes for legitimizing German efforts to undermine the treaty in the 1920s and 1930s and for laying the groundwork for appeasement in the 1930s.[14] This was partly true: German leaders took advantage of Keynes's book in their campaign to discredit the treaty. Nevertheless, his critics have overstated the influence of the book. It did not wreck the treaty or create German resistance to it or cause the disorders of the 1920s and 1930s. More fundamental forces were at work; and farsighted though Keynes may have been, he could not have anticipated all of these outcomes. In any case, he wrote from a wish to see the treaty revised but not entirely discarded.[15]

But his critics had a point. Keynes's manifesto was an exaggerated production in several important respects. Written in the form of an indictment, it was a one-sided brief against the treaty, focused excessively on the reparations issue. The central idea was that the reparations regime would cripple Germany financially and unleash forces that might set off a revolution or another war. While such events did unfold during the 1920s and 1930s, it is not true that reparations or the treaty was their primary cause.

To a significant degree, the Allied representatives in Paris presented Germany with a bill designed to placate anti-German sentiment at home, a point that Keynes did not fully appreciate.[16] By 1921, the reparations commission set up by the Allies scaled back the levies to $33 billion (about 132 billion gold marks) to be paid at interest over thirty or so years, a sum that was lower than Keynes's initial estimates but still much higher than he thought Germany could afford to pay. Nearly two-thirds of this sum was assessed in the form of "C bonds," which carried no interest and would be due at an indeterminate date when the commission decreed that the Weimar government could pay it. The C bonds were, as many said at the time, a phantom assessment. Thus the commission, bowing to economic reality, effectively slashed the reparations down to a level close to what Keynes estimated that Germany could afford.

Even at these reduced rates, however, the German government balked at making payments because the German people regarded reparations as a national humiliation—although Germany had imposed a war indemnity upon France at the conclusion of the Franco-Prussian War only fifty years earlier. The payments were made erratically until they were deferred after the stock market crash and then canceled when Hitler took power in 1933.

Scholars estimate that between 1920 and 1930 Germany paid approximately 20 billion gold marks in reparations, a fraction of the amount assessed, and a figure that was dwarfed by loans that poured into Germany from primarily American sources.[17] At these levels, the reparations could not have caused all of the problems attributed to them: the German hyperinflation in 1923, the stock market collapse, or Hitler's rise to power. The reparations in the end were more of a throbbing political problem that discredited the Weimar government within Germany and impeded international economic cooperation across Europe. Economists who have looked at these figures generally agree that the Germans could have afforded to pay the levies—that is, the 50 billion gold marks—if they had wanted to do so.[18] As events proved, the massive debts run up by the belligerent powers during the war were far more consequential than German reparations in destabilizing the international economy in the 1920s.

Nor was it accurate for Keynes to claim that the treaty imposed a "Carthaginian Peace" upon Germany, because while the German army collapsed in the field in the autumn of 1918 and the German government disintegrated into chaos at home, German territory was never occupied by Allied troops and the country suffered little actual war damage. The war ended in an armistice rather than in national capitulation. Most of the war damage was localized in areas of Belgium and northern France. This was the basic problem: Germany was never subjected to the tribulations of foreign occupation and plunder that usually accompany defeat in war. For this reason, Germans never fully accepted the fact that they had lost the war. The Allies imposed harsh terms on Germany but set up no mechanism to enforce them against a recalcitrant government and population. Once the United States rejected the treaty and Great Britain withdrew from continental affairs, France was left alone to enforce the treaty against a larger and potentially more powerful adversary. As the years passed, Germany felt free to ignore the terms of the treaty, secure in the belief that they could not be enforced.

Keynes's grand solution—a reduction of reparations linked to the cancellation of inter-ally war debts—may be considered a statement of British financial interest as much as an expression of sympathy for the German position. He wrote that the payment of interest on those loans was an oppressive prospect for Great Britain and the other debtor countries. Nevertheless, the United States, given its history and its relationship to the European powers at that time, was not going to absorb the costs of a European war that it had no role in starting. Public opinion in America would have rebelled against any such solution. It was not a realistic proposal, nor was Keynes's plea for another international loan from the United States after he had called for the cancellation of already existing debts. "Does he think we are financial simpletons?" asked one American reviewer of the book.

Keynes was also wrong to think that Wilson's vision should or could have controlled the peace conference or that Germany would have accepted a treaty that fully incorporated his Fourteen Points. Here Keynes's argument was more than a little illogical, for he wrote that "when it came to practice [Wilson's] ideas were nebulous and incomplete. He had no plan, no scheme, no constructive ideas whatever for clothing with the flesh of life the commandments which he had thundered from the White House." In that circumstance, it is hard to see why he thought that Wilson's vision could have set the agenda for the conference. In addition, France and Great Britain had legitimate financial and security interests that could not be swept aside in the postwar negotiations, even by Wilson. The treaty that emerged from those negotiations was inevitably going to contain a bundle of compromises that gave each of the major powers some but not all of what it asked for.[19] Public opinion in France and Great Britain would have recoiled against a "slap on the wrist" treaty in regard to German responsibility for the war. It is also probable that Germany would have recoiled against a thoroughly Wilsonian treaty, inasmuch as one of the Fourteen Points called for an independent Polish state to be carved out of the Polish populations on the eastern border of Germany, assured of free and secure access to the sea. That was a sore point for Germany, and one whose inclusion might have undermined any treaty that emerged from the Paris negotiations. Two decades later, the Second World War began on the day that Hitler moved to reverse that particular provision of the Treaty of Versailles.

In his own way, Keynes may have been as utopian as Wilson was in envisioning the postwar order. Wilson looked to transcend the balance-of-power politics that characterized the prewar regime in favor of a system of collective security as institutionalized in the League of

Nations. That was judged by nearly everyone, including Keynes, to be a utopian vision and one that was unworkable under the conditions of the time. In much the same way, Keynes proposed a vision of European economic cooperation and integration that was equally implausible in a situation in which national rivalries and resentments had been inflamed by the deaths, damage, and overall suffering of the war. Keynes, in effect, was asking the warring parties of Europe to set aside their differences and forget past humiliations in the interests of mutual cooperation and economic progress, with the financial burden for that solution to be carried by the United States. None of the parties was willing to do that in 1919, and few people at the time thought that such a prospect was possible. The weight of history was still too great to allow for either the Wilsonian or the Keynesian solution.

It would take another war before such a vision could be seriously considered, this time under the supervision and patronage of the United States, motivated in large measure by the emergence of the Soviet Union as a potential adversary. As the Second World War approached an end, American and British planners sought to avoid the missteps of 1918 and 1919. This required in the first place the unconditional surrender of German forces and the Allied occupation of German territory. The remedies that Keynes proposed in 1919—relief, reconstruction, renewal of trade, cancellation of debts, limited reparations, stabilization of currencies, and integration of the vanquished into the postwar order—were generally accepted in 1945 as guideposts for the postwar order. Keynes, as the British representative at the Bretton Woods conference in 1944, played an important role in designing the institutional foundations of the postwar economic order: the World Bank, the International Monetary Fund, and an international currency regime pegged to the U.S. dollar. These policies and institutions, much in contrast to those adopted in 1919, established a basis for postwar security and prosperity across Western Europe and North America.

CHAPTER TWO

The Keynesian Revolution in Political Economy

Keynes attacked the Treaty of Versailles on political grounds, bluntly asserting that the negotiators addressed the wrong problems and held a mistaken vision of the postwar order. A consistent theme in his career as an economist is that he was a *political* economist. This was true in at least three senses: first, he understood that economic ideas had to be communicated to the public in a manner designed to persuade; second, he saw that the policies of the state had to be grounded in sound economics; third, he knew that the organization of the economy could not in the end be separated from the institutions of the state.

From this arises a central irony of the Keynesian revolution in economic policy: while Keynes was a *political* economist, assigning new responsibilities to the state to stabilize the economy, academic economists who followed his lead turned their discipline into a technical enterprise entirely separate from politics. The distinguished tradition of political economy largely faded away as Keynes's revolution unfolded in the postwar era. This development has served to conceal an intriguing possibility—that Keynes's enterprise is vulnerable not primarily because the economic theory is flawed, but because it cannot be made to work from a political point of view.

In *The Economic Consequences of the Peace*, Keynes declared that the old order of political economy in Europe had come to an end with the First World War. He took this theme further in *The General Theory of Employment, Interest, and Money*, where he argued, against the backdrop of the Great Depression, that the nineteenth-century theory of free markets and limited government was inadequate to modern conditions. His prescriptions for setting capitalism on a new foundation launched the "Keynesian revolution." A key question today is whether evolving conditions in the political economy of capitalism are in the process of making the Keynesian synthesis ineffective and obsolete in its turn.

*   *   *

The Great Depression, more than any previous economic crisis, ignited a fundamental rethinking of the future of capitalism. What had gone wrong with the market system to cause such an unprecedented collapse? Was there a way to tame its "boom and bust" cycles? Could the capitalist system survive? Did it even deserve to survive; and if so, on what terms? The victories of communism in Russia and fascism in Germany suggested that capitalism would soon give way to one or the other of these extreme alternatives.

The Depression era produced three influential but widely diverging statements about the future of capitalism: Keynes's *General Theory* (1936), Joseph Schumpeter's *Capitalism, Socialism, and Democracy* (1942), and Friedrich Hayek's *The Road to Serfdom* (1944). Each was a work of political economy in the broad sense, weaving together the interconnected subjects of politics, culture, institutions, and economic theory. Each had long been gestating in the mind of its author and expressed his considered reflections on the world crisis of the time. All three of these economists were well known in academic and policy circles long before these particular works appeared. To some extent, then, each developed his ideas in answer to theoretical challenges posed by the others.

Today, more than seventy years since they were first published, these three works continue to stand as seminal statements of influential public doctrines: Keynes's *General Theory* for orthodox liberalism, *The Road to Serfdom* for market liberalism, and *Capitalism, Socialism, and Democracy* for conservatism and neoconservatism, or for the belief that culture is decisive for the survival of capitalism. For this reason, some have called their authors the "political philosophers" of the twentieth century. Among them, Keynes exercised by far the greatest influence in the post-Depression and postwar era. More than Hayek, Schumpeter, or any other economist of the time, Keynes went beyond diagnosis to offer practical remedies for the economic crisis of the 1930s. His *General Theory* did not arrive in time to be of much use during the Depression, but his insights revolutionized economic policymaking and the study of economics in the postwar era.

The evolution of "managed economies" in the postwar era owed a great deal to the writings of Keynes in which he assigned responsibility to governments for stabilizing economies. For Keynes, achieving full employment was the principal goal of economic policy, and he provided policymakers with a set of fiscal tools for smoothing out the booms and busts of the business cycle. This was the "middle way" that he tried to steer between the extremes of communism and fascism, and between state planning and free-market capitalism. From a political point of view, Keynes was among the liberal reformers of that time who sought to "tame" capitalism by giving new managerial duties to national governments.

Many attributed the rapid growth in America's postwar economy to the application of Keynes's theories. One economist called the postwar era "the age of Keynes."[1] *Time* magazine took note of his vast influence by publishing a cover story in 1965 under the title "We Are

All Keynesians Now." As the magazine acknowledged, "Keynes and his ideas, though they still make some people nervous, have been so widely accepted that they constitute both the new orthodoxy in the universities and the touchstone of economic management in Washington." Though Keynes's theories were temporarily in retreat in Washington and London during the 1980s and 1990s, they never really lost currency among academic economists, and the recent financial crisis provided a new occasion for their application. We have not yet evolved beyond "the age of Keynes."

* * *

In *The General Theory*, Keynes worked out the premises for a conclusion he had already reached. This is evident in a series of essays that he wrote during the 1920s and into 1930, which are collected into a single volume under the title *Essays in Persuasion* (1931). Here he reflected on the evolution of the capitalist order from its origins in the eighteenth century and on the significant changes in the international system brought on by the war. He maintained that rapid changes in the economic order required parallel changes in political and economic institutions, and corresponding adjustments in political and economic theory.

"The End of Laissez-Faire" (1926) is an essay in which Keynes rejected the principles of natural liberty and enlightened self-interest that lay at the heart of Adam Smith's economics of free markets. "The world is not so governed from above that private and social interest always coincide," he wrote. "It is not a correct deduction from the principles of economics that enlightened self-interest always operates in the public interest. Nor is it true that self-interest generally is enlightened."[2] This was rather a caricature of the foundational assumptions of market economics, which did not insist that enlightened self-interest always operates in the general interest, but that it will do so more reliably than other forms of economic organization. Nevertheless, Keynes rejected these principles for two reasons: first, he considered them to be far too abstract to offer solutions to practical problems; second, he judged them to be increasingly obsolete in the modern world of institutional capitalism shaped by large corporations, labor unions, and not-for-profit institutions. At this time he began to consider (as he wrote) "possible improvements in the technique of modern capitalism by means of collective action."

In that essay, Keynes focused on the organizational evolution of capitalist economies as a factor that altered or undermined the operation of free and competitive markets. An important phenomenon of modern life, he wrote, is the tendency for large enterprises to socialize themselves—or, in other words, to pursue social as opposed to purely private objectives. He suggested that "A point arrives in the growth of a big institution—a big railway or public utility enterprise but also a bank or insurance company—at which the owners of capital are almost entirely dissociated from the management, with the result that the direct personal interest of the owners (the shareholders) becomes quite secondary."[3] As organizations reach a certain size, managers become interested in other goals besides profit, such as stability, security of employment, reputation, and independence. Keynes also welcomed the development of semiautonomous not-for-profit institutions such as universities and scientific societies that promote the general interest in different spheres of activity.

Keynes envisioned an emerging system of capitalism in which large business enterprises and not-for profit institutions operated alongside government in common efforts to promote the public interest. The friction between the public and private spheres, so much an aspect of the old order of liberalism, was giving way to a new order of cooperation among large institutions. Keynes's corporatist vision of the capitalist order represented an evolution of liberalism beyond its nineteenth-century emphasis on individuals, competition, and suspicion of the state.

The separation of ownership and control in large organizations implied that expert managers might assume new powers in the direction of political institutions and of private corporations, a concept that Keynes first broached in *The Economic Consequences of the Peace*. While this seems like a modern technocratic concept, it also had a traditional aristocratic pedigree, at least for Keynes. Roy Harrod, his friend and biographer, suggested that Keynes assumed that important economic decisions would always be in the hands of experts operating in the public interest, much in the way that central bankers are allowed to control interest rates and the supply of money without close political supervision. As a member of his country's intellectual aristocracy, Keynes "tended to think of the really important decisions being reached by a small group of intelligent people, like the group that [later] fashioned the Bretton Woods plan."[4] Keynes, according to Harrod, approved of this as a normative matter; he also thought it to be an element in the evolution of modern capitalism as experts inherited control of the system from entrepreneurs.

Keynes pointed out two areas where the state could and should intervene to improve the operation of the capitalist order. The first was in the area of money and credit, where he called for deliberate control and planning by a central institution—that is, by a central bank with powers sufficient to regulate the supply of currency and credit toward the goal of full employment and stable prices. This was an implicit attack on the gold standard, which Keynes regarded as an archaic inheritance from the nineteenth century, and as an ineffective instrument for regulating money and credit in the wake of the war.

He had several longstanding objections to the gold standard. The main problem was that it required nations to expand or contract money and credit in order to maintain the exchange value of their currencies, while Keynes believed that monetary policy should assign priority to domestic employment and stable internal prices. His second objection was that the United States now held the lion's share of the world's gold reserves, mainly due to wartime loans, and this circumstance allowed the U.S. central bank to dictate interest-rate policy to the rest of the world. Keynes vehemently opposed Britain's return to the gold standard in 1926, predicting that it would lead to deflation, rising real interest rates, added burdens to debtors, and domestic unemployment. He cheered when Britain abandoned the gold standard in 1931, after his forecasts were borne out, in favor of central bank management of monetary policy. On this subject, Keynes proved to be farsighted. After many fits and starts during the 1930s and in the postwar era, the world abandoned the gold standard for good in the 1970s in favor of a system of fiat currencies managed by central banks.

Keynes's second innovation was to call for public control over investment such that the state would replace banks, investment houses, and wealthy individuals as the major supplier of investment capital. In the modern world, he pointed out, "savers" and "investors" were now different people and institutions; their decisions had to be coordinated by private intermediaries that took in savings and directed them toward new and hopefully profitable enterprises. Keynes had little faith that this process could be carried out seamlessly in the public interest, and so he looked to the state as the institution where the investment function could be carried out rationally in the interests of society as a whole. He returned to this theme again and again in the 1930s, and in *The General Theory* he argued in great detail for public investment as a means of rescuing the world from the Depression.

This is an area in which (fortunately) the Keynesian revolution never fully took hold, despite Keynes's great influence and the growth of state spending in the postwar era. Banks and investment houses are still in private hands and our stock markets still allocate capital through private channels. Today we understand something that Keynes did not—namely, that modern governments, because they respond to constituent pressures, lobbyists, and campaign donors, are incapable of allocating capital on a rational or disinterested basis; they allocate funds on the basis of political rather than economic signals. Private investors, whatever their flaws, do a far better job of allocating capital than modern governments could ever do. Yet Keynes, writing in the midst of the Depression, focused far more on the failures of private markets than on the possible defects of democratic governments.

In 1930 he was still optimistic that the economic slump was but a temporary lapse in the onward march of capitalist development; he dismissed claims that it marked the end of prosperity or the collapse of capitalism. The system had "magneto trouble," he wrote in "The Great Slump of 1930," suggesting thereby that something had gone wrong with the starting mechanism of the capitalist machine. The system was not corrupt or fundamentally broken, as socialists and communists claimed; the machine only required a fix to make it run more smoothly and reliably. Keynes went on in that essay to identify the problem, writing, "If I am right, the fundamental cause of the trouble is the lack of new enterprise due to an unsatisfactory market for capital investment."[5] Investors and entrepreneurs were not putting capital to work because, in the midst of the slump, they saw no market for machines, factories, new employees, and the like. At that moment, Keynes thought the slump could be reversed if the central banks in Britain, France, and the United States could coordinate monetary policy to increase the flow of credit internationally. Such a play might have worked, but it was never seriously attempted.

The tone is even more optimistic in "Economic Possibilities for Our Grandchildren" (1930), an essay in which Keynes characterized the current economic difficulties as a transitional period from the age of laissez-faire to the age of institutional capitalism. "We are suffering, not from the rheumatics of old age," he wrote, "but from the growing pains of over-rapid changes, from the painfulness of readjustment between one economic period and another."[6] Keynes calculated that over the previous one hundred years the standard of living of the average European and American had grown at least fourfold, and predicted that over the next one hundred years it would improve between fourfold and eightfold again.* Within two or three generations, he suggested, the necessities of a comfortable life would be available to all, and mankind's long struggle for survival in the face of scarcity would be near an end.

Keynes thought that the values of work, thrift, and moneymaking were erroneously associated with capitalism; he believed they are instead called forth by scarcity, poverty, and need. He speculated that these values would be rendered obsolete when, through capitalist enterprise, scarcity was eventually overcome, at which point mankind would be able to turn its attention to activities that make life worthwhile: art, music, literature, and philosophy. This, according to Keynes, would establish the final stage of capitalism—an end of history—when advanced societies would be able to live off their accumulated capital. Capitalism, with its moneymaking preoccupations, would then "wither away," much as Karl Marx had predicted, but through a peaceful and evolutionary process.

Like many other thinkers of his time, Keynes regarded the political and moral principles associated with market capitalism as degrading and in need of replacement by a more humane set of ideals. There was an evolutionary or historical element in his thought: he claimed that capitalism developed in historical stages and also in a morally favorable direction. Institutional capitalism was an improvement over the "classical" system of the nineteenth century, but still a stepping-

---

* As things turned out, Keynes was not far off in this prediction. In the United States, per capita income increased about sevenfold from 1945 to the present time. Yet there is no thought today that the "economic problem" has been solved.

stone on a path to the final phase of capitalist development, when the "economic problem" would be solved once and for all.

* * *

Keynes published his collected *Essays in Persuasion* during an economic slump that he thought would soon end. Like everyone else, he expected the world's economies to bounce back quickly from the crash in the United States, just as it had done on many occasions in the past, most recently in 1920 and 1921. Keynes was as surprised as anyone by the severity of the slump, and in fact he lost a fair amount of money in the crash of the world's stock markets.

The industrial economies had gone through recessions and even depressions in the past, but none as deep and prolonged as the collapse in the 1930s. In the United States, where the slump began, industrial production declined by a third between 1929 and 1933 and unemployment exploded from 3 percent to 25 percent of the workforce. More than a third of the country's banks failed between 1931 and 1933, leaving depositors broke and the credit system badly damaged. In Great Britain the decline was not as steep, in part because the country's economy had never fully recovered from the war. Nevertheless, economic output declined by a third there as well, exports declined by more than half, and unemployment rose to about 20 percent of the workforce in 1932. It was a global catastrophe that bottomed out only when the world's economic machinery ground to a halt in 1933.

Disasters of this magnitude were not supposed to happen in market economies, which were thought to possess self-correcting features. When the slump dragged on, Keynes concluded that there was something wrong with the adjustment mechanisms of the market that was not accounted for in the standard economic theories. Much like the Great War, for Keynes the Great Depression called into question the received wisdom of the time.

This was the background for his *General Theory*, where he laid out the theoretical case for countercyclical government spending policies that proved to be so influential in the postwar era. Like *The Economic Consequences of the Peace*, this book too was widely discussed and reviewed when it first appeared, frequently in newspapers and magazines that catered to policymakers and intelligent laymen. But whereas the former set out a lucid argument that no one could misunderstand, *The General Theory* contained a bewildering mix of new concepts and arguments, critiques of old theories, and loosely related excursions into subjects like stock market speculation and mercantilist theories, all of which led to confusion among readers as to what the central point actually was. Paul Samuelson, one of Keynes's American expositors, found it to be "a badly written book," full of "mares' nests of confusions," where flashes of insight were interspersed with arguments that seemed to lead nowhere.[7] Keynes developed a meandering argument in his tour de force and left it to others to work out the implications.

In *The General Theory*, Keynes mounted an attack on what he called the "classical" school of economics, the doctrine of free and self-adjusting markets developed by the political economists of the previous century. The classical theory, he suggested, is not a *general* theory but rather a special theory applicable to a condition of full employment and to an economy of small producers, independent workers, and competitive markets—circumstances that no longer obtained in modern economies, increasingly dominated by large institutions and by labor unions. A central theme of Keynes's theory, and of Keynesian economics in general, is that market economies do not automatically adjust to systemic shocks like stock market crashes, widespread bank failures, famines, and wars. A second is that the market system, left on its own, will operate most of the time at levels below full employment and potential output.

In an early chapter, he set down and rejected three postulates of "classical" political economy that (he claimed) were central to the theory of self-correcting markets. The first was Say's Law, named for Jean-Baptiste Say, a nineteenth-century economist who held that aggregate supply creates its own aggregate demand, or as Say put it, "The general demand for products is brisk in proportion to the activity of production." Thus, a general glut across the entire economy ought never to occur because demand should always be sufficient to soak up the goods produced. The second principle, and one related to Say's Law, was that widespread unemployment should never occur because workers, even during slumps, should find employment by adjusting their wage demands downward to levels where employers will hire them. A third was that savings are a form of deferred consumption that are put to work in the form of investment for the production of future goods, with the interest rate regulating the general volume of savings and investment at any particular moment. The flexible movement of prices, wages, and interest rates allows the market to adjust quickly to changes in production, the demand for labor, and increases or decreases in saving.

Keynes rejected these postulates as either wrong or inapplicable to the new world of institutional capitalism in which corporate managers had replaced entrepreneurs, labor unions now intervened to negotiate on behalf of workers, and banks and investment houses emerged to act as intermediaries between savers and investors. As for Say's Law, Keynes thought that the existence of widespread unemployment contradicted the hypothesis that supply creates its own demand. He pointed out that producers and consumers act independently and not necessarily according to the same calculations. For these reasons, Keynes rejected Say's Law and asserted the reverse: that it is consumer demand that calls producers into action. As for wages, he observed that there were unemployed laborers more than willing to work for prevailing wages, which meant that they were not "voluntarily" unemployed but were out of work because they had no offers of employment. To complicate matters, Keynes rejected the assumption that employers could easily reduce wage rates during slumps. Wage rates, he argued, were "sticky" rather than fluid (as the classical economists supposed) in a downward direction. The existence of labor unions ready to defend labor contracts or to call worker strikes made it even more difficult for employers to cut wages during slumps. (They typically cut production and employment instead.) In addition, wage cutting across the economy has deflationary effects, so it is possible for the price level to fall faster than wages, leaving the real wage as high or higher than when the process started.

As for saving and investment, Keynes again emphasized that savers and investors were no longer the same parties as they may have been in the previous century, but rather independent actors in the economy, operating on different views of the future. Now, savings and investment had to be brought together by financial intermediaries. He went further to argue that savings are a "leakage" from consumer demand and therefore tend to draw down investment as well, since investors respond to the ups and downs of consumer demand. Consumers change their rate of saving, and businesses and entrepreneurs their level of investment, for reasons largely independent of the interest rate. This means that there is no automatic mechanism to direct the flow of savings into investment and to maintain the two quantities at roughly equal levels.

Keynes concluded that there was no obvious process of adjustment in wages, prices, and interest rates that would correct the slide in employment and output. Under certain circumstances, there could be a general overproduction of goods, widespread unemployment, hoarding of money by consumers, and a collapse of investment—all occurring at the same time and in response to one another. This meant that the market might reach equilibrium at levels well below full employment; and Keynes argued that this was in fact what had happened in the 1930s. Wage demands could remain above the level where businesses are prepared to hire, especially in times of deflation. There might be times when low or even negative interest rates would prove insufficient to induce people to spend and invest. As incomes fall, so also do savings and the purchasing power of consumers. Those with jobs and incomes, seeing what is happening around them, hold back on purchases, further worsening the situation. Where there is weak consumer demand, there will be little investment, and thus no expansion in employment and incomes, and no progress in society. For all these reasons, slumps can be self-perpetuating and need not correct themselves by the natural operation of market processes. In that case, some external intervention is required to restore consumer demand, investment, and employment.

Having rejected the economic principles of the "classical" school, Keynes went on to attack its moral postulates as well. The virtue of thrift, for example, was not as socially beneficial as many claimed. Thrift, which might make sense for individuals, results in general harm when it is too widely practiced because it leads to the withdrawal of consumption from the marketplace and a consequent reduction in consumer demand. Since savings are not automatically used up in investment in times of slack consumer demand, increased savings can lead to a reduction in the wealth of the community and an acceleration of the downward economic spiral. This was his "paradox of thrift," a not-so-subtle attack on the nineteenth-century proposition that thrift and deferred consumption are the foundations for order and progress.* Keynes reversed the traditional for-

---

* In an addendum to *The General Theory* (chap. 23), Keynes approvingly cited Mandeville's *Fable of the Bees*, which suggested that frugality and virtue carried to excess lead to general impoverishment. Keynes's point was that his theory about consumer spending and consumer demand was not novel but had an ancient pedigree in the history of economic thought.

mula, insisting that consumption and debt, rather than thrift and saving, are the keys to prosperity.

The basic problem according to Keynes, and the reason that market economies so often fall short of potential output and "overshoot" on both the up and down sides, is that investors and businesses must make calculations about spending and hiring in the face of a fundamentally uncertain future. Investors are the "prime movers" of the economy, and also the source of market volatility. Consumers, by contrast, behave fairly predictably, spending a stable percentage of their incomes on goods and services of various kinds, except on occasions when fear and panic lead them to reduce expenditures and increase savings. Investors, on the other hand, must allocate funds based upon uncertain assessments of conditions many years into the future. "Our knowledge of the factors that will govern the yield of an investment some years hence is usually very slight and often negligible," Keynes wrote in *The General Theory*. To complicate matters further, the evolution of stock markets requires investors to make judgments about how other investors assess the future—since those assessments, when added up, determine the value of stocks.

Keynes pointed to the distinction between risk and uncertainty. Risks are subject to calculation but uncertainties are not. Investors, Keynes argued, confront an unknowable future—that is, an uncertain future—when they commit funds for five, ten, or thirty years. They cannot know if a war, inflation, a natural disaster or some other unpredictable event will intervene to undermine their investments. In a rational universe, investors might keep their funds on the sidelines permanently due to the impossibility of knowing what the future holds. In the world as it is, Keynes suggested, investors are moved not by calculations of risk but by alternating moods of confidence and pessimism that are socially contagious but loosely grounded in real conditions. These are the "animal spirits" that at bottom drive the market economy. Keynes thought that investor uncertainty was a factor that kept interest rates too high because it required lenders to demand a premium on loans. Uncertainty also cut in the other direction: from the standpoint of businessmen, future profits may appear too uncertain to justify the loans required to expand or start their enterprises. In times of pessimism, uncertainty was one of the factors that drove the economy along in a downward spiral. This element of Keynes's theory pointed in the direction of central bank policy to maintain interest rates at low levels to eliminate the "uncertainty premium," even if such a policy risked inflation or weakening of the currency.

Keynes thus drew a portrait of the market economy that was very close to the opposite of that drawn by his eighteenth- and nineteenth-century predecessors. They saw a system that operated like a machine with its various parts working together to keep it moving forward even in the face of external shocks, which might slow it down but could not knock it off course for very long. In their view, entrepreneurs and investors were the rational and calculating participants that kept the economic machine moving. Keynes described a system that was inherently prone to booms and busts because its various parts did not work in harmony and because it was greatly influenced by shifting investor moods. In his theory, investors and entrepreneurs were the dynamic but capricious elements, putting their funds into play and withdrawing them according to those shifting moods about future prospects and in response to the spending and saving decisions of consumers.

Thus, consumers and investors increased or reduced their spending in a reciprocal dynamic, creating a "pro-cyclical" bias in the system and giving the market its boom-and-bust character. Keynes looked to government spending and borrowing as a countercyclical factor that might stabilize the system, particularly during slumps when consumer hoarding and investor pessimism sent the economy into a downward spiral. This new role for government may have represented his most radical departure from his nineteenth-century predecessors.

Keynes was by no means the first economist or public figure to call for public spending or public works projects to reduce unemployment during slumps. Spending on public works was a common theme in political platforms in the United States and Great Britain during the 1920s and 1930s, though the proposals were generally set forth as emergency measures, not as a systemic means of stabilizing the economy over the long term. Keynes recommended public works projects to President Roosevelt when the two met in Washington in 1933, before Keynes worked out the details of his general theory. Keynes had also called for a larger role for the state in the management of the economy during the 1920s when there was no immediate crisis of unemployment. In 1925, for example, he urged the Liberal Party to adopt a platform in which the state would take a large role in "directing economic forces in the interests of justice and social stability."[8] Like many other liberals of the time, Keynes wanted the state to take on greater powers over the economy, with or without a broad theoretical rationale.

What was novel about his call for public spending in *The General Theory* was the broad theoretical case that he advanced for it, with public spending used as an antidote to the failure of the marketplace and as a means to restimulate private economic activity. In effect, Keynes developed a technical or instrumental case for the expansion of state powers, rather than a political or ideological one. This was another way in which he saw the state as a potential partner with the business sector instead of a rival or competitor. Keynes envisioned a new order of capitalism in which the state would act to reduce the uncertainty that he felt was a source of instability in the marketplace.

The state could manage its spending and borrowing policies toward the goal of stabilizing consumer demand, which would reduce the uncertainty faced by investors and thereby smooth out the boom-and-bust cycle of the capitalist order. Keynes pointed out that when individuals hold back on consumption or cannot spend because they lose income during slumps, and when investors defer spending because they lose confidence, government can step in to borrow and spend as a means of maintaining demand and generating investment, instead of waiting for the market to make adjustments that may take a long time to occur. Every dollar or pound spent by governments in times of slack demand would be multiplied by some fraction as it is spent and passed through the economy by consumers. In Keynes's simplified model, domestic output is determined by these three factors: consumption plus investment plus government spending (plus net exports).

While in recessions or depressions it would be preferable for governments to spend on useful and needed projects, Keynes said that any form of spending would be preferable to a policy of inaction. As recovery takes place, government budgets might be brought back into balance and debts incurred during slumps can be paid down. Keynes argued that his approach represented a middle path, or a third way, between the failures of laissez-faire and the excesses of socialism because it was a policy of gradualism that left intact the institutions of private property and representative government.

In terms of short-term policy, there were several attractive features to the approach he outlined. First, there was the proposal to balance public spending over the business cycle in order to bring public budgets into phase with the natural ups and downs of the market economy, which meant that Keynes was not departing all that far from the principles of fiscal rectitude. In addition, he called for public borrowing mainly when interest rates were at their lowest point during the business cycle. Second, he provided policymakers with new tools to deal with slumps as alternatives to beggar-thy-neighbor trade policies like tariffs and currency devaluations, and also as alternatives to central bank credit policies that he judged to be ineffective during slumps. Third, his recommendations involved (at least from his point of view) only limited interventions into the market system. He wrote, "Apart from the necessity of central controls to bring about an adjustment between the propensity to consume and the inducement to invest, there is no more reason to socialize economic life than there was before.... It is in determining the volume, not the direction, of actual employment that the existing system has broken down."[9] Policymakers need not direct spending into this or that area of the marketplace, but simply control the general volume of spending to support consumer demand and maintain full employment. (What Keynes overlooked is that officials cannot help but direct money to particular areas of the economy when they allocate funds.)

* * *

So far, this is the "conservative" Keynes who called for modest government interventions into the economy in order to reverse slumps and to maintain full employment. He did not mount a moral attack on the market system but rather recommended adjustments to make it run more efficiently. He did not advocate nationalization of industry, the redistribution of incomes, or even the vast accumulation of government debt. He cautioned against government interventions that undermined investor confidence or interfered with investors' willingness to put money to work. He criticized President Roosevelt's National Industrial Recovery Act because he saw it as a bureaucratic interference into wage and price decisions that was likely to scare off investors. Keynes urged FDR instead to emphasize policies that stimulated consumer demand. When he was first presented with the Beveridge Report in 1942, Keynes worried about how the costly pension and welfare programs it advocated would be paid for. Surprisingly, Keynes was not a "big spender" or an advocate of expensive welfare programs. He did not immediately see that his calls for activist fiscal policy might be paired with calls coming from other directions for public spending on old-age pensions, relief for the poor, and more public services. He saw fiscal policy as an instrument to stabilize the economy and to promote full employment, but not much more.

On the other hand, *The General Theory* also contained a more radical message in regard to the relationship between the state and the private market. Keynes was already on record in earlier writings as criticizing the "moneymaking" preoccupations of investors and entrepreneurs and the moral values of thrift and work associated with market capitalism. In *The General Theory*, he might have stopped with his short-run prescriptions for dealing with business-cycle slumps. But he went from there to suggest that the state should maintain a continuously active fiscal policy to prevent slumps from happening in the first place. He went even further to argue that the state should take control of investment in order to rectify the shortage of capital that he identified as an endemic weakness of market capitalism. In his view, uncertainty would always be too great and likely returns too low to induce private investors to part with their funds at levels needed to sustain robust growth and full employment. Thus he believed that "a somewhat comprehensive socialization of investment will prove the only means of securing an approximation to full employment." Keynes looked forward to "the death of the rentier," the private investor, and he saw the state, unlike individual investors or businessmen, as being in a position "to calculate the marginal efficiency of capital goods on long views and on general social advantage."[10] The state could act (he thought) as both the "saver" and the "investor" at one and the same time, much as the wealthy entrepreneurs acted in the prewar era, thereby eliminating the need for financial intermediaries and the intricate process of translating savings into investment.

These speculations were at odds with the overall tenor of his theory, which he tried to cast as a moderate approach for correcting endemic problems in the capitalist system. Some have suggested that Keynes viewed this as an end state that would gradually be reached through systematic efforts to apply his theory. That may have been true. In any case, his statement that the state can act on the basis of "long views and the general social advantage" revealed how little he understood about the operations of democratic governments and the short-term outlook of most popularly elected politicians.

By and large, in the United States at least, it was the "conservative" Keynes that carried the day in postwar economic policy and the practice of economics in colleges and universities. Robert Lekachman called it "commercial" Keynesianism because it emphasized growth over redistribution, and he distinguished it from "liberal" Keynesianism as advanced by economists like John Kenneth Galbraith who saw Keynes's doctrine as an opportunity to expand the welfare state and tame the business sector. In the 1960s, Lekachman could write that, "In the calm which has followed a new national consensus, it is possible to see that Keynesian economics is not conservative, liberal, or radical. The techniques of economic stimulation and stabilization are simply neutral administrative tools. Keynes's personal history and the early affiliation of liberals and radicals with Keynesian doctrine have obscured this vital point."[11] This was undoubtedly an overstatement and an oversimplification, particularly in view of what happened later, but it was a sound expression of the intellectual and political consensus of the time.

The postwar boom in the United States contributed immensely to the momentum behind the "Keynesian revolution" both in public policy and in academic economics. Partly for this reason, Keynes achieved greater influence in the United States in the postwar period than in any other Western nation.[12] Keynesian ideas spread first through the economics profession in the 1940s and 1950s before fully taking hold in the political world when John F. Kennedy entered the presidency in 1961. It was a fortuitous juxtaposition of circumstances that allowed economists to work out the macro-economic details and implications of Keynes's treatise at the same time that policymakers had the resources at their disposal to put his policies into action. Economists and policymakers facilitated the revolution by emphasizing goals about which everyone agreed: economic growth and full employment. This is one reason why many economists could claim that Keynesianism was a neutral administrative tool.

By the mid-1960s, when the editors of *Time* wrote that "We are all Keynesians now," the revolution was essentially complete. Keynesians had largely taken over the economics profession, and the Kennedy-Johnson administration was busy putting Keynesian policies into operation at the national level. Even Richard Nixon could announce that he was "a Keynesian in economics" as he slapped wage and price controls on the U.S. economy in 1971.

The Keynesian consensus began to come apart in the 1960s, first when some influential liberals (Galbraith most prominently among them) began to question growth and production for their own sake, and then more dramatically in the 1970s when inflation and unemployment provided openings for conservatives and market-oriented economists to question the effectiveness of Keynesian policies and point to "big government" as a cause of the nation's economic troubles. In that decade, both Friedrich Hayek and Milton Friedman won Nobel Prizes in economics for work that challenged Keynes's theories and the consensus that had formed around them. Margaret Thatcher and Ronald Reagan moved that debate to a higher plane in the 1980s as they implemented policies to reduce marginal tax rates and free up the British and American economies from regulatory burdens. During that period, Keynesian advisers were largely absent from influential government posts in the United States.

The success of those measures tended to polarize the economic debate, as advocates of Keynesian and "classical" free-market theories moved into rival political parties, think tanks, and academic departments. This is one of the elements of the polarized politics of the present time. The so-called "classical" theory, which many thought Keynes had buried in the 1930s, returned in full force in the 1980s as an alternative to the Keynesian consensus. As things turned out, the financial crisis of 2008 did not end the debate, as many thought it should have, but rather intensified it by providing a new occasion for quarrels over stimulus packages, taxes, and regulation. The financial crisis and the policy response to it proved that the "age of Keynes" had not yet run its course, in large part because Keynes's ideas were now woven into the fabric of national politics and the American state. At this point, extricating them would probably require a "revolution" similar to that which occurred in the 1930s and 1940s.

* * *

In making his economic case, Keynes meant to overturn not just the "classical" theory of economics but also the doctrine of limited government linked to it. In economics and economic policy he emphasized consumption, debt, and public spending as foundations for growth, rather than thrift, saving, and laissez-faire. In opposition to Schumpeter, he argued that if capitalism was to be saved, it had to be placed on a modern moral foundation in which spending, consumption, and debt were no longer seen as vices. He looked forward to a stage of capitalism when scarcity would be overcome, along with the harsh moral principles associated with it. Keynes understood that the revolution he proposed in economics had to be accompanied by corresponding breakthroughs in morality, culture, and political institutions.

The political economists of the eighteenth and nineteenth centuries saw a strictly limited state as an elemental feature of an efficiently operating market system. It was for this purpose that they devised the constitutional rules and institutional checks that we associate with the liberal states of that time. The architects of this classical liberal order saw the state as a threat to liberty and therefore tried to tie it down through various constitutional, legal, and political constraints. The new roles that Keynes assigned to the state were precisely the kind that liberal constitutions were designed to preclude: large public expenditures, public borrowing, and political management of economic affairs. In challenging the classical theory of economics, Keynes also challenged the political doctrine of classical liberalism to which it was attached.

Keynes never spelled out a theory of the state to correspond to his economic theory of public spending and investment. He did acknowledge in the final chapter of *The General Theory* that in order to maintain full employment the state would have to take on functions never envisioned by those earlier proponents of liberal government. These would include setting tax rates to promote consumption and directing investment to productive and socially useful goals. Yet he was never specific about how the state should organize itself to carry out these functions.

There is one obvious requirement for a Keynesian-style system: the state must command resources at a level commensurate with its responsibility to stabilize the economy. This condition was never met through most of the history of the United States. From 1800 to 1932, the U.S. federal government never had a budget that exceeded 3 percent of GDP except in times of war, when it exceeded that percentage for brief periods. During that long period, the federal government had few responsibilities beyond national defense and running the postal service, and relied mainly on the tariff to fund its operations. In 1930, at the onset of the Depression, the federal government spent about 2.5 percent of GDP, a proportion far too small to enable it to leverage enough debt to stimulate consumer demand across the economy. Federal spending increased to 10 percent of GDP by 1940, on the eve of World War II, then increased four- or fivefold during the war years, before stabilizing throughout the postwar era at around 20 percent of GDP—or at a level large enough to finance Keynesian-style policies.

The Keynesian revolution, in order to succeed, also had to push back against inherited suspicions about government debt. In 1932, both President Hoover and FDR campaigned for the presidency in favor of a balanced federal budget. Throughout the nineteenth century, leaders of both political parties in the United States expressed horror at the prospect of a permanent public debt. After the Civil War, Republican Party platforms consistently inveighed against government debt and in favor of the tariff to finance limited federal operations. From 1800 to 1932, total U.S. government debt never surpassed 20 percent of national GDP except during wars, after which the debts were rapidly paid off. But by 1940, total federal debt approached 40 percent of GDP and then increased to more than 100 percent of GDP by the end of the war. Rapid growth in the postwar period enabled the government to reduce that total back to about 40 percent of GDP by the late 1960s, after which time it began to grow again as a result of slowing economic growth and the burdens of increasing expenditures to pay for Great Society programs. From the late 1960s to the present, the U.S. government has achieved budget surpluses on only two occasions, notwithstanding the general prosperity of the period. Today, total federal debt (public and private) exceeds 100 percent of annual GDP and continues to grow steadily in the aftermath of the financial crisis. In 2009 and 2010, due to efforts by the Obama administration to engineer a Keynesian-style recovery from the crisis, the federal government ran budget deficits that amounted to more than 10 percent of GDP.

The most problematic element of the Keynesian state turns on the forms of political organization required to sustain it. Here, too, it stands in contrast to the classical liberal state. The dominant political parties in the United States from 1800 to the 1930s—the Democratic Party before the Civil War and the Republican Party afterward—were organized around the dispersion of political power in order to protect local or private interests. State and local governments jealously guarded their rights and privileges under the federal system. In the modern age, the fiscal power of the federal government has drawn all major interests into a national orbit, including state and local governments, whose representatives make routine pilgrimages to Washington in search of funds to cover their budgets. Both political parties—but especially the Democratic Party—organize constituent groups with interests in the federal budget, and enterprising politicians learned long ago that they could organize new voting blocs with promises of federal funds. This kind of politics—"Keynesian politics"—maintains a continuous demand for federal spending that facilitates Keynesian-style economic policies.

Yet this kind of politics also creates inflexibilities in public budgets that make it difficult to adjust fiscal policy to movements in the business cycle. Politicians have found it all too easy to increase spending and to approve stimulus programs during slumps; but those expenditures, once made, are difficult to scale back during subsequent recoveries. Every item of expenditure on the public budget develops an interest group whose main purpose is to keep it going. Under those circumstances, it is not hard to understand how and why political leaders can gradually lose control of public budgets.

Nearly eighty years after the publication of *The General Theory*, the problems that Keynes diagnosed of too much saving and obsessive thrift have given way to the opposite problems of exploding debt and uncontrolled spending. With the United States and the developed world facing new challenges of public debt and insolvent governments, the question arises as to how and on what terms the system of political economy that Keynes helped to design can be maintained in political and economic circumstances that superficially resemble those of the 1930s but in fact are far different.

* * *

There have not been all that many clear-cut cases in which efforts to apply Keynesian fiscal policies have rescued modern economies from recession or depression. FDR's spending policies during the 1930s are sometimes cited in this connection, but those policies were too inconsistent, quixotic, and uncertain in their effects to be judged as Keynesian successes. The Kennedy tax cut of 1964 is more plausibly cited as a triumph of Keynesian policy, since it was explicitly crafted by Kennedy's advisers as a demand-side stimulus and it did produce a boom, at least for a short time. It is of special interest that this effect was achieved by cutting taxes rather than by increasing expenditures. There is also the argument that our modern political economy incorporates built-in stabilizers such that recessions create automatic and self-correcting deficits; in other words, we have constructed a Keynesian system that automatically prevents or corrects for slumps. From this point of view, Keynes no longer stands for a set of policy prescriptions but rather for a fiscal system that is built into the structure of governance.

On the other hand, there are several contrary cases that must be considered, such as the British experience in the 1960s, when Keynesian policies led to a major devaluation, and the American experience in the 1970s, when similar policies resulted in "stagflation." For the past twenty-five years, since the collapse of its real estate and stock markets, Japan has tried various Keynesian-type policies, including major stimulus packages and public works programs, with little success in producing sustained growth but leaving a public debt roughly twice the size of the annual gross domestic product. The United States also enacted a Keynesian stimulus package in 2009 to deal with a major recession, but the results were disappointing. Once the funds were spent, the expansion slowed and unemployment rates began to creep up again, provoking calls for further stimulus spending. Meanwhile, government debt levels in the United States now exceed annual GDP, a condition that is manageable only so long as the nation's central bank can maintain interest rates at low levels. In the United States, Japan, and several European countries, governments have come close to expending whatever Keynesian ammunition they once had.

For a theory of such longstanding influence, this one has had decidedly mixed results when applied to real-world economies.[13] Of course, there are many economists who claim that his approach does not work at all or that the market economy adjusts much more smoothly to shocks than Keynes or his followers contend. There are others who suggest that recent experiences in Japan and the United States show the growth effects of Keynesian policies to be getting weaker with the passage of time.

One possible reason for this weakening may be that political processes in Western democracies lead gradually to an allocation of public resources that does not contribute to economic expansion but may instead hinder it. In such a situation, Keynesian spending policies might actually interfere with necessary adjustments in the economy, thereby slowing down rather than speeding up economic growth. If this is so, then the problem lies more with the political economy of Keynes than with the economics of Keynes.

This case was first advanced in 1982 by Mancur Olson in *The Rise and Decline of Nations: Economic Growth, Stagflation, and Social Rigidities.*[14] In this insightful book, Olson tried to account for the "stagflation" of the 1970s and the failure of Keynesian theories to explain it. He argued that democratic nations over time develop political rigidities that permit strategically placed interest groups to block breakthroughs in policy and to exploit political influence in order to seize shares of national income that they have neither earned nor produced. These "distributional coalitions," in Olson's terminology, are organized around struggles over "the distribution of income and wealth rather than over the production of additional output."[15] Often called "rent-seeking" coalitions, they include cartels or special-interest groups like trade or industrial unions, public employee unions, trade associations, advocacy organizations, or corporations that try to increase the incomes of their members by lobbying for legislation "to raise some price or wage or to tax some types of income at lower rates than other types of income."[16]

As rent-seeking groups accumulate and multiply their influence, they win more advantages for themselves but impose ever-greater burdens on the private economy, by blocking change or disinvestment in old industries and by diverting resources from wealth-creating to wealth-consuming uses. When an economy reaches a point where distributional coalitions are pervasive, it loses the flexibility to respond to shocks, recessions, or unanticipated changes in price levels. "The economy that has a dense network of narrow special-interest organizations will be susceptible during periods of deflation or disinflation to depression or stagflation," Olson writes.[17] The reason for this is that an unexpected deflation will expose above-market incomes and prices in the "fixed-price" sector, forcing movement out of that sector and into the "flexprice" sector where incomes, wages, and prices are set by market competition. Many will resist such moves, or not know how to accomplish them; queuing and searching costs will be high; the adjustments will force prices to fall further in the flexprice sector, reducing overall demand in the economy. An extended period of stagnation will follow as the marketplace adjusts to the distortions caused by distributional coalitions.

One might suggest that the government should then step in with the standard Keynesian remedy, borrowing money and incurring debt to arrest the deflation and to allocate funds to maintain the

above-market prices and incomes in the fixed-price sector. This in fact looks very much like what the U.S. government tried to accomplish with its $800 billion stimulus package in 2009, which was allocated disproportionately to public employee unions, university research programs, energy companies that could not get loans from banks, and bankrupt auto companies and their labor unions.*
Olson's reply might be that such remedies will have only a temporary effect because they empower distributional coalitions that do not produce wealth and growth but seek to maintain their advantages at the expense of the economy as a whole. Keynesian spending policies run up debt that everyone is obliged to repay in order to underwrite above-market incomes and prices for groups whose activities impede economic growth.

This is the reason, Olson suggests, that new states grow more rapidly than long-established ones: because new states have yet to develop rent-seeking coalitions. Thus, the United States economy grew rapidly during the nineteenth century, and the economies of Japan and West Germany similarly expanded in the two or three decades after World War II. These economies all had extended periods in which markets were free to operate and interest groups had not organized to obstruct change or to claim rents; they were open to investment and entrepreneurship, and as a consequence they enjoyed historically high rates of growth. Olson emphasizes that all three countries had gone through traumatic wars and revolutions that had the salutary effect of cleaning out existing rent-seeking groups. In the United States, such groups were wiped out by revolution and then restrained by constitutional rules that limited the power of the central government; in Germany and

---

* The General Motors (and United Auto Workers) bailout was paid for out of the Troubled Asset Relief Program, the $750 billion program adopted to allow the federal government to recapitalize banks and insurance companies by purchasing "troubled" assets.

Japan, they were eliminated by war, so that these countries started over with clean political slates. But growth and affluence led over time to the formation of rent-seeking groups that created obstacles to further expansion.

Olson has been criticized for suggesting that such rigidities are usually cleaned out by wars and revolutions—upheavals that are far worse than the problem they would solve. In the modern age, these are obviously off the table as solutions to this economic problem. Of course, the business cycle might operate in market economies to disperse at least some distributional coalitions by making above-market prices and wages more expensive for others to bear. Yet the objective of Keynes's approach was to "smooth out" the business cycle, which allows distributional coalitions to persist over the long run, even as new ones are forming. The fact that some governments (like that of the United States) can incur debt almost without limit means that this process of underwriting distributional coalitions by government spending can be extended well into the future, or at least until that borrowing capacity is called into question. But the distributional coalitions and the debt are both burdens on future growth.

Thus, in an economy where distributional coalitions are numerous and powerful, the Keynesian remedies (or at least spending remedies) may be ineffectual in restoring consumer demand, private sector investment, and economic growth. Keynesian spending policies may in fact encourage the formation of distributional coalitions that eventually render those policies less effective. In the process, political friction builds between influential rent-seeking groups and those who are compelled to fund their benefits. This is the political flaw hidden within Keynes's theory.*

---

* The consequences for party politics are further discussed in Chapter 5 below.

* * *

The "age of Keynes" has now lasted about seventy-five years, or roughly as long as the "age of laissez-faire" that preceded it. Is this era approaching an end under the pressures of the long recession, the financial crisis, accumulating public debt, the demands of distributional coalitions and the political tensions they generate? Keynes himself argued that the capitalist system evolves through stages by the development of new organizational forms and by its dynamic process of invention and destruction. There is thus no reason to assume that the "age of Keynes" represents a permanent or final stage in the evolution of capitalism. One prospect is likely: the United States, and advanced economies in general, are in the early stages of an upheaval that will test the Keynesian system to its limits.

CHAPTER THREE

The New Deal Metaphor

Much as generals make the mistake of fighting the last war, politicians are prone to recycle old nostrums that were previously successful in getting us (and them) out of one crisis or another. The financial meltdown of 2008 thus led to a revival of Keynesian public-spending remedies and the dream of replaying FDR's New Deal. So strong is the hold of the New Deal over the liberal imagination that few people stop to consider how different the world is today from the one that Franklin Roosevelt faced when he took office in 1933 at the very bottom of the Great Depression.

It was not surprising, following Barack Obama's election in 2008, to hear liberal pundits and Democrats in Congress calling for another New Deal and a rerun of Roosevelt's "first hundred days," but even more ambitious this time. One influential columnist called our new president "Franklin Delano Obama," while lamenting that the original New Deal was far too modest and lacking in vision to achieve reform on the required scale. Shortly after the election, an issue of *Time* magazine carried on its cover an image of the president-elect's face merged into a famous photo of FDR in a convertible, wearing a fedora and a wide smile. Accompanying the image was an article titled "The New New Deal," drawing parallels between Roosevelt's leadership during the Depression and the opportunities now arrayed before Obama. Many said (with much relief) that the financial collapse combined with Democratic electoral sweeps marked the end of the Reagan–Thatcher era with its focus on free markets, open trade, and low taxes.

President Obama and his advisers have been of two minds about these associations with FDR, at times embracing them to burnish his image as a reformer and at others rebuffing them out of concern that he may not be able to fulfill the hopes thereby ignited. They did, however, adopt the concept of a New Deal–type stimulus package including funds for public works programs, "clean" sources of energy, and other projects designed to stimulate consumer demand and create new jobs. The *Wall Street Journal* reported, "President-elect Obama is promising to intervene in the economy in ways that Washington hasn't tried since the 1970s, favoring some industries and products while hobbling others." It is sobering to recall that the policy experiments of the 1970s, which gave us a decade of alternating recession and inflation, were modeled on the New Deal. There was little reason to expect that they would work any better today.

The New Deal metaphor in wide circulation today is based on a misconception: the belief that the kind of interventions that were effective during the Great Depression are the right medicine for dealing with a financial crisis and a stagnant economy today. This misconception rests in turn on a faulty analysis of the recent past: the notion that the market-oriented policies of the past quarter century were a great mistake and should be replaced by a more coordinated set of policies that (it is argued) will yield more stable growth and a fairer distribution of income. Thus the New Deal metaphor is now invoked as a call to overturn the free-market revolution of the 1980s, just as the New Deal threw overboard the Wall Street–favored policies of the 1920s. Such hopes are based on a fairytale version of the New Deal and a highly ideological interpretation of recent history.

*   *   *

The New Deal was erected in an unprecedented calamity, with the American economy at a near standstill. Between 1929 and 1933, unemployment rose from 3 to 25 percent of the workforce, national output fell by more than 30 percent, the dollar value of U.S. exports fell by more than two-thirds, the stock market dropped close to 90 percent, and more than a third of the nation's banks failed. The Great Depression, as it came to be called to distinguish it from the mini-depressions of the 1870s and 1890s, was a catastrophe on a scale far beyond what anyone previously thought was possible. No one knew what to do about it, certainly not Franklin Roosevelt, who had campaigned on a platform calling for a balanced budget.

When FDR took office, things were about as bad as they could possibly get, and there was little reason to worry about what we would today call "downside risk." Thus, Roosevelt took an experimental approach to the crisis, adopting various contradictory policies in the hope that some of them might work to reverse the slide. He also had more room to maneuver than is the case with policymakers now, operating as he did in an environment in which the federal government spent (in 1932) only about 3 percent of GDP, by contrast with today's 20-plus percent. There were no social programs to speak of. The economic collapse removed the traditional political restraints on federal spending, while international factors of trade and exchange rates did not significantly restrict Roosevelt's options after he took the United States off the gold standard. Thus there was much room to increase federal spending, and, by blaming the rich for the catastrophe, FDR had a justification for raising their taxes.

At that time, however, the federal government did not command a large enough share of the economy to "prime the pump" with Keynesian-style deficits. (That would come later.) Since most workers were employed on farms or in factories, they could be diverted in a time of high unemployment to public works programs, building roads, bridges, and schools. FDR did not have to worry about putting hordes of unemployed investment bankers, lawyers, or accountants back to work; nor did he have to worry about environmental regulations or cumbersome permitting rules of the kind that hold up road and bridge building today. Any public works program proposed on the model of Roosevelt's Works Progress Administration would now have to be tailored to the characteristics of the unemployed in a service economy, to the current regulatory environment, and to the objections of public sector unions.

Some of the most constructive and long-lasting features of the New Deal are those that today's would-be reformers ignore when calculating its achievements—most particularly, the broad financial reforms that FDR implemented during his first hundred days. He moved quickly in 1933 to address the failures in the financial system that were obvious sources of the continuing deflation and downward spiral in the economy, immediately declaring a bank "holiday" (to stop bank panics) and removing the United States from the gold standard to free the Federal Reserve from its deflationary restrictions. In short order, Congress approved a series of reforms that created a system of deposit insurance, brought more banks under the supervision of the Treasury and the Federal Reserve, established standards of transparency in the public sale of securities, and built a wall of separation between commercial and investment banks in order to curtail the speculation with bank deposits that many saw as a cause of bank failures. Roosevelt also effectively devalued the U.S. dollar in relation to gold, raising the exchange value from $21 to $35 per ounce. In combination, these measures stopped the slide and re-established the banking system on a stronger and more stable foundation. Most of them continue to function today as underpinnings of the financial system (save for the split between commercial and investment banks, which was repealed in 1999).

At the same time, many of the New Deal measures most favored by reformers today were either unhelpful or counterproductive in addressing the economic crisis. FDR's farm programs, designed to raise prices by cutting agricultural production, may have helped some farmers, but they did not promote farm exports nor did they help consumers with tight family budgets. In a misguided effort to raise prices, New Deal functionaries destroyed meat and produce and took cropland out of production even as hungry Americans stood in bread lines. The National Industrial Recovery Act (NIRA), designed to bring unions and corporations together to set prices, production levels, and working conditions, proved to be a bureaucratic tangle as businessmen tried to use it to guarantee profits, unions to drive up wages, and government officials to expand public power. Through its complex codes, NIRA succeeded not only in raising prices—a dubious achievement—but also in sowing confusion throughout the economy as to what business practices were and were not permitted. It was soon declared unconstitutional by the Supreme Court and FDR never tried to revive it.

The main elements of the so-called Second New Deal—the Social Security Act, the National Labor Relations Act, and the Revenue Act of 1935—added new burdens to business in the form of payroll taxes, higher corporate taxes, and collective bargaining for labor unions. Whatever their long-term benefits, these measures did not improve the climate for investment and job creation in the 1930s. The NLRA, predictably, led to more union organization and to a spike in industrial strikes. The passage of these measures was accompanied by a good deal of antibusiness rhetoric, which was not helpful either. Indeed, the Revenue Act, because it raised the highest marginal tax rate to 78 percent, was sometimes called the "soak-the-rich tax." When a severe recession followed in 1937 and 1938, sending the unemployment rate from 14 percent to 19 percent, FDR attributed the crisis to a "capital strike" engineered by business leaders exercising "monopoly power." Such demagoguery may have succeeded as a political strategy in deflecting blame from the administration to the business community, but it failed miserably as an approach to economic growth, as Amity Shlaes argued in *The Forgotten Man*, her counterestablishment history of the Depression era. Unemployment remained high throughout Roosevelt's second term, never going below 14 percent until the nation began to mobilize for war in 1941.

The antibusiness rhetoric of the New Dealers had its source in a misguided understanding of the causes of the Depression, which they located in industrial concentration and monopoly and an overproduction of goods that drove down prices after the stock market crash of 1929. Lurking behind all these ills, supposedly, were the rich bankers and industrialists whose speculation and abuse of monopoly power caused the entire system to collapse. But none of these factors, as economists now agree, could have caused a collapse on the scale of the Great Depression, nor could they have accounted for the generalized deflation that occurred. By April 1930, moreover, stocks had regained much of the value that had been lost in the meltdown of the previous October.

The real causes of the Depression are to be found elsewhere, and they are instructive for today's economic problems. Though economists and historians still debate the subject, several interconnected factors appear to have combined to turn a serious stock market correction in late 1929 into a full-scale depression by 1932: (1) An ill-advised tariff policy passed by Congress in 1930 to protect U.S. manufacturers had the unintended effect of shutting down international trade and U.S. exports. (2) A monetary policy adopted by the Federal Reserve raised the discount rate and allowed the money supply to shrink through 1932 even as the economy faltered.

(3) A cascade of bank failures wiped out savings and credit for large swaths of the economy. (4) A mountain of international war debt destabilized exchange rates, undermined the prewar gold standard, and impeded economic growth in debtor countries. These factors worked together in a reinforcing process from 1930 to 1933 to send the world economy into a downward spiral.

The economic collapse was thus accelerated by policy errors made by Congress and especially by monetary authorities that did nothing as the money supply contracted and banks failed. All those involved had failed to take into account and make accommodations for the unprecedented international situation created by the war. Today's financial authorities, apparently mindful of history's lessons, seem determined to prevent a replay of the falling dominoes of the 1930s. To the extent we avoid that experience, it will undoubtedly be through the use of monetary levers that were untried, unknown, or unavailable at that time.

* * *

Admirers of the New Deal point to the prosperity of the 1950s and 1960s as evidence that FDR's reforms, rather than undermining American capitalism, actually smoothed out its rough edges and permitted it to operate more efficiently. FDR himself claimed that his New Deal had saved market capitalism from its own inherent excesses. That is the case he made to critics from the business community during a campaign speech in Chicago on October 14, 1936: "It was this administration which saved the system of private profit and free enterprise after it had been dragged to the brink of ruin by these same leaders who now try to scare you." Many mainstream economists and historians have elaborated upon FDR's claims. John Kenneth Galbraith, for example, argued in *American Capitalism* (1952), *The Affluent Society* (1958), and *The New Industrial State* (1967) that the New Deal put into place a modern economy in which large corporations and labor unions control markets and work with government to maintain demand for products and to set wages and prices. Such a system, he contended, was required by technological advances that called for large business enterprises, which in turn needed to be regulated by government in the public interest.

The corporatist ideal, along with a bipartisan foreign policy, was a pillar of the governing consensus during the Eisenhower and Kennedy–Johnson years. Conservative Republicans were sorely disappointed when Eisenhower maintained the essential contours of the New Deal following his landslide election. Richard Nixon also endorsed that consensus, declaring in January 1971 that he was "now a Keynesian in economics." That year, he removed the dollar from the international gold standard and imposed wage and price controls in the hope of battling inflation. By the mid-1970s, though, it was clear that the policy prescriptions of the New Deal—stimulus packages, loose money, job training programs, bailouts of bankrupt cities and corporations—had failed to stem the accelerating "stagflation."

The postwar governing consensus was built upon a temporary and artificial situation in which America's chief competitors in Asia and Europe were on the sidelines as a result of the war. It took at least two decades for those economies to recover (with American aid) to the point where they could compete with American industry in fields like automobiles, steel, and energy. The U.S. economy operated at high levels during the 1950s and 1960s, exporting products around the world and maintaining balance-of-payments surpluses, notwithstanding the high personal and corporate taxes, the regulatory structure, and the adversarial labor unions that were the legacies of the New Deal.

That system came under increasing stress in the 1970s as the global economy began to impinge on those comfortable postwar arrangements, as European and Japanese companies challenged our industrial supremacy with high-quality and efficiently produced exports, and as the oil shocks of 1973 and 1979 caused energy prices to soar. By early 1980, unemployment was running at 7.5 percent, inflation at 14 percent, and interest rates at 21 percent—marking a decade of slow growth and inflation.

Liberals have often criticized Ronald Reagan's policies of low marginal tax rates, deregulation of business, and free trade as an ideologically motivated attack on key features of the New Deal. It would be more accurate, though, to view those policies as adaptations to a changing global economy and as remedies for a severe and prolonged economic crisis. Some such measures would have had to be adopted sooner or later to break the cycle of inflation and unemployment. Those adjustments in policy have been ratified not only by two decades of robust growth but also by the tacit endorsement of leading Democrats. After all, despite much weeping and wailing, prominent Democrats gradually accommodated themselves to the new framework, much as President Eisenhower adapted his administration to the New Deal reforms. President Clinton, after being elected to reverse the Reagan-era policies, instead signed the North American Free Trade Agreement, kept marginal tax rates low, did little to promote unionization, and signed a welfare reform bill that dismantled a main feature of FDR's Social Security Act of 1935. As a consequence of these steps, Clinton left office with a strong economic record.

* * *

The desire to overturn the market revolution that began in the 1980s and replace it with an updated version of the New Deal was thus the ultimate snare for Democrats when the Obama administration began. High marginal and corporate tax rates, managed trade and protectionism, the undoing of NAFTA and other trade agreements, private sector unionization, new health-care mandates on business, subsidies for politically favored industries, increases in public sector employment—all of which have been enacted or proposed in one form or another during the Obama presidency—are a recipe for an extended period of slow growth and stagnation. The recovery from the recession of 2008 has thus been the most anemic of all postwar recoveries, with annual growth rates rarely exceeding 2 percent. President Obama's decision to embrace a "government agenda" rather than a "growth agenda" is largely responsible for this unfortunate outcome, which is discrediting Democrats once again as ham-fisted on the great question of economic growth. While this approach has been much to the advantage of Republicans, it has done immeasurable harm to the country, which may take decades to repair.

A wiser though less exciting course would have been to accept the inherited framework of policy with its emphasis on growth rather than redistribution, while finding other avenues by which to address Democratic priorities. More than six years into the Obama presidency, it is now far too late to reverse course. The Obama years are destined to be recalled as a time of wasted opportunity and stagnation for the American economy. One hopes that things will not get worse over his final two years in office, though that possibility cannot be discounted. If the president and his supporters wanted to find inspiration in the New Deal, they could have done worse than to look to FDR's successful efforts to modernize the financial system as a foundation for economic recovery. FDR understood, even if many of his aides and advisers did not, that if a party in power cannot deliver economic growth, there is little else that it can hope to accomplish.

⤜

A version of this chapter appeared in *The Weekly Standard*, January 19, 2009.

CHAPTER FOUR

American Capitalism and the 'Inequality Crisis'

Just as the Great Depression launched an expansion of government powers and programs, and the financial crisis of 2008 led to calls for another New Deal, liberals and progressives over the past five decades have announced a variety of other "crises" as reasons to raise taxes, adopt expensive government programs, impose new regulations on business, or, perhaps, to increase their own influence. In the 1960s they gave us the "poverty crisis" and the "urban crisis," followed in the 1970s and 1980s by the "environmental crisis," the "energy crisis," and the "homeless crisis." More recently we have had the "health-care crisis" and a civilization-threatening "global warming crisis," now rebaptized as a "climate crisis." Some progressives have found it useful to turn multifaceted problems into crises in order to stampede the voters into supporting policies they might otherwise (quite sensibly) reject.

Today, the issue of the hour is the "inequality crisis," another complex subject that is being seized upon in some quarters as an opportunity to raise taxes, attack "the rich," and discredit policies that gave us three decades of prosperity, booming real estate and stock markets, and an expanding global economy. In recent years, journalists and academics have been turning out books and manifestos bearing such titles as *The New Gilded Age*; *The Killing Fields of Inequality*; *The Great Divergence: America's Growing Inequality Crisis and What We Can Do About It*; and *The Price of Inequality: How Today's Divided Society Endangers Our Future*—to list just a few of the many dozens on the subject. The common message of these books is not subtle: "the rich" have manipulated the political system to lay claim to wealth they have not earned and do not deserve, and they have done so at the expense of everyone else.

In the past, those who wrote about inequality focused on poverty and the challenge of elevating the poor into the working and middle classes. No more. Today they are preoccupied with "the rich" and with schemes to redistribute their wealth downward through the population, as if it were possible to raise the living standards of the bottom "99 percent" by raising taxes on the top "1 percent." Many of the new egalitarians—professors at Ivy League universities, well-paid journalists, or heirs to family wealth—are themselves materially comfortable by any reasonable standard. Their complaints about "the rich" or "the 1 percent" call to mind Samuel Johnson's barbed comment about the reformers of his day: "Sir," he said, "your levelers wish to level down as far as themselves; but they cannot bear leveling up to themselves." Judging by recent polls, the wider public has not bought into this new crisis. In essence, members of the top 2 or 3 percent of the income distribution are waging class warfare against the top 1 percent while everyone else looks on from a distance, apparently feeling that the new class struggle has little to do with their own circumstances.

* * *

The controversy over inequality gained more fuel in 2014 with the publication of Thomas Piketty's *Capital in the Twenty-First Century*,* a

---

* Translated by Arthur Goldhammer, Belknap Press (Harvard University), 2014.

dense and data-filled work of economic history that makes the case against inequality far more extensively and exhaustively than any that has appeared heretofore. The book quickly climbed to the top of the bestseller lists and remained there for several weeks. All the attention quickly turned Piketty, a scholarly-looking professor at the Paris School of Economics, into something of a literary celebrity and made his treatise a rallying point for those favoring income redistribution and higher taxes on "the rich."

The *New York Times* called Piketty "the newest version of a now-familiar specimen: the overnight intellectual sensation whose stardom reflects the fashions and feelings of the moment." Paul Krugman, in a review essay in the *New York Review of Books*, called the book "magnificent" and wrote that "it will change both the way we think about society and the way we do economics." Martin Wolf of the *Financial Times* described it as "extraordinarily important," while a reviewer for the *Economist* suggested that Piketty's book is likely to change the way we understand the past two centuries of economic history. The *Nation* called it "the most important study of inequality in over fifty years." Not since the 1950s and 1960s when John Kenneth Galbraith published *The Affluent Society* and *The New Industrial State* has an economist written a book that has garnered so much public attention and critical praise.

Liberals and progressives have hailed *Capital in the Twenty-First Century* as the indictment of free-market capitalism they have been waiting decades to hear. The market revolutions of the last three decades have placed them on defense in public debates over taxation, regulation, and inequality, and Piketty's book provides them with intellectual ammunition to fight back. It documents their belief that inequalities of income and wealth have grown rapidly in recent decades in the United States and across the industrial world, and it portrays our own time as a new "gilded age" of concentrated wealth and out-of-control capitalism. It suggests that things are getting worse for nearly everyone, save for a narrow slice of the population that lives off exploding returns to capital. It pointedly supports the progressive agenda of redistributive taxation.

Some reviewers have compared *Capital in the Twenty-First Century* to Karl Marx's *Das Kapital*, both for its similarity in title and for its updated analysis of the historical dynamics of the capitalist system. Though Piketty deliberately chose his title to promote the association with Marx's tome, he is not a Marxist or a socialist, as he reminds the reader throughout the book. He does not endorse collective ownership of the means of production, historical materialism, class struggle, the labor theory of value, or the inevitability of revolution. He readily acknowledges that communism and socialism are failed systems. He wants to reform capitalism, not destroy it.

At the same time, he shares Marx's assumption that returns to capital are the dynamic force in modern economies, and like Marx he claims that such returns lead ineluctably to concentrations of wealth in fewer and fewer hands. For Piketty, as for Marx, capitalism is all about "capital," and not much more. Along the same lines, he also argues that there is an intrinsic conflict between capital and labor in market systems so that higher returns to capital must come at the expense of wages and salaries. This, in his view, is the central problem of the capitalist process: returns to capital grow more rapidly than returns to labor. Rather like Marx in this respect, he advances an interpretation of market systems that revolves around just a few factors: the differential returns to capital and labor, and the distribution of wealth and income through the population.

Though he borrows some ideas from Marx, Piketty writes more from the perspective of a modern progressive or social democrat. His book, written in French but translated into English, bears many features of that ideological perspective, particularly in its focus on the distribution rather than the creation of wealth, in its emphasis on progressive taxation as the solution to the inequality problem, and in the confidence it expresses that governments can manage modern economies in the interests of a more equal distribution of incomes. Piketty is worried mainly about equality and economic security, much less so about freedom, innovation, and economic growth.

The popularity of his book is another sign that established ideas never really die but go in and out of fashion with changing circumstances. Liberals, progressives, and social democrats were shocked by the comeback of free-market ideas in the 1980s after they assumed those ideas had been buried once and for all by the Great Depression. In a similar vein, free-market and "small government" advocates are now surprised by the return of social-democratic doctrines that they assumed had been refuted by the "stagflation" of the 1970s and the success of low-tax policies in the 1980s and 1990s. Piketty's book has garnered so much attention because it is the best statement we have had in some time of the redistributionist point of view.

* * *

For all the attention and praise it has received, the book is a flawed production in at least three important respects. First, it mischaracterizes the past three or four decades as a time of false rather than real prosperity, and it distorts the overall history of American and European capitalism by judging it in terms of the single criterion of equality versus inequality. Second, it misunderstands the sources of the "new inequality." Third, the solutions it proposes will make matters worse for everyone—the wealthy, the middle class, and the poor alike. The broader problem with the book is that it advances a narrow understanding of the market system, singling out returns to capital as its central feature and ignoring the really important factors that account for its success over a period of two and a half centuries.

Piketty addresses an old question dating back to the nineteenth century: Does the capitalist process tend over time to produce more equality or more inequality in incomes and wealth?

The consensus view throughout the nineteenth century was that rising inequality was an inevitable byproduct of the capitalist system. In the United States, Thomas Jefferson tried to preserve an agricultural society for as long as possible in the belief that the industrial system would destroy the promise of equality upon which the new nation was based. In Great Britain early in the nineteenth century, David Ricardo argued that because agricultural land was scarce and finite, landowners would inevitably claim larger shares of national wealth at the expense of laborers and factory owners. Later, as the industrial process gained steam, Marx argued that competition among capitalists would lead to ownership of capital in the form of factories and machinery becoming concentrated in fewer and fewer hands, while workers continued to be paid subsistence wages. Marx did not foresee that productivity-enhancing innovations, perhaps together with the unionization of workers, would cause wages to rise and thereby allow workers to enjoy more of the fruits of capitalism.

Perspectives on the inequality issue changed in the twentieth century due to rising incomes for workers, continued improvements in worker productivity, the expansion of the service sector and the welfare state, and the general prosperity of the postwar era. In addition, the Great Depression and two world wars tended to wipe out the accumulated capital that had sustained the lifestyles of the upper classes. In the 1950s, Simon Kuznets, a prominent American economist, showed that wealth and income disparities leveled out in the United States between 1913 and 1952. On the basis of his research, he proposed the so-called "Kuznets Curve" to illustrate his conclusion that inequalities naturally increased in the early phases of the industrial process but then declined as the process matured, as workers relocated from farms to cities, and as "human capital" replaced physical capital as a source of income and wealth. His thesis suggested that modern capitalism would gradually produce a middle-class society in which incomes did not vary greatly from the mean. This optimistic outlook was nicely expressed in John F. Kennedy's oft-quoted remark that "a rising tide lifts all boats."

From the perspective of 2014, Piketty makes the case that Marx was far closer to being right than Kuznets. In his view, Kuznets was simply looking at data from a short period of history and made the error of extrapolating his findings into the future. Piketty argues that capitalism, left to its own devices, creates a situation in which returns to capital grow more rapidly than returns to labor and the overall growth in the economy.

This is Piketty's central point, which he takes to be a basic descriptive theorem of the capitalist order. He tries to show that when returns to capital exceed growth in the economy for many decades or generations, wealth and income accrue disproportionately to owners of capital, and capital assets gradually claim larger shares of national wealth, generally at the expense of labor. This, he maintains, is something close to an "iron law" of the capitalist order.

He estimates on the basis of his research that since 1970 the market value of capital assets has grown steadily in relation to national income in all major European and North American economies. In the United States, for example, the ratio increased from almost 4:1 in 1970 to nearly 5:1 today, in Great Britain from 4:1 to about 6:1, and in France from 4:1 to 7:1. Measured from a different angle, income from capital also grew throughout this period as a share of national income. From 1980 to the present, income from capital grew in the United States from 20 to 25 percent of the national total, in Great Britain from 18 to nearly 30 percent, and in France from 18 to about 25 percent. These changes weigh heavily in

Piketty's narrative, which stresses the outsized role that capital has seized in recent decades in relation to labor income.

There is nothing original or radical in the proposition that returns to capital generally exceed economic growth. Economists and investors regard it as a truism, at least over the long run. For example, the long-term returns on the U.S. stock market are said to be around 7 percent per annum (minus taxes and inflation) while real growth in the overall economy has been closer to 3 percent. This is generally thought to be a good thing, since returns to capital encourage investment, and this in turn drives innovation, productivity, and economic growth.

But it does not follow that returns to capital, even if they are greater than overall growth in incomes, must be concentrated in a few hands instead of being distributed widely in pension funds, retirement accounts, college and university endowments, individual savings, dividends, and the like. Nor is it true that higher returns to capital must come at the expense of labor, since growing productivity advances the standard of living for everyone; workers benefit along with everyone else when their savings or pensions grow with increasing returns to capital. The low and still falling interest rates of recent decades suggest that returns for at least some forms of capital are similarly falling. There is also a natural check on the concentration of capital: owners of capital die sooner or later, at which time their assets are disbursed through estate taxes, charitable gifts, and bequests to heirs.

Why, then, has capital grown in recent decades as a share of national income and in relation to labor income? The answer is to some extent embedded in Piketty's definition of "capital." He defines "capital" in a broad way to include not only inputs into the production process, like factories, equipment, and machinery, but also stocks, bonds, personal bank deposits, university and foundation endowments, and residential real estate—all assets that are subject to substantial year-to-year fluctuations in market value. In his measure of "capital," then, Piketty is undoubtedly incorporating the explosion in asset prices that has occurred since the early 1980s, especially in stocks and to a lesser degree in real estate as well.

Many reviewers of *Capital in the Twenty-First Century* have slighted Piketty's larger themes of the "iron law" of capitalism, the increasing returns to capital, and the competition between labor and capital for shares of national income. Instead, every major review of the book dwells at length on its documentation of rising inequality and its call for new and higher taxes on the wealthy. Piketty sees inequality as an inevitable byproduct of modern capitalism, and substantially higher taxes as the only means of remedying it.

He has assembled a wealth of data that allow him to trace the distribution of wealth and incomes in the United States and Western Europe from late in the nineteenth century to the present day. His analysis yields a series of U-shaped charts showing that the shares of wealth and income claimed by the top 1 percent or 10 percent of households peaked between 1910 and 1930, then declined and stabilized during the middle decades of the century, and then began to rise again after 1980.

In the United States in the decades before the Great Depression, the top 1 percent received around 18 percent of total income and owned about 45 percent of total wealth. Those figures fell to around 10 percent (share of income) and 30 percent (share of wealth) between 1930 and 1980, at which point these shares started to grow again. As of 2010, the top 1 percent in the United States received nearly 18 percent of total incomes and owned about 35 percent of the total wealth. The pattern is similar for the top 10 percent of the income and wealth distributions. Before the Great Depression, from 1910 to 1930, this group claimed about 45 percent of national income and between 80 percent of the wealth; between 1930 and 1980, those shares fell to roughly 30 percent (income) and 65 percent (wealth); and from 1980 to 2010 their shares increased again to between 40 and 50 percent (income) and 70 percent (wealth). Piketty also shows that the super-rich, the top one-tenth of 1 percent of the income distribution (about 100,000 households in 2010), increased their share of national income from about 2 percent in 1980 to nearly 8 percent in 2010. The patterns are similar in the other Anglo-Saxon countries—Great Britain, Canada, and Australia—but very different in continental Europe, where the wealthiest groups have not been able to reclaim the shares of income and wealth that they enjoyed before World War I.

There is little mystery as to the sources of the U-shaped curves in income and wealth distribution in the United States and the flatter curves in continental Europe. In Europe in particular, the two great wars of the first half of the twentieth century, combined with effects of the Great Depression, wiped out capital assets to an unprecedented degree, while progressive taxes enacted during and after World War II made it difficult for the wealthiest groups to accumulate capital at the same rates as before. In the United States, the Depression wiped out owners of stocks, and high marginal income tax rates (as high as 91 percent in the 1940s and 1950s) similarly made it difficult for "the rich" to accumulate capital. Beginning in the 1980s, as rates were reduced on incomes and capital gains, especially in the United States and Great Britain, those old patterns began to reappear.

Piketty highlights a new factor in wealth distribution since the 1980s: the dramatic rise in salaries for "supermanagers," which he defines as "top executives of large firms who have managed to obtain extremely high and historically unprecedented compensation packages for their labor." This group also includes highly compensated presidents and senior executives of major colleges, universities, private foundations, and charitable institutions, who often earn well in excess of $500,000 per year. Surprisingly, then, "the rich" today are likely to be salaried executives and managers, rather than the "coupon clippers" of a century ago who lived off returns from stocks, bonds, and real estate. "The 1 percent," in other words, are people who work for a living.

Piketty doubts that these supermanagers earn their generous salaries on the basis of merit or contributions to business profits. He also rejects the possibility that these salaries are in any way linked to the rapidly growing stock markets of recent decades. He points instead to cozy and self-serving relationships that executives establish with their boards of directors. In a sense, he suggests, they are in a position to set their own salaries as members of a "club" alongside wealthy directors and trustees.

To alleviate the growing inequality problem, Piketty advocates a return to the old regime of much higher marginal tax rates in the United States and Europe. He thinks that marginal rates in the United States could be increased to 80 percent (from 39.5 percent today) on the very rich and to 60 percent on those with incomes between $200,000 and $500,000 per year without reducing their productive efforts in any substantial way. Such taxes would hit the so-called supermanagers who earn incomes from high salaries, though it would not touch the owners of capital who take but a small fraction of their holdings in annual income.

As a remedy for this problem, Piketty advocates a global "wealth tax" on the super-rich, levied against assets in stocks, bonds, and real estate. He acknowledges that such a tax has little chance of being imposed globally, though he hopes that at some point it might be applied in the European Union. Several European countries—Germany, Finland, and Sweden among them—had a wealth tax in the past but have discontinued it. France currently has a wealth tax that tops out at a rate of 1.5 percent on assets in excess of ten million euros (or about $14 million). The United States has never had such a tax, and in fact it may not be allowed under the Constitution (which authorizes taxes on incomes).

Wealth taxes are notoriously difficult to collect, and they encourage capital flight, hiding of assets, and disputes over pricing of assets. They require individuals to sell assets to pay taxes, thereby causing asset values to fall. Piketty thinks that a capital tax would have to be global in scope to guard against capital flight and the hiding of assets in foreign accounts. It would also necessitate a new international banking regime under which major banks would be required to disclose account information to national treasuries. Under this scheme, a sliding-scale tax would be imposed, beginning at 1 percent on modest fortunes (roughly between $1.5 and $7 million) and perhaps reaching as high as 10 percent on fortunes in excess of $1 billion. Wealthy individuals like Bill Gates and Warren Buffett, with total assets in excess of $70 billion each, might have to pay as much as $7 billion annually in national wealth taxes. In the United States, with household wealth currently at around $80 trillion, such a tax, levied even at low rates of 1 or 2 percent, might yield as much as $500 billion annually. The purpose of the tax, it should be stressed, is to reduce inequality, not to spend the new revenues on beneficial public purposes.

Piketty implies that reductions in taxes over the past three decades have allowed "the rich" to accumulate money while avoiding their fair share of taxes. This is not the case at all, at least not in the United States. As income taxes and capital gains taxes were reduced in the United States beginning in the 1980s, the share of federal taxes paid by "the rich" steadily went up. From 1980 to 2010, as the top 1 percent increased their share of before-tax income from 9 to 15 percent, their share of the individual income tax soared from 17 to 39 percent of the total paid. Their share of total federal taxes more than doubled during a period when the highest marginal tax rate was cut in half, from 70 to 35.5 percent. The wealthy, in short, are already paying more than their fair share of taxes, and the growth in their wealth and incomes has had nothing to do with tax avoidance or deflecting the tax burden onto the middle class.

* * *

Piketty's estimates of wealth and income shares over the decades are probably as reliable and accurate as he or anyone else could make them, but even so they are estimates based on imperfect and inexact data often interpolated or extrapolated from entries in government records. This is especially true of his information on wealth, since governments have long maintained records on incomes (to collect taxes on incomes) but not on individual wealth. Following the publication of his book, many analysts challenged the accuracy of his data on the distribution of wealth in Great Britain and the United States. It will take some time to sort out these criticisms as other researchers attempt to replicate his analysis and as Piketty himself replies to his critics.

Even where Piketty's numbers may be accurate, they can still lead to faulty conclusions. As some critics have pointed out, he uses statistics on national income as denominators for his calculations of shares of income claimed by various groups of the population, but these figures exclude transfers from government such as Social Security payments, food stamps, rent supplements, and the like, which constitute a growing portion of incomes for many middle- and working-class people. If those transfers were included in the calculations, then the shares of income claimed by the top 1 percent or the top 10 percent would undoubtedly decline, and the shares of other groups would correspondingly increase.

Leaving these controversies aside, and accepting Piketty's data as valid for the time being, there are nevertheless good reasons to question his basic conclusions about capitalism in the twentieth century. He claims that inequality has increased since 1980, especially in the United States and Great Britain, that this kind of inequality is built into the nature of capitalism, and that it has been exacerbated by new tax policies that have cut the levies on high incomes and great wealth. These claims are greatly exaggerated.

The inequality that he measures is essentially a byproduct of the stock market boom of the last three decades. Since the early 1980s, the U.S. stock market, measured by the Dow Jones Industrial Average, has grown twentyfold; the British stock market, as measured by the FTSE 100, nearly tenfold; and the German market, measured on the DAX 30, by more than a factor of fifteen. The capitalization of world stock markets has grown from about $2 trillion in 1980 to about $60 trillion today. We have lived through an unprecedented three-decade-long bull market in stocks that no one foresaw in the 1970s. It would be surprising if such an escalation in market prices did not have a significant influence on the distribution of wealth and incomes; and it would be hazardous to forecast that such a pattern must continue indefinitely into the future.

The chart below makes the point more clearly that rising inequality is closely linked to stock market returns. The chart illustrates the strong association from 1957 to 2012 between shares of income claimed by the top 1 percent in the United States and parallel changes in the Dow Jones Industrial Average and the Standard & Poor's 500 stock index. The income data are taken from a paper published by Piketty and Emmanuel Saez and posted on Saez's website; the stock market data are taken from tables published by the St. Louis Federal Reserve Bank. For ease of illustration and comparison, the three measures are indexed to 100 in 1957; the values for the top 1 percent are shown on the left axis and the stock market values on the right. The broken line at the top charts the growth in income shares of the top 1 percent, while the dark line measures changes in the S&P 500 and the lighter line below it tracks changes in the Dow Jones Industrial Average.

Top 1% Share of National Income vs. Stock Market Performance
(1957 = 100)

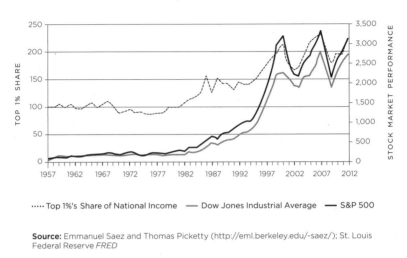

····· Top 1%'s Share of National Income   ── Dow Jones Industrial Average   ── S&P 500

Source: Emmanuel Saez and Thomas Picketty (http://eml.berkeley.edu/~saez/); St. Louis Federal Reserve *FRED*

The key point is that all three lines move in the same pattern, remaining roughly flat and stable from 1957 to 1982, then trending upward in tandem thereafter, with peaks and valleys corresponding to booms and busts in the stock markets. Inequality began to tick upward after 1980 and accelerated in the 1990s as the stock markets heated up. As the chart shows, income inequality dropped most rapidly and dramatically when the stock markets faltered, as they did in 2000 with the technology bust and, more spectacularly, in 2008 with the financial crisis. Measured statistically, there is a 0.95 correlation between changes in the income shares of the top "1 percent" and changes in the S&P 500; and a 0.96 correlation with changes in the Dow Jones Industrial Average.

These patterns strongly suggest that changes in inequality in the United States have been closely linked to the three-decade-long boom in world stock markets. When inequality rises as a result of such a boom, it is far less socially damaging than when it is caused by a bust, as in the Great Depression. Nor, in a circumstance like this, can anyone say that the owners of such assets have "stolen" their wealth from the poor or gained it through the exploitation of workers. In many cases, owners have benefited by investing in enterprises that have yielded profits and, therefore, benefits to consumers. In addition, willing buyers are driving these asset prices forward in the belief that they will yield income or that those prices will continue to increase over the long haul.

One could raise the question as to why the financial markets in the United States and elsewhere suddenly took off in the early 1980s and continued their upward movement for three-plus decades. A few possibilities suggest themselves. The period that began in 1981 or 1982 has been one of falling interest rates and disinflation, two developments that are especially beneficial to stock and real estate prices. The elimination of trade barriers, the end of the Cold War, and the entry of China, India, and various Asian countries into the world economy were also beneficial developments that reinforced the booming stock markets, but perhaps disadvantaged American workers who were now forced to compete in a global marketplace. The official termination of the gold standard paved the way for a rapid expansion of credit and debt in the 1980s. Cuts in tax rates may have played a role in the rise in stock prices, but certainly not a dominant one. No one should want to "solve" the inequality problem in the same way that it was "solved" in the 1930s—by erecting trade barriers, shutting down international trade, and crashing the stock markets.

* * *

In the broader message of his book, Professor Piketty argues that we are living through a new "gilded age" of extravagant wealth and lavish expenditures enjoyed by a narrow elite at the expense of everyone else. As with the original Gilded Age of the late nineteenth century, the wealth accruing to the few gives the illusion of progress and prosperity, but conceals growing hardships and economic difficulties endured by the rest of the population. Much of Piketty's thesis rests upon the proposition that we are living in a time of faux prosperity—a claim that is subject to debate.

Piketty divides the history of modern capitalism into three phases. First is the original Gilded Age, running in Europe from roughly 1870 to the outbreak of World War I in 1914 (a period he often calls the Belle Époque), and in the United States from the end of the Civil War to the stock market crash in 1929. The second is the golden age of social democracy, from 1930 to 1980, when progressive tax regimes and welfare programs were installed in most industrial countries. Finally there is the new "gilded age," beginning in 1980 and running to the present, a period in which those tax regimes were dismantled, marginal rates and capital gains taxes were reduced, and wealth and income began to flow once again to the very rich. Piketty documents these three historical phases with data and charts showing that the shares of wealth and income claimed by the top 1 percent or top 10 percent of households peaked in the early decades of the twentieth century, then declined and stabilized in the middle decades of the century, and then began to rise again after 1980.

This argument makes sense only if one accepts the narrow premise that these multifaceted regimes can be assessed on the basis of the single criterion of wealth and income distribution, or that the essence of the capitalist order is found solely in returns to capital and in the distribution of wealth and incomes rather than in rising living standards, innovation, and the spread of modern civilization. In each of these three eras, there was much more going on than simply the rearranging of wealth and incomes.

No less an authority than John Maynard Keynes, as we have seen, looked back on the decades leading up to World War I in Europe as a golden age of capitalism, "an extraordinary episode in the economic progress of man." Following the unification of Germany in 1871, trade accelerated across the European continent as industry expanded and population swelled. At the same time, rapid growth, stable prices, and high real wages in the United States drew millions of immigrants from Europe to build railroads and work in factories. Far-reaching innovations—electricity, the telegraph, mass-produced steel, and motorcars—drove the industrial process forward and made a few people very rich. It was the first era of globalization and open trade. Innovation, emigration toward emerging centers of wealth, and widening circles of trade have been key elements of "golden ages" throughout history, and especially in the modern age of capitalism. This particular golden age ended in 1914 in Europe and in 1929 in the United States.

As for the golden age of social democracy that followed, there is much to commend it; one should not gainsay the genuine economic and social progress achieved in the United States and elsewhere during the middle decades of the century. Nevertheless, the virtues of that time can be overstated. As Piketty acknowledges, much of the accumulated capital of the preceding era was wiped out by war and depression. Confiscatory tax rates—with marginal rates as high as 91 percent in the United States in the 1940s and 1950s—may have equalized incomes to some degree, but they also discouraged enterprise, risk taking, and innovation. The impressive growth rates of the 1950s and 1960s developed from a depressed base and by building out innovations from the earlier period. Labor unions grew and won substantial wage gains for members, but mainly because (in the United States) they were bargaining with domestic oligopolies in the auto, steel, railroad, aluminum, and other industries. The structure of American industry was highly concentrated, a circumstance that, in the opinion of some, impeded innovation. John Kenneth Galbraith wrote that cartelization was a permanent feature of the U.S. economy. There was little immigration into the

United States and Western Europe between 1930 and 1970. Most importantly for the distribution of wealth, the U.S. stock market barely moved in real terms between 1930 and 1980; in 1980, the Dow Jones Industrial Average was at a lower level (adjusted for inflation) than at its peak in 1929.

The high-tax regime collapsed in the 1970s, not because "the rich" dismantled it, but because government spending and regulation brought with them more crime, dependency, and disorder, along with simultaneously growing rates of unemployment and inflation. It was Jimmy Carter who first led the charge to deregulate the airline, railroad, trucking, and communications industries. Democrats and Republicans agreed that the U.S. economy was suffering from a shortage of capital, and that tax rates should be reduced to promote capital formation. That approach succeeded. At the same time, U.S. leaders pushed successfully for the elimination of trade barriers and a more open international trading system.

Keynes's comments about the prewar era in Europe might just as well be applied to the era from the 1980s to the present. This was the "age of Reagan," defined by the tax and regulatory reforms that President Reagan set in place. Far from being a "gilded age," it appears from a broader perspective to have been a new golden age of capitalism, marked by life-changing innovations in technology, globalized markets and widening circles of trade, unprecedented levels of immigration into centers of prosperity, the absence of major wars, rising living standards around the world, falling inflation and interest rates, and a thirty-year bull market in stocks, bonds, and real estate. The prosperity of the period sustained the major social programs of the New Deal and the Great Society. At the same time, the boom in financial assets and real estate has also enriched the endowments of colleges, universities, and foundations, along with pension and retirement funds upon which millions of households depend.

These developments broke up the concentrated structure of the

U.S. economy, making it more open, competitive, and innovative. At the same time, corporate profits are far higher now than in the age of industrial concentration and oligopoly. The end of the Cold War and the entrance of China into the world economy similarly broke open the structure of world politics and finance that dominated the middle decades of the century. Meanwhile, levels of poverty and inequality around the world have declined dramatically over the past three decades. Though some individuals have won incredible riches in this new age of capitalism, they have done so by developing new products and technologies of benefit to everyone or by investing in enterprises that earn profits by satisfying customers. The inequality that we see today is interwoven into this regime of innovation, globalization, and rising stock prices. It cannot be eliminated or even substantially ameliorated without also taking out the whole regime.

Keynes once remarked that the challenge in such a situation is to keep the boom going—not bring it to a premature end in the superstitious belief that those who have prospered must be punished by high taxes and stifling regulations. Those errors have been made in the past, most spectacularly in the 1930s, and it isn't only the rich who are punished. The most recent golden age of capitalism is bound to end sooner or later, but if Professor Piketty and his supporters have their way, it will be sooner.

CHAPTER FIVE

America's Fourth Revolution

The acclaim that greeted *Capital in the Twenty-First Century* reflected a widespread agreement with Thomas Piketty's belief that the industrial world generally and the United States particularly are heading for a crisis of inequality and that government action is required to mitigate it. Barack Obama and many others in the Democratic Party share this view. According to Obama, economic inequality means that our system of free-market capitalism "has never worked," and for many people the financial meltdown of 2008 added weight to that argument. Several years later, there are signs that our system may indeed be on the verge of a new crisis, but the revolution may not occur as Piketty and Obama envision it.

If there is an upheaval in the near future, it will not be unprecedented in our nation's history. The United States has been shaped by three far-reaching political revolutions since its founding: Jefferson's "revolution of 1800," the Civil War, and the New Deal. Each of these upheavals concluded with lasting institutional and cultural adjustments that set the stage for new phases of political and economic development. The United States could not have developed into the multiracial, multiethnic superpower that we know today without the upheavals that facilitated territorial expansion in the early 1800s, ended slavery in the 1860s, and laid the basis for the regulatory and entitlement state in the 1930s and 1940s. If we are approaching a "fourth revolution," what kind will it be?

Barack Obama likes to think of himself as a revolutionary or transformational figure on the order of Abraham Lincoln and Franklin Delano Roosevelt. After his re-election, he and his supporters had more reason to see their multicultural coalition as the wave of the future in American politics, and there are demographic trends to support that interpretation. At the same time, there are also political forces working in the opposite direction, such as the "Tea Party" movement, the unpopularity of "Obamacare," and a gathering mood among voters to rein in the powers and privileges of public sector unions. Many of those voters understand the ineluctable economic and financial realities of the current regime. The U.S. government has already borrowed to the hilt, the baby-boom generation is retiring, and the American economy is no longer growing at the rates of a few decades ago—certainly not at the rates of the 1950s and 1960s, when most of our costly entitlement programs were conceived and sold to the public. It is hard to see how any new government programs can be paid for; indeed, it is hard to see how those already in place will be paid for. In this light, the Obama presidency may represent the end of an era rather than the beginning of a new one.

Some people may find it difficult to imagine that our present system of social programs and entitlements might be undone because it is widely assumed that the welfare state is a historical destination with no further political possibilities beyond it—that we have at length reached the "end of history," where the future is simply a gradually improving extension of the present. This is the conventional view, and for many of us it is a comforting expectation. When systems have been in place for a long time, there is a tendency to believe that they are natural or permanent, even as their foundations may be crumbling underfoot. We should bear in mind that something similar was believed not so long ago about other deeply rooted institutions, such as slavery, the gold standard, and the British Empire.

An uprooting of long-established institutions may be rare, but that is not the same as impossible. Rare events of low probability, moreover, have disproportionate effects on our lives, as Nassim Nicholas Taleb writes in *The Black Swan*: "Almost everything in social life is produced by rare but consequential shocks and jumps, while almost everything studied about social life focuses on the 'normal,'..." We have been fortunate to live in a time when most change happens in gradual and incremental steps. But not always: many wise heads have gone wrong by making projections from current trends, as when Norman Angell wrote in 1910 that a war among the European powers was inconceivable, or when the economist Irving Fisher said in 1929 that stocks had reached a permanently high plateau, or when John Kenneth Galbraith said in the 1980s that the Soviet Union was as stable as the United States.

A "fourth revolution" in the American political system is not inconceivable; neither does it have to mean a decline of civilization or the end of America. Quite the opposite—it could launch a new phase of growth and dynamism in the American experiment.

* * *

Notwithstanding its reputation for stability and continuity, the United States seems to resolve its deepest problems in relatively brief periods of intense and destabilizing conflict. These events are what some historians have called America's "surrogates for revolution" because, rather than overthrowing the constitutional order, they adjust it to developing circumstances and insert into it new forms and meanings. More than simply electoral realignments, they are fundamental changes in the national regime—a "regime" being defined as a system of law and policy sustained over time by a durable coalition of supporters, generally organized by a political party or parties.

There are many reasons why the American system adjusts in this discontinuous fashion. The constitutional system, with its dispersed powers and competing institutional interests, resists preemptive and overarching solutions to accumulating problems. Hard decisions are finessed or postponed, "kicked down the road," to use a contemporary term. At the same time, America's dynamic economy and mobile society continuously present new challenges to which the political system cannot easily respond. At times these challenges have mounted to a point where the differences between parties and interests have been so fundamental as to defy efforts to resolve them through the established channels of party competition. New institutions must be invented or new coalitions assembled to address them. That is a point we may be approaching today.

Over the course of its 227-year history under the Constitution, the United States has been governed by three distinct regimes, each with one party dominating:

1. A Democratic-expansionist regime from 1800 until 1860, when it dissolved in the midst of the slavery and secession crisis.
2. A Republican-capitalist regime from 1865 until 1930, when it was brought down by the Great Depression.
3. A Democratic-welfare regime from 1932 until the present, albeit with faltering support after 1980.

These regimes were organized around quite different principles of national development and ended through quite different kinds of events. By and large, they achieved important goals for themselves and the nation, at least for a time. The Jefferson-Jackson regime promoted democracy (for whites), localism, and westward expansion in successive conflicts with France, Spain, Great Britain, and Mexico; it foundered on the issues of slavery in the territories and Southern nationalism. The Republican regime from the 1860s onward orchestrated the industrialization of the nation based on the concepts of economic liberty, the protective tariff, and the gold standard. The Democratic-welfare regime tried to provide economic security for the middle and working classes through social insurance, support for labor unions, and stabilization of the economy by federal spending.

There are parallels in the birth and life of these regimes that may provide clues to what we might expect in any new upheaval. The pivotal events that gave rise to each regime—Jefferson's revolution, the sectional conflict, and the crisis of the 1930s and 1940s—extended over several election cycles. The political settlements that emerged from those upheavals lasted for roughly a lifetime—sixty or seventy years—before they began to unravel under the pressure of new developments. Each cycle of conflict ended with the ouster of the party that had dominated the system during the previous era, and each change in party regime brought in a new set of governing elites representing newly empowered electoral groups. In each situation, the newly dominant party had an early run of success that permitted it to implement its agenda and thus to change the course of national politics. Jefferson's Democratic Party won six straight presidential elections from 1800 to 1820; Republicans similarly won six straight elections from 1860 through 1880, aided by the defection of Southern states; and Democrats won five straight elections from 1932 through 1948.

More fundamentally, each of these realignments was carried out and then maintained by one dominant political party. Following the election of 1800, Jefferson's (and later Jackson's) Democratic Party defined the parameters of political competition until the outbreak of the sectional crisis in the 1850s. The Republican Party led the nation through the Civil War and maintained its dominant status throughout the postbellum age of industrial development. In the midst of the Great Depression, FDR's Democratic Party organized the modern system around the politics of public spending and national regulation. The Democrats completed this revolution after World War II when the U.S. government began to assume responsibilities in the international arena commensurate with those it had already assumed in the domestic economy. The New Deal revolution of the 1930s would have been incomplete without the settlement of the war that ended with the United States as the West's dominant power, Europe and Japan on their backs, and the U.S. dollar as the international system's reserve currency.

The dominant party in each of these eras might be called the "regime party" because it was able to use its political strength to implement and carry forward the basic themes around which the political settlement was organized. Jefferson's party pushed forward the themes of localism, democracy, and expansion; Lincoln's the themes of union, freedom, and capitalism; FDR's the themes of national regulation, public spending, and internationalism. In this sense, the United States has rarely had a two-party system, but rather a system of one and one-half parties: a "regime party" and a competitor forced to accept a subordinate position. These competitors—the Whigs in the 1840s, the Democrats after the Civil War, and the Republicans in the postwar era—occasionally won national elections, but only after accepting the legitimacy of the basic political themes established by the regime party.

These systems come apart when issues develop that cannot be addressed within the existing structure of party politics, or that resist resolution by the remedies that have worked in the past. Such issues—like slavery in the western territories or the Great Depression—tear apart or discredit established parties and the interests associated with them, while at the same time they promote a new politics of invention and creativity. Thomas Jefferson and James Madison invented the mass political party as the instrument by which they sought to defeat Alexander Hamilton and his mercantile system—though they expected that parties would wither away once this was accomplished. In trying to resolve the issue of slavery in the territories, Democratic leaders in the 1850s inadvertently broke apart the coalition between southerners and western farmers upon which Jefferson and Jackson had built the party. In 1930 and 1931, Republicans may have made the economic slump worse by doubling down on the tariff and the gold standard, two key elements of their post–Civil War policy that had proved successful in the past but were of doubtful efficacy in the new circumstances prevailing after the Great War. This is not unusual: political leaders will typically go back to what has worked in the past, often unaware that the conditions that allowed those measures to work no longer exist.

Are we now approaching a point where the ruling Democratic-welfare regime will exhaust itself in trying to resolve a new crisis with outdated policies, much as those earlier systems had expired when they could no longer offer effective solutions?

* * *

The Democratic Party emerged in the 1930s and 1940s as the "regime party" in American politics by building majorities around the claims that it pulled the country out of the Depression and won the war against fascism. These were momentous achievements. Democrats not only won five consecutive presidential elections from 1932 to 1948, but also maintained control over both houses of the U.S. Congress throughout the period from the 1930s into the 1980s. This electoral strength gave the Democrats solid control over the institutions of the national government. Within a few years they gained control of the Supreme Court, which for more than three decades used its influence to ratify and extend the party's agenda. The major policy achievements of the New Deal and the Great Society—Social Security, Medicare, and Medicaid—are still intact and widely popular, though ever more difficult for the country to afford.

Given the popularity of FDR and the New Deal, Republicans had little choice but to accept the general contours of the new regime. Following their landslide defeat in 1936, Republicans nominated a succession of presidential candidates—Willkie, Dewey, Eisenhower, and Nixon—who did not challenge New Deal programs but promised only to administer them more effectively. Among Republican candidates between 1940 and 1980, only Barry Goldwater sought to roll back the New Deal, and his defeat in 1964 was taken as evidence of the futility of that approach.

Some argue that the New Deal alignment came apart in the 1960s and was eventually replaced by Ronald Reagan's conservative coalition in the 1980s. The protesters of the 1960s, however, were not in revolt against the welfare state or even against the Democratic Party, but rather against the Johnson administration's Cold War policies. Many of the leaders of that movement, like John Kerry or Bill and Hillary Clinton, eventually settled down as conventional liberal Democrats. As for the Reagan administration, its success in reviving the U.S. economy may have given the New Deal system another lease on life, while the end of the Cold War took the national security issue off the table, much to the advantage of Democratic presidential candidates like Bill Clinton and Barack Obama. In effect, conservatives saved the Democrat-welfare regime in the 1980s.

It is true that Republicans have achieved rough electoral parity with the Democrats since 1980, winning five of nine presidential elections and winning control of the House and Senate in approximately half of the elections that have taken place since then. Still,

Republicans never managed to reverse the flow of political power to Washington and failed to eliminate or even substantially reduce any of the New Deal or Great Society social programs. Federal spending on domestic programs grew nearly as quickly under Republican as under Democratic administrations. Republicans have on occasion tried to balance the budget or tinker with Social Security and Medicare but have never succeeded in doing much to rein in their costs. These programs have always been too popular to allow for any serious changes. Republican governors and mayors, like their Democratic counterparts, continue to make their pilgrimages to Washington in search of grant money and subsidies for their states and cities, just as members of Congress from both parties run for re-election by pointing to the federal funds they have brought back to their states and districts.

Nor have Republicans had much success in penetrating leading cultural and educational institutions on behalf of ideas that have wide support among voters. College faculties and editorial boards are more resolutely Democratic and liberal today than they were in the 1960s. Republicans have so far been unable to parlay their considerable electoral success into commensurate influence over existing cultural, journalistic, and educational institutions. Instead, conservative Republicans have done something altogether different: to circulate their ideas, they have created their own newspapers, magazines, think tanks and research institutes, and colleges and schools. In effect, they have formed their own "counterestablishment" through which they communicate with their supporters and wage ideological warfare against Democrats. The two parties increasingly live in their own political and philosophical worlds, drifting further apart and finding compromises ever more difficult to achieve.

The parties are sorting themselves out into different states and regions where they can proceed to implement their respective visions of social and economic policy. Walter Russell Mead has introduced a useful distinction between the "blue state" and "red state" models of political organization to describe this process. The "blue state" model—the current Democratic model—takes its inspiration from the New Deal and is based on the concept that governments can underwrite working-class and middle-class incomes by a regime of higher taxes and aggressive public spending on education, health care, welfare, and public employment. The "red state" model as implemented in various Republican states calls for a regime of low taxes and reduced public spending as a means of attracting business and promoting economic growth. California, Illinois, and New York are prototypes of the "blue state" model; Texas, Arizona, and Indiana are prototypes of the "red state" model.

This sorting process has resulted in a volatile and potentially destabilizing alignment between the two major parties, one rooted in the public sector and the other in the private sector, and each communicating mainly with its own supporters. In the past, political parties were coalitions of private interests seeking influence over government in order to facilitate their growth within the private economy. This was true of early party conflicts that set commerce against agriculture, or slavery against free labor, or business against organized labor. The regional and sectional conflicts of the past were also of this character. This was in keeping with the small-government bias of the Constitution, in which the government itself was never supposed to emerge as a political interest in its own right. But the party conflict today between Democrats and Republicans pits public sector unions, government employees and contractors, and beneficiaries of government programs against middle-class taxpayers and business interests large and small.

When these dynamics are added up across the nation, they result in something close to a stalemate in national politics. That, at least, has been the pattern in recent decades. Is the stalemate about to be broken? As Mead points out, the "blue state" model is collapsing because of its high costs and the detrimental effects of the taxes needed to maintain it. If the "blue state" model is in fact dying, that may signal the end of the regime of public spending with which it is associated.

*   *   *

There are three reasons for thinking that America's third regime is in the process of fading out or collapsing: debt, demography, and slowing economic growth, compounded by political polarization and inertia. Within a decade, these factors may overwhelm the system of politics under which we have lived since the 1930s.

1) From 2001 to 2011, federal spending grew at twice the rate of economic growth. In 2014, the U.S. government spent around $3.8 trillion, of which about one-sixth was borrowed. The national debt (as of 2014) stands at nearly $18 trillion, a sum slightly greater than the nation's annual gross domestic product. The debt owed to the public exceeds $12.5 trillion, about half of which is held abroad by foreign governments and funds that could decide at any time to cut back on purchases of U.S. debt or demand higher interest rates on those loans. The U.S. government currently spends about $300 billion per year on interest payments on the debt, or about 8 percent of federal spending, a sum that will increase if and when interest rates go up from their historic lows. A large share of the intragovernmental debt (about $5 trillion) is owed to the Social Security Trust Fund, and it must be repaid in the future out of general revenues. Much of today's debt was accumulated during years of prosperity when, it was sometimes said, the government could afford to pay back the debt—though it never does.

America's current situation is in no way comparable to that of the 1940s when the nation borrowed large sums to finance World War II. During the war years, national debt grew to an amount

nearly equal to the nation's annual GDP; but once the war ended, Congress cut spending and more or less stopped borrowing,
at which point the U.S. economy proceeded to grow at more than
4 percent per year in real terms for the next twenty years. Today,
everything points in the other direction: demands for spending
will accelerate; borrowing will probably increase; and interest rates
have nowhere to go but up. State and local governments also rely
upon federal transfers to balance their books; and many of those
jurisdictions are dealing with public retirement systems that are
badly underfunded. No reasonable person today believes that
spending is likely to be cut or that public debt will be paid down as
a proportion of GDP.

2) The demographic trends now unfolding are likely to make a
difficult situation worse. According to the 2010 census, there are
about 40 million Americans age 65 and over; this year (2014)
there are about 48 million people drawing benefits from Medicare and about 58 million drawing Social Security benefits of one
kind or another. Those are large numbers, which these systems are
absorbing with some difficulty. The census also counts nearly 80
million baby boomers, born between 1946 and 1963, and estimates
that in a dozen or so years there will be 72 million Americans age
65 and over. If we add an increment to account for those under
age 65 drawing survivors' or disability benefits, then we could easily have between 80 and 90 million people drawing benefits in
twelve to fifteen years. This does not include the 66 million or so
people now drawing Medicaid, a number that may increase by as
much as a third over the next decade because of the health-care
legislation passed in 2010.

No one should blame these beneficiaries for the financial squeeze
the nation is facing. The decisions to launch and expand these programs were made collectively. For the most part, the beneficiaries

depend upon these programs for support and services. Leaving Social Security aside, beneficiaries receive services, not money, from the programs. The money lands in the pockets of the providers: doctors, hospitals, and pharmaceutical companies.

How will these programs be paid for? The U.S. census tells us that there are about 160 million people in the U.S. workforce, of whom about 142 million are currently employed and perhaps 120 million have full-time jobs paying the full panoply of payroll taxes. The U.S. workforce is expected to expand by 0.6 percent per year over the next decade, or by about one million per year. This means that the workforce will grow by one million people per year on average in the coming years, while the number of people turning age 65 will expand at close to twice that rate. Even if we assume an expanding economy and a declining unemployment rate, the nation will eventually reach a point where there are perhaps 150 or 160 million people working and paying payroll taxes to support more than 80 million people drawing benefits from Social Security and Medicare.

One might ask why our government has not made preparations for a development that has been in the making for the past sixty-five years. Far from preparing for this event, the political authorities have done several things in recent years to make the problem even more acute. In 2001, Congress passed an expensive prescription benefit program for seniors without providing funds to pay for it. Many blame President Bush and the Republican Congress for this, but it was not entirely their fault, since the Democrats in Congress proposed an even more expensive program than the one that was eventually passed. In 2009, President Obama and a Democratic Congress passed a new health-care entitlement program to guarantee coverage for the 40 million or so Americans without health insurance, but paid for it by taking $50 billion per year from Medicare, thus further stretching a system that was already on the path to insolvency. In addition, the U.S. government has taken annual surpluses from the Social Security Trust Fund and applied them to deficits arising in the overall federal budget. This accounts for most of the $5 trillion or so in debt held internally by the government. Beginning in 2009, the Social Security Trust Fund began to run a deficit, and it will remain in deficit for at least another twenty years, until the baby-boom generation passes through the system. From this point forward, the U.S. government will have to pay back the money it has borrowed from the trust fund out of annual tax revenues.

3) On top of all this, there is the problem of slowing economic growth, which is the most fundamental challenge of all. The United States needs a rapidly growing economy to produce the wealth to pay for its expensive social programs and to stabilize its debt, but growth has been slowing down decade by decade. During the 1950s and 1960s, real GDP grew by an average of 4.3 percent per year; during the 1970s that rate fell to 3.7 percent. It fell to 3.5 percent in the 1980s, and to 3.2 percent during the 1990s. Following the technology bust and recession of 2000, GDP grew from 2000 to 2008 by a rate of 2.6 percent per year, but if we factor in the recession of 2008 and 2009, GDP grew at a rate of 1.7 percent per year for the whole decade of 2000 through 2009. In the subsequent five years, the U.S. economy climbed out of a deep recession with tepid growth rates of around 2 or 2.5 percent per year. Forecasters expect this trend to continue at least through 2015 or 2016. There is some divergence of opinion as to what is likely to happen beyond that point. No one really knows, but the long-term pattern is one of slowing growth.

This point is illustrated more clearly in the chart below, which displays the pattern of real GDP per capita economic growth from 1950 through 2013. The pattern is displayed in five-year moving averages in order to remove the "noise" of year-to-year changes so that the long-term trend can be seen more clearly. As the chart suggests, the U.S. economy has gone through three extended boom periods over the past sixty-plus years, the first in the 1960s, the second in the 1980s, and a third in the 1990s. Yet each boom period has been less robust in GDP growth than its predecessor: during the 1960s growth exceeded 4 percent, in the 1980s it reached 3.5 percent, and in the 1990s about 3 percent. In between, the nation has gone through periods of sluggish growth, including an extended one in the 1970s that set the stage for the Reagan revolution. From the late 1990s onward, the pattern has been steadily downward, and much more sharply and for much longer than in previous sluggish periods.

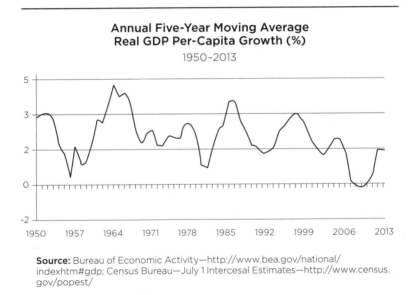

**Annual Five-Year Moving Average
Real GDP Per-Capita Growth (%)**
1950-2013

Source: Bureau of Economic Activity—http://www.bea.gov/national/indexhtm#gdp; Census Bureau—July 1 Intercesal Estimates—http://www.census.gov/popest/

What difference does it make for an economy to grow at, say, 2 percent versus 4 percent per year over an extended period of time? The chart below illustrates the different paths that the U.S. economy would follow between 2013 and 2030 at various annual rates of GDP growth, using 2013 GDP of about $16 trillion as the baseline.

The top line displays the growth path of GDP over the seven-teen-year period with annual growth rates of 4 percent, while the second line from the bottom displays that path with annual growth rates of 2 percent (which is close to what we have seen in recent years). The difference in GDP at the end of the period is large, approximately $32 trillion in 2030 under the 4 percent scenario and just under $23 trillion under the 2 percent growth path. That difference of $9 trillion in GDP would yield $2 trillion more in available federal spending with a 4 percent growth rate versus the 2 percent rate (assuming federal spending to be roughly 21 percent

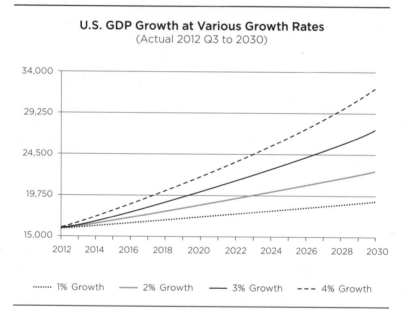

U.S. GDP Growth at Various Growth Rates
(Actual 2012 Q3 to 2030)

······· 1% Growth   —— 2% Growth   —— 3% Growth   – – – 4% Growth

of GDP). An annual growth rate of 4 percent over the next two decades, similar to what the United States experienced in the 1950s and 1960s, might allow the nation to "grow its way" out of its fiscal challenges. In the slow-growth scenario, there is little chance that the U.S. government could pay the pledges it has made. That would also apply to various states and cities in the federal system.

Those who think the U.S. economy can absorb the rising costs of government generally assume that real economic growth will return to a pre-crash trend of 3 to 4 percent per year. The Obama administration's 2013 economic report, for example, anticipates that the economy will grow at more than 3 percent per year from 2014 to 2017 and at a 4.5 percent clip (real GDP growth) for several years thereafter—in other words, at rates we have not seen on a consistent basis since the 1960s. That is a hopeful view, unsupported by data and contradicted by the patterns displayed above. Even if the rosy scenario plays out, the United States will still face some real fiscal challenges, though perhaps ones that can be managed without the elimination of popular programs.

Robert J. Gordon of Northwestern University suggests that the U.S. economy is unlikely to expand at rates of earlier decades due to various headwinds, including a slowdown in innovation, the dissipating effects of the computer and technology revolution, the demographic trends noted earlier, rising inequality, the leveling off of the educational attainment of the U.S. population, and the burdens imposed by rising household and government debt. Taking these headwinds into account, Gordon thinks that the U.S. economy may grow in the future in real terms at a rate of less than 0.5 percent per year—obviously a nightmare scenario. At that rate, the U.S. economy in total would not generate anywhere close to enough revenues to cover growing government commitments. That is a pessimistic view, so let us assume that future rates of growth will fall somewhere between the rosy and nightmare scenarios. That was the case between 2000 and 2007—and those growth rates still resulted in substantial deficits, and without the demographic complications the nation is now beginning to encounter.

There are larger questions at stake here. Writing in the 1950s in his book *People of Plenty: Economic Abundance and the American Character*, the historian David M. Potter argued that economic abundance was the key factor in the success of America's experiment in democracy and limited government. Of course, he was far from the first or the only historian to make that case. Alexis de Tocqueville observed in the 1830s that the abundance of open land in America created an equality of condition that was favorable to the political ideal of equality. That was true during the nineteenth century; in the twentieth century, it was economic growth through innovation that reinforced and extended the ideals of independence, achievement, and democracy. Americans have never favored radical schemes to redistribute income because of their faith in social mobility and the belief that they can get ahead on their own. A stagnant America, lacking growth and broad opportunities for advancement and achievement, would represent something entirely new and dangerous for a nation whose ideals and institutions have been built upon a foundation of abundance.

*   *   *

Isn't it possible for Congress and the president to formulate a strategy to deal with these problems now, before they reach the point of crisis? Various proposals have been set forth, such as the Bowles-Simpson plan, for example, and other plans to reduce the budget deficit over a ten-year period. Representative Paul Ryan, along with other Republicans in Congress, has offered plans to reform entitlement programs and to rewrite the tax code so that it encourages economic growth. Pundits and think tank scholars have offered their own plans for budget and entitlement reform.

Such proposals might make sense on paper, but they are unlikely to be adopted anytime soon. For one thing, the problems are too large to be remedied by modest incremental reforms. The prospect of cutting the federal budget by any amount is impossible to contemplate for politicians who have grown up in an environment of abundance and who have won elections by promising ever more benefits to voters. It is unrealistic to look to our political process to solve a problem that it has been instrumental in creating.

The clearest obstacle to any preemptive solution is the polarization of the two major political parties. Scholars have found that Republican voters and officeholders have become more conservative since the 1980s, while Democrats are increasingly liberal. From the late 1930s to the late 1950s, roughly half the members of the House and Senate were "moderates" as measured by their voting records. The existence of a large body of moderates in Congress facilitated compromise and a fair degree of consensus between the two parties, and so all the major legislation of that period was approved via bipartisan majorities. Since that time, the number of moderates has steadily declined as the parties have moved in opposite ideological directions, dividing into liberal and conservative camps. In the early 1980s, the proportion of moderates dropped below 40 percent, and by the late 1990s it had fallen below 20 percent. Today less than 10 percent of the members of Congress are moderates on the liberal–conservative scale. Through the same process, the ideological distance between the two congressional parties has grown as Democrats have moved leftward and Republicans rightward. Students of public opinion have observed a similar pattern among voters in recent decades: they are now sharply polarized between liberals and conservatives, express strong dislike for the opposing party and its voters, and generally do not trust the government to enact policies in the public interest. A polarized and distrustful political system will never yield the compromises needed to address the serious fiscal challenges ahead.

Polarization is characteristic of regimes as they begin to tear themselves apart in conflicts that defy resolution within the existing structure of politics. Such was the case in the United States during the 1850s as the slavery controversy cut across every other important issue and complicated efforts by the Congress to address even minor problems. As noted above, the Great Depression, World War II, and the Cold War produced a surprising degree of consensus in U.S. politics. That was a time when both parties had their conservative, moderate, and progressive wings, and it was possible to craft bipartisan coalitions. That pattern, too, is characteristic of the early years of a regime when the settlement of a crisis results in broad agreement to move forward instead of refighting old battles. It is now late in the day for America's postwar regime, and the increasing polarization is one obvious sign that it is coming apart.

Behind this polarization among officeholders and voters alike is another factor of greater importance. The growth of government and its expansion into so many areas has given rise to myriad groups seeking state or federal funding for their enterprises, and these demands for public dollars have paralyzed the political process and driven governments to the edge of insolvency. These "rent-seeking" groups (as economists call them) are widely varied: trade associations, educational lobbies, public employee unions, government contractors, ideological and advocacy organizations, health-care providers, hospital associations that earn revenues from Medicare and Medicaid programs, and the like. As we saw in Chapter 2, the economist Mancur Olson called them "distributional coalitions" because they are concerned with the distribution rather than the production of wealth.* They have strong incentives to organize around the state because the incomes of their members depend on state expenditures.

Distributional coalitions are not necessarily redistributive in the sense that they transfer income from the wealthy to the poor; rather, they transfer income from the less to the more politically influential. Universities, symphony orchestras, museums, energy companies, and even state and local governments lobby the federal government for special appropriations. These groups or coalitions win benefits for their members not only at the expense of taxpayers but also at the cost of reduced overall economic output, as

---

* Mancur Olson, *The Rise and Decline of Nations: Economic Growth, Stagflation, and Social Rigidities* (New Haven: Yale University Press, 1982).

their demands produce an inefficient allocation of national income.

Rent-seeking coalitions have little interest in moderating their demands for the sake of the broader economy. The leaders of the various constituent groups reason that the economy will be little affected by the small share of it to which they are laying claim, and they calculate that if *they* do not take the public money, someone else surely will, so they are not inclined to be "fools for the public interest." But since the leaders of all rent-seeking groups think this way, the interest-group system as a whole operates with little concern for the requirements of economic growth and wealth production. This is the main reason why, in times of crisis, rent-seeking coalitions demand tax increases to pay for their programs instead of recommending fiscal policies designed to accelerate growth.

These groups are highly influential in the political process because they invest large sums in lobbying and election campaigns in order to protect their sources of income. A focus on distributional claims in a society tends to increase the divisiveness of political life by bringing issues to the fore in which some can gain only at the expense of others. If distributional coalitions are small or narrow in relation to the economy as a whole, these divisive effects will not be great; but as the coalitions become more numerous and influential, they make political life more contentious because increasing numbers of voters will see their livelihoods at stake in elections or in debates over legislation. These conflicts are more easily contained during periods of rapid growth, when the advantages gained by distributional coalitions may not appear to be won at the expense of others. During recessions, and especially in times of deflation or disinflation, these privileges are more clearly recognized and resented by taxpayers who must fund them, often on falling incomes, and who thus have reason to support divisive political campaigns to scale back the privileges.

This general problem has become more intractable since Olson described it in 1982, at least in the United States and probably in other countries as well. Two or three decades of prosperity have permitted government budgets to grow and more distributional coalitions to form in order to lay claim to these expanding resources. Interest groups seeking to block development or trying to gain tax or regulatory benefits are now well represented in Washington, D.C. Indeed, many of the environmental groups that oppose oil and natural gas development rely on federal grants to fund their operations. Distributional coalitions have also banded together into broader coalitions built on a shared interest in the government spending and regulation that sustain their incomes.

While rent-seeking groups can be found in both political parties, the largest and most influential of them (at least on the spending side) have congregated within the Democratic Party, which at this point may fairly be described as a coalition of rent-seeking groups: private and public sector labor unions and beneficiaries of public spending and regulation. The Republican Party, with its low-tax and small-government constituencies, may be viewed as a coalition formed with an eye to dismantling some of those privileges. This is the new look of the party conflict in the United States, an unprecedented formation that pits one party rooted in the public sector against a rival with its base in the private economy—a distributional coalition against its mirror image. Our constitutional system gives each party an effective veto power over the other, such that neither can be defeated or dislodged without some fundamental shock equivalent to, say, the Civil War or the Great Depression.

Political paralysis and economic stagnation are characteristic of political systems captured by rent-seeking coalitions. Operating collectively, these groups can thwart efforts to cut spending or to address the problem of accumulating debt. The system, in short, is unlikely to be set right by any preemptive fix. That is where the United States is today: a mature industrial society experiencing slow economic growth in the face of mounting public commitments and a stalemated political system. The demands on government have grown far more rapidly than has the underlying economy that must finance them. This process is cumulative and self-perpetuating. It will continue unless brought to a halt by events that call into question the availability of resources to underwrite it.

Any number of events or developments could throw the system into a terminal crisis—another recession perhaps, a stock market crash, the bankruptcy of a large city or financial institution, a war in the Middle East, or any far-reaching event that destabilizes the international economy. Such a development would make it difficult for the U.S. government to pay off the commitments it has made to seniors, the poor and unemployed, students, federal contractors, state and local governments, and various other groups and institutions that depend on payments from the government. In that circumstance, the voters would face a choice of either watching the various interests fight it out for shares of dwindling resources or getting behind a party or candidate that could bypass the interest-group system in order to implement policies to restore economic growth. Either of these outcomes—stagnation or upheaval—is possible.

Such an upheaval, a "fourth revolution," need not result in the end of America, but only the end of the political regime that took shape in the 1930s and 1940s. It would be a difficult and painful process for Americans to go through, just as were the revolutions of the early 1800s, the 1860s, and the 1930s. As in the past, the United States will be forced to renew itself in the face of crisis, and to identify a political coalition that can guide the nation into a new cycle of growth and development. If there is anything to be learned from America's three previous revolutions, it is that the nation may well emerge from the next one as strong or stronger than before.

⟨⟨⟨

Adapted from "The Fourth Revolution," *The New Criterion*, June 2012.

PART TWO

Liberalism and Conservatism

CHAPTER SIX

Liberalism at High Tide

As the 1960s began, liberalism was unquestionably the most creative and vital force in American politics. The liberal movement rode a wave of accomplishment that started in the Progressive Era and ran through the New Deal into the postwar period. John F. Kennedy had just been elected to the presidency, and though there were many doubts as to the depth of his commitment to liberal doctrine, there was little doubt that his administration would advance the unfinished agenda of liberal reform. Liberals looked ahead to a future defined by their ideas of progress through the expansion of democracy and the welfare state; and they assumed that the United States would play a decisive role in spreading these hopes and expectations to other lands. By the end of the decade, however, liberal doctrine was in disarray, with many of its central assumptions broken by events of the preceding years. Liberals may have been too optimistic and complacent to absorb the tragic and unexpected events of the decade.

In the previous decade, thoughtful liberals had come to understand that for the first time they represented the political establishment in the United States. Liberals had been in power for the two eventful decades from 1933 to 1953, and to them went the credit for the domestic experiments of the New Deal, the victory over fascism in World War II, and the creation of the postwar international order. As a consequence of these achievements, liberalism had earned its designation as the public philosophy of the nation. Even Republican leaders like Dewey, Eisenhower, and Nixon were obliged to accept the liberal framework of ideas, to which they added the claim that they could carry it out more efficiently.

The reformers and critics of the previous generation were now insiders, placed in the position of defending their status and accomplishments. Liberalism thus began to absorb some of the intellectual characteristics of conservatism: a due regard for tradition and continuity, a sense that progress must be built incrementally, an awareness of the threat from Soviet totalitarianism, and a conviction that its domestic opponents were radicals bent on undoing its hard-won achievements. Richard Hofstadter, Columbia University's prizewinning historian, expressed this mood very well in *The Age of Reform* (1955), his influential account of the reform movement from the 1890s through the New Deal: "For the first time since the 1880's, there are signs that liberals are beginning to find it both natural and expedient to explore the merits and employ the rhetoric of conservatism. They are far more conscious of those things they would like to preserve than they are of those things they would like to change."[1]

Liberal thinkers in the postwar era were convinced that liberalism provided the only rational doctrine of progress available to the American people. At the same time, they feared that irrational and atavistic elements in the American polity would roll back the liberal accomplishments of previous generations.

* * *

The mood described by Hofstadter called forth a distinctly new chapter in the history of liberal reform, one that stood in contrast with the ethos of the Progressive and New Deal movements before it. These earlier movements were both confident that they represented the views and interests of a majority of Americans; both sought to mobilize the public against the special interests intent on taking advantage of the common man. The leaders of these movements were happy to embrace the labels of liberalism and reform. Woodrow Wilson was proud to call himself a liberal and claimed that liberalism was the philosophy of all thinking men. Roosevelt and Truman said much the same thing. These leaders never found it "expedient to explore the merits and employ the rhetoric of conservatism," as Hofstadter put it. In varying degrees, they accepted the idea of liberalism that developed late in the nineteenth century, which held that the conflict between the individual and the state in a struggle for liberty had been replaced by one that pitted the individual against large corporations and an entrenched political machine. In this new struggle, it was argued, the state was obliged to take the side of the individual and the common man against the new aggregations of power.

The Progressives believed that they spoke for the masses of Americans when they fought the trusts, the bosses, and the special interests that they claimed had insinuated themselves into the machinery of American government. They advanced their reform agenda from two distinct directions. First, they aimed to circumvent the influence of special interests by returning power back to the people in the form of the direct primary, initiatives and referenda, and the direct election of United States senators. At the same time, they advocated a host of new regulatory bodies, such as the Food and Drug Administration, the Federal Reserve Board, and the Federal Trade Commission, all of which were to be administered by disinterested experts acting in the public interest. The first reform reflected a traditional theme in American life according to which nefarious interests had infiltrated the temples of government; the second reflected the reality of new industrial combinations that had to be regulated in the public interest. Thus, liberal reformism began a century ago with the conflicting propositions that the people must rule but that in many areas they can do so only through the agency of disinterested judges, commissioners, and regulators.[2]

The Progressives were animated, as Hofstadter and others argued, by a moral impulse that aimed to restore the influence in American life of the independent worker, the farmer, and the small businessman. The nation had been built on its faith in such people, but acting on their own they had little chance of competing successfully against the emerging urban political machines, labor unions, and large commercial enterprises. The sense among Progressives that they were trying to shore up the traditional foundations of American democracy gave their movement a certain crusading and moralistic character. They disdained a politics of interest or faction because of its suggestions of partisanship and corruption. They followed instead a politics of moral uplift with appeals to democracy, law, and disinterested leadership. When the arch-Progressive Woodrow Wilson led the nation to war in 1917 he did so not on the basis of national interest but rather to make the world safe for democracy. As Hofstadter wrote in relation to the moralistic aspects of progressivism, "It is hardly an accident that the generation that wanted to bring about direct popular rule, break up the political machines, and circumvent representative government was the same generation that imposed Prohibition on the country and proposed to make the world safe for democracy."[3]

The New Deal introduced a kind of reform politics that was less moralistic and more programmatic than progressivism. In contrast to progressivism, the New Deal developed in an atmosphere of profound crisis. For this reason, FDR and his supporters were far less interested in process and procedural issues than the Progressives had been; the New Dealers focused almost entirely on substantive measures that might restore the economy to productive functioning and relieve the distress caused by the Depression.

Unlike progressivism, which had friends and foes in both political parties, the New Deal was entirely associated with the Democratic Party, which henceforth became the vehicle for liberal reform in American politics. Whereas progressivism was largely a middle-class movement, the New Deal represented the working man and encouraged labor unions. President Roosevelt established a broad base of popular support for New Deal measures that would guarantee their survival far beyond his time in office. In perhaps the most important departure from progressivism, the New Deal accepted the reality of modern industrial organization and sought to respond to it, not by restoring the influence of the individual farmer, worker, and businessman, but by building a parallel capacity in the national government to regulate and direct industry.[4]

The New Deal, in contrast to progressivism, institutionalized itself in government and in the party system. As a consequence, a destructive world war only augmented the appeal of the New Deal after 1945, whereas the previous world war had killed the spirit of progressivism in 1918. The New Deal represented a victory of party politics and administration, and to some extent a fusion of the two impulses that the Progressives had felt to be in tension. The New Dealers saw party politics as a means of advancing and representing the interests of the broad public rather than as an avenue for corruption, patronage, and special-interest favors. The spirit of New Deal liberalism was more administrative and experimental than moralistic; it sought to establish new levers of power in the American system more than to reinvigorate old ones.

In a matter of a few years, Roosevelt and the Democrats managed to build the foundations of the American welfare state in the form of old-age insurance, bank deposit insurance, securities regulation, collective bargaining for unions, price supports for farmers,

welfare for widows and orphans, and much more—all administered through a now vastly enlarged national government. When
he was finished with his domestic agenda, Roosevelt next led the
nation into a world war against fascist tyranny that ended with the
United States as the undisputed leader of the democratic world.
Most importantly, Roosevelt and the New Deal, in the minds of
many, had saved the liberal order itself from the chaos of the 1930s
and the totalitarian ideologies that claimed to own the future. By
1945, liberalism, now identified with the Democratic Party and
personified by FDR, had guided the nation through depression
and war, along the way laying the foundations for the welfare state
and establishing the United States as the leader of the postwar international order.

* * *

For the postwar liberals, the programmatic ethos of the New Deal
was more appealing than the moralistic and procedural approach
of the Progressives. Their champion in politics was FDR rather
than Woodrow Wilson. Liberalism was now a philosophy more
attuned to the challenges of governance than to those of opposition. Postwar liberals saw in the New Deal something to be defended, but also a roadway into the future through further acts
of reform. Hofstadter put it well when he said that the liberals of
the postwar period looked more to things they wished to preserve
than to those they wished to change. Critics on the left, by contrast, denounced postwar liberalism (or Cold War liberalism, as
they called it) on precisely these grounds—as being too pragmatic
and technocratic, as placing too much faith in incremental reform
instead of radical change, as far too detached from the struggles
of workers and the poor, and as inappropriately preoccupied with
communism and the Cold War. In their view, the liberals of the
1950s and early 1960s were "too conservative."[5]

The influence of FDR and the New Deal, along with the hopes and expectations of American liberals at the end of the war, were on display in *The Vital Center* (1949), an early and influential liberal manifesto of the postwar era by Arthur Schlesinger Jr. Written before Joseph McCarthy appeared on the scene, the book urged a continuation of New Deal liberalism as the most effective alternative to communism abroad and stagnation at home. In Schlesinger's view, big-business conservatism, or "plutocracy" as he called it, had discredited itself in the 1920s because it placed private interests above the public interest, an attitude that led ultimately to the stock market collapse and to the Great Depression. The opposition of business interests to price controls and regulation, he wrote, continued to damn them in the eyes of the average citizen.

As a consequence, business-oriented conservatism, with its faith in free markets and individualism, could not hope to govern effectively or win the support of a public that had enthusiastically endorsed the programs of the New Deal. On the left, progressivism had discredited itself because it was soft and sentimental, because it sought to restore ideals now buried in the past, and because it tended to view politics as a stage on which to work out emotional grievances rather than as a means of developing practical programs that might make life better for the masses of citizens. Genuine liberalism, Schlesinger argued, requires both a vision of the possible and a practical sense of how it may be achieved.

Schlesinger's critique of conservatism and progressivism was particularly telling because it pointed toward the kind of practical reform implemented so successfully in the New Deal, with government administrators supervising the decisions made by corporate boards:

> We are changing from a market society to an administrative
> society; and the problem is which set of administrators is to
> rule. If the decisions are to be made in a directors' boardroom

or in a government agency, then the political process permits
us a measure of access to a government agency. Big government, for all its dangers, remains democracy's only effective
response to big business.[6]

Here Schlesinger, no doubt exaggerating the responsiveness of
bureaucracy to popular will, expressed some of the fundamental
ideas of New Deal reformism—that large organizations are inex-
tricable elements of modern life, and that government, because it
is responsive to the public will, must regulate business and other
private centers of power in the public interest. This was the "vital
center" of American politics, an alternative both to self-interested
conservatism and to sentimental and ineffective progressivism.

The Vital Center, it should be acknowledged, contained a powerful denunciation of communism and a condemnation of the
Soviet Union as a totalitarian state. Schlesinger left little doubt
that he, along with liberals in general, regarded the Soviet Union
as a threat to the United States and its allies in Europe. Indeed,
writing in the early years of the Cold War, he argued that the Soviet Union, not the United States, was responsible for stirring up
tensions. Stalin (as Schlesinger wrote) decided even before World
War II was over that the wartime partnership with the West was
no longer necessary to advance Soviet interests. Soviet occupation
of Eastern Europe and the imposition of undemocratic governments in that region were aggressive moves that provoked a reaction in the West, setting the Cold War in motion.[7]

It was the rise of Joseph McCarthy and the anticommunist
movement after 1950 that more than anything else contributed
to a new conservative mood among postwar liberals. Schlesinger,
because he wrote his book immediately after the war and before
McCarthy burst onto the scene, wrote with a sense of optimism
about the American public and its continued support for liberal

initiatives. He could not foresee the implications of McCarthy and the anticommunist movement for the ethos of postwar liberalism. McCarthy, because of his obvious popular support, demonstrated plainly that liberalism was vulnerable to populist attacks and that, indeed, liberalism was not necessarily the preferred philosophy of the masses after all (as Schlesinger and other New Dealers thought it was). The accepted wisdom of the previous generation had now reversed itself: liberalism was about to become the doctrine of the elites and the establishment, while the masses of Americans seemed to be animated by reactionary impulses. The challenge to postwar liberalism was to make sense of this reversal while maintaining its democratic ideals.

McCarthy came to public attention with his controversial speech at Wheeling, West Virginia, in early 1950, when he declared that he held a list of 205 employees of the State Department who were members of the Communist Party—a number that he would repeatedly change and adjust in subsequent weeks and months in response to demands for evidence to document his accusations. McCarthy's speech, which created a national sensation, came just weeks after Alger Hiss, a former State Department official and devoted New Dealer, had been convicted of perjury for denying in sworn congressional testimony that he had known Whittaker Chambers as a member of the communist underground during the 1930s. Hiss's conviction, along with revelations by various ex-communists of Soviet espionage activities in the United States, provided ammunition for McCarthy's claim that communism was advancing in the world because it had been aided and abetted by traitors in our own government. McCarthy said in his speech:

> The reason we find ourselves in a position of impotency is not because our powerful enemy has sent men to invade our shores but rather because of the traitorous actions of those who have been

treated so well by this nation. It has not been the less fortunate
or members of minority groups who have been traitorous to this
nation, but rather those who have had all the benefits that the
wealthiest nation on earth has to offer, the finest homes, the finest
college education and the finest jobs in government we can give.[8]

With this stroke, McCarthy turned the tables on the liberals
and Progressives who had earlier made political headway by attacking "special interests" and "malefactors of great wealth" in
the name of an aroused and outraged public. The liberals had
viewed themselves as spokesmen for the common man, seeking
to improve his condition through government action, but the rise
of McCarthy confused matters considerably. Now McCarthy
himself sought to turn the wrath of the people against the liberal
veterans of the New Deal who, he claimed, had looked the other way as communists infiltrated the government. With these attacks, McCarthy and other anticommunists were able to steal the
mantle of populism from the liberal New Dealers. Their targets,
as Daniel Bell later wrote, were elite groups like "intellectuals,
Harvard, Anglophiles, internationalists, and the Army."[9]

From this point forward through the 1950s and into the 1960s,
liberals were aware that their most pressing challenges came not
from domestic radicals or from communism abroad, but rather
from the far right at home in the form of anticommunist extremism and allied causes, including especially Protestant fundamentalism and religious and racial bigotry. Such movements seemed
to represent, in the context of the time, a collection of forces that
might easily overwhelm the liberal establishment and perhaps
even begin to repeal the landmark legislation of the New Deal.

In the minds of some, the tactics and rhetoric of these extremists threatened the democratic order itself. According to Bell, "the
ideology of the right wing in America threatens the politics of

civility. Its commitment and methods threaten to disrupt the fragile consensus that underlies the American political system." While most Americans at the time believed that the greatest threats to the nation came from the Soviet Union and international communism, the liberals argued something altogether different: that the fundamental challenge to liberal institutions came from extremists on the right. Though this was an overreaction to McCarthy and his allies (as became clear later by the collapse of the far right in the 1960s), it nonetheless reflected an awareness of real threats and vulnerabilities.

The danger arose because right-wing spokesmen manipulated the incendiary rhetoric of "treason" and "betrayal" to rouse the population against New Deal policies and necessary accommodations with the Soviet Union. Adlai Stevenson, a favorite of liberals because of his facility with ideas and the spoken word, described during the 1952 campaign the paradoxical situation in which liberals now found themselves:

> The strange alchemy of time has somehow converted the Democrats into the truly conservative party in the country— the party dedicated to conserving all that is best and building solidly and safely on these foundations. The Republicans, by contrast, are behaving like the radical party—the party of the reckless and embittered bent on dismantling institutions that have been built solidly into our social fabric.[10]

Stevenson's astute observation reflected the awareness among liberals that they now had a responsibility to defend the institutions and policies their movement had built. There was also the strong implication in these comments, and in liberal writings of the period, that there existed no rational opposition to liberalism—that such opposition as did exist was irrational, extremist, and delusional.

* * *

The liberal movement was fortunate to have had during this time a group of intellectual spokesmen whose output in the form of influential books and articles compares favorably with any previous generation of thinkers in the United States with the exception of the Founding Fathers. Richard Hofstadter, Arthur Schlesinger Jr., and Daniel Bell, who have already been mentioned, but also Louis Hartz, Lionel Trilling, David Riesman, and Seymour Martin Lipset—these were the writers who shaped the new liberalism and sought to adapt it to its new circumstances. All wrote or edited important books that contributed to the repositioning of American liberalism as a doctrine of continuity, tradition, and practical reform. Most were academics. One thus finds in their writings an effort to use the theories of historians and social scientists to understand their immediate situation. Their persistent focus was on the dangers to the nation, as they saw them, arising from the American right. In contrast to their Progressive and New Deal predecessors, who thought mainly in terms of change, reform, and new policy, these writers focused more on consolidating earlier gains, defending them against new challenges, and reconciling their ideas with the American democratic tradition.

Hartz, a professor of government at Harvard University, offered the most comprehensive statement of the revised liberal outlook in his 1955 book, *The Liberal Tradition in America*, which argued that the American nation was built around liberal assumptions and that, moreover, these are the only ideals that Americans really know or understand. Hartz thus emphasized the broad consensus around liberal ideals that shaped the development of the American nation, in contrast to the Progressive historians, like Charles Beard and Frederick Jackson Turner, who saw the conflict between democracy and capitalism as the animating source of national development and progress. The use of the term "tradition" in the title was deliberate, as it implied that there was also a conservative dimension to liberalism.[11]

Hartz's consensus theory of American politics, as it was called, was built upon the historical fact that the United States lacked a feudal background such as in Europe gave rise to class divisions and ideological conflicts. The United States, by contrast, was "born free," as Tocqueville had observed, with neither a privileged aristocracy nor a powerful established church. There was thus no need here for a bloody revolution to demolish aristocratic privilege, as occurred in France, England, and elsewhere. America had its own revolution, to be sure, but it was a liberal revolution that reiterated principles about which nearly everyone agreed. As a consequence, Americans inherited liberal ideals as a kind of birthright without having had to fight for them. Since there was little opposition to these ideals, they advanced here in isolation from the forces that challenged and inhibited them in Europe.

This unique historical background created a polity that enjoyed a near universal consensus around the liberal ideas of liberty, private property, and representative government. Yet at the same time, Americans were prone to a loss of perspective owing to their isolation from conflicting philosophies or ideologies. This meant to Hartz and others that Americans were inclined to moralism in politics, precisely because they understood their ideals as universal moral imperatives that cannot be legitimately opposed. Such moralism, they pointed out, can be dangerous or self-defeating when it leads to a phenomenon like McCarthyism or to conflicting urges either to withdraw from the world (as in isolationism) or to declare war against it (as in efforts to "roll back" communism).[12]

It followed from Hartz's thesis that the United States lacked an authentic conservative tradition that might be called upon to restrain radical impulses from the right. Without a feudal tradition, Hartz said, America also lacked a true conservatism of the kind found in Europe, which defended established institutions in the name of continuity and experience. (For the same reason, the United States lacked a class-based socialist movement as found in Europe.) Conservatism, Hartz argued, had no genuine roots in American history and culture, and therefore had little chance of building substantial popular appeal. In America, therefore, attacks on liberalism tended to be radical or populist in nature, rather than conservative in the traditional sense.

This is why attacks on liberalism from religious fundamentalists and anticommunists like McCarthy expressed a kind of radicalism that showed little regard either for the practicality of their proposals or for the give-and-take that is essential to democratic politics. Moreover, the rhetoric and literature of the far right came from those who felt weak and dispossessed by modern life, not from groups in possession of power and authority who had traditionally carried the conservative point of view. It was, as Hofstadter wrote, "a literature of resentment, profoundly anti-establishment in its impulses."

Daniel Bell referred to this collection of forces as the "radical right" and, indeed, employed this term as the title of a book of essays that he edited on the subject.[13] Hofstadter, in one of his essays from the period later collected in that book, preferred the term "pseudo-conservative," which he borrowed from Theodore Adorno, the German sociologist, to describe those "who employ the rhetoric of conservatism, [but] show signs of a serious and restless dissatisfaction with American life, traditions, and institutions. They have little in common with the temperate and compromising spirit of true conservatism in the classical sense of the word." Hofstadter went on to say of the pseudo-conservatives that "their political reactions express rather a profound if largely unconscious hatred of our society and its ways—a hatred one would hesitate to impute to them if one did not have suggestive clinical evidence."[14] If liberalism defined the American creed, as Hartz and others believed, then the pseudo-conservatives, with their overwrought attacks on liberal traditions, were guilty of a right-wing form of anti-Americanism.

The far right, Hofstadter and Bell reminded everyone, developed out of the politics of prosperity rather than from depression or stagnation. The politics of the 1950s was something far different from the politics of the 1930s. "During depressions," Hofstadter wrote, "the dominant motif in dissent takes expression in proposals for reform or in panaceas. Dissent then tends to be highly programmatic. It is also future-oriented and forward-looking in that it looks to a time when the adoption of this or that program will materially alleviate or eliminate discontents." On the other hand, in times of prosperity, when status politics becomes more important, "there is a tendency to embody discontent not so much in legislative proposals as in grousing. Therefore, it is the tendency of status politics to be expressed more in vindictiveness, in sour memories, in the search for scapegoats than in realistic proposals for positive action."[15] Status politics is often irrational in that it involves the projection into the political world of private and personal anxieties that cannot be relieved by the implementation of any practical program. There was thus in this analysis the suggestion that there was something else bothering the radical rightists other than the concerns they expressed about communists in government and U.S. policy toward the Soviet Union.

Hofstadter argued that the radical right was a product of the "rootlessness" of American life and the constant movement of Americans from place to place and up and down the ladders of class and status.[16] Where people are uncertain of their status in the community or fear that they and the cultural groups to which they belong are losing status to other groups, they are prone to blame their situation on powerful symbols like "the establishment" or "Wall Street bankers." Supporters of the radical right, he suggested, are those who are most uncertain of their status in a changing society or who fear they are losing out to new groups that have more recently appeared on the scene. Bell argued along similar lines, suggesting that support for the far right came from "the dispossessed," that is, the "old middle class" of farmers and small-town businessmen whose values predominated in the nineteenth century but came under relentless attack in the twentieth century by trends such as industrialization, immigration, the rise of the welfare state, and the erosion of religious convictions.[17] Viewed from this perspective, it seemed that the real grievance of the far right was with modernity itself.

The postwar historians saw a link running back from the radical right of the 1950s to other extremist movements in the American past, such as the Know-Nothings of the 1850s, the Populists of the 1890s, the Ku Klux Klan in the 1920s, and the followers of Huey Long and Father Coughlin in the 1930s. All these, argued Hofstadter, Bell, and others, were a product of the dynamism of American life, which gives birth to a new array of winners and losers every generation or so. Here was a novel historical interpretation, one put forth most convincingly by Hofstadter in *The Age of Reform* but also developed in some of the essays in *The Radical Right*: the claim that extremist groups in America, whether expressing left-wing or right-wing ideas, arise in response to challenges to their status caused by the forward movement of American life.[18]

Such movements, while developing out of different conditions, had some obvious features in common—in particular, the conviction that their people had been "sold out" by a conspiracy of Wall Street financiers, traitors in the government, or some other sinister group. Such conspiracies are put forward as a readymade explanation for the loss of status and influence in society. As Bell put it in his introductory essay in *The Radical Right*, "The theme of conspiracy haunts the mind of the radical rightist."[19] This conspiratorial cast of mind, he argued, accounted for the central delusion of McCarthy and the anticommunists: the belief that communism was not merely an external threat to the United States but a grave domestic threat as well.

This thought—the notion that the far right was unhinged from reality—was developed most memorably in Hofstadter's influential essay "The Paranoid Style in American Politics," published in *Harper's* magazine in 1964 but based on a lecture he delivered at Oxford University in 1963 just days before President Kennedy was assassinated. The concept of the "paranoid style" seems to have seeped into our political lexicon to the point where it is applied to any number of hyperbolic statements or accusations. Hofstadter, however, tried to capture a broader phenomenon that he saw at work in the rhetoric of the radical right. He was impressed not simply with the wilder statements emanating from such quarters (for example, the claim by the head of the John Birch Society that President Eisenhower was a communist or that Senator Robert Taft, who died of cancer, was actually killed by a radium tube placed in his Senate chair), but by a style of argument that seemed to begin with feelings of persecution and concluded with a recital of elaborate plots against the nation and its way of life.

Communism was a repetitive theme in the rhetoric of the far right, but Hofstadter also cited paranoid fears about fluoride in the drinking water, efforts to control the sale of guns, federal aid to education, and other (usually) liberal initiatives. The paranoid style is one that inclines toward a belief in plots and conspiracies as explanations for complex phenomena.[20] The paranoid mind is one that is predisposed to see the world in terms of conspiracies.

The exemplars of the paranoid style—men like McCarthy, Joseph Welch of the Birch Society, and the fundamentalist ministers heard over the radio—may not have seemed irrational to the casual observer because they documented their theories with facts and footnotes, which gave a patina of respectability to their accusations of treason and betrayal. "The entire right-wing movement of our time," Hofstadter wrote, "is a parade of experts, study groups, monographs, footnotes, and bibliographies."[21] Yet, as he argued, such recitals of facts, statistics, and expert judgments merely laid the groundwork for imaginative leaps to bring together apparently disparate events into the form of vast and sinister conspiracies. Though there are conspiracies in history, Hofstadter acknowledged, the paranoid style is one that views conspiracy as the driving force of history. From this standpoint, then, it seems entirely reasonable to ask questions like "Who lost China?" or "Who sold out Eastern Europe?" Important events never happen through coincidence, circumstance, or the unfolding of complex processes, but by the actions of malevolent powers.

With this analysis, Hofstadter brought to the surface some assumptions that had long been implicit in the liberal assessment of the far right—namely, that it represented a form of lunacy or irrationality that is best understood in psychological or sociological terms rather than as an ideology or a point of view that might be challenged by rational argument. Unfortunately, in the revised version of his lecture that appeared in *Harper's* after the 1964 election, Hofstadter described Barry Goldwater and his conservative followers as contemporary manifestations of the paranoid style, thereby bringing the Republican Party and the conservative movement generally under indictment for irrationality and paranoia.[22] If this were a valid judgment (which it was not), then it would follow that any opposition to the liberal worldview was irrational at best, and possibly delusional and dangerous.

Hofstadter's essay is an illustration of the preoccupation of the postwar liberals with "the politics of irrationality" and with the psychological underside of politics. The emergence and coming to power of fascism in Europe in the 1920s and 1930s permanently altered their political outlook, as did the rise of McCarthyism and the radical right in the United States after the war. Such developments proved clearly enough, to their minds anyway, that the great challenge to liberal democratic life came not so much from competing ideologies framed in rational terms as from irrational and emotional forces turned loose in the arena of politics.

Hofstadter developed this theme further in another influential book of the period, *Anti-Intellectualism in American Life* (1964), in which he argued that American culture has been consistently hostile to intellectuals and the life of the mind, and that such prejudices have had unwelcome political consequences, most particularly in persistent efforts to mandate conformity, to shut down dissent, or to emphasize practicality at the expense of academic learning.[23] If the Progressive historians viewed American history as a continuing battle between capitalism and democracy, Hofstadter and his liberal colleagues portrayed a different kind of conflict, one in which the national psyche was divided between a commitment to liberal rationality on the one side and the temptation to engage in emotional and counterproductive tantrums on the other. They tried to show how one or another of these tendencies has temporarily gained the upper hand at different times in our past, producing a cyclical pattern in which periods of reform are followed by periods of reaction, much of it driven by resentment or irrational yearnings.

* * *

Having framed the issues in this way, the postwar liberals came to view ideological thinking, whether of the left or of the right, as an expression of the irrational in politics and thus as something to be discouraged and criticized. Bell made this case most explicitly in an essay titled "The End of Ideology in the West," the final chapter of a book of essays suitably subtitled "On the Exhaustion of Political Ideas in the 1950s." Here he argued that the ideological alternatives to liberal capitalism had been discredited by the horrifying realities of Hitlerism and Soviet communism. The radical passions of the previous generation had been spent in the failed enthusiasms of the 1930s. They could not now be revived except in new and completely different forms.

Politics would henceforth proceed along a more mundane and orderly path marked out by the assumptions of postwar liberalism. "In the Western world," Bell wrote, "there is rough consensus among intellectuals on political issues: the acceptance of the welfare state; the desirability of decentralized power; a system of mixed economy and political pluralism."[24] He dismissed socialism and communism as failed alternatives to liberalism but dismissed also those who said that the welfare state placed us on "the road to serfdom," a clear reference to Friedrich Hayek's critique of socialism and the welfare state from a free-market point of view. The liberal framework thus seemed to define the boundaries both of the possible and of the rational in politics.

There was, however, a disquieting aspect to the postwar situation: the end of ideology, as Bell and others suggested, meant that politics would now become a rather boring affair, reduced to questions centering on the minimum wage, old-age pensions, the price of bread and milk, and the like. Such an agenda, Bell recognized, cannot provide a unifying appeal to those who seek more from politics than stability, incremental reforms, and material progress. Affluence and prosperity had changed the focus of intellectual criticism from economics and class conflict, the paramount issues of the 1930s, to concerns about cultural issues that do not lend themselves to political solutions. Here he had in mind issues relating to mass taste, conformism, and relations between the sexes. The very success of liberalism in overcoming basic economic conflicts might, paradoxically, lead to new expressions of the radical impulse centering on cultural questions that had hitherto been kept out of the political arena.

Notwithstanding the skepticism of the postwar liberals regarding the popular mind, the liberal reformers from the Progressive Era through the postwar period generally accepted an American version of what Herbert Butterfield called "the Whig interpretation of history": the idea that history is a tale of steady progress in the direction of liberty and democracy. He referred to those British historians of the nineteenth and twentieth centuries who tended "to write on the side of Protestants and Whigs, to praise revolutions provided they have been successful, to emphasize certain principles of progress in the past and to produce a story which is the ratification if not the glorification of the present."[25] The Whig historian, according to Butterfield, sets himself up as the arbiter of past controversies, identifying winners and losers according to their roles in bringing about the present state of affairs. Orwell wrote that this approach to history encourages a complacent attitude toward the present and the future. "Nourished for hundreds of years on a literature in which right invariably triumphs in the last chapter," he wrote in one of his wartime essays, "we believe half-instinctively that evil always defeats itself in the long run." The belief that everything turns out all right in the end takes away from the past much of its genuine complexity and open-endedness. Things might have turned out differently—and they yet may.[26]

The Progressives viewed American history as a continuing battle between the forces of democracy and those of capitalism, while the postwar liberals tended to emphasize the ongoing struggle between liberalism and the counterproductive and irrational responses to its successes. It may be true (as Butterfield suggested) that the Whig interpretation, and variations on its themes, represents an ideological view of the past in that it takes sides on past controversies in favor of those whose positions point toward the present. Yet it is also true that every modern political movement has developed its own view of history in order to identify itself as the crucial link between past

and future. This is as true of liberalism as it is of Marxism or conservatism—all doctrines that understand the past in terms of their
unique struggles, whether in behalf of liberty, or the proletariat, or
religious authority. Butterfield makes a case for dispassionate and
objective history that does not take sides on the great controversies
of the past and avoids association with any of the present political
parties or interests. His advice, though often cited, is most difficult
to follow, not simply because historians have political biases, but because political movements have need of their own distinctive histories. In America, as in England, history as often as not has found
itself placed in the service of political parties or social movements.

Many of the leading theorists of the reform tradition were historians who tried to place that tradition in a historical context, thereby lending it greater legitimacy and momentum. Progressivism,
though focused on political reform, developed its own version of
the American past that focused on the emerging commercial forces
that it sought to understand and control. The rise of progressivism
as a political movement was greatly aided by the work of an influential group of Progressive historians, led by such luminaries as
Charles Beard, Frederick Jackson Turner, and Vernon Louis Parrington, who, in Hofstadter's words, "moved the thinking of American historians . . . into the controversial world of the new century
and into the intellectual orbit of the Progressive movement."[27]

During the 1940s, Schlesinger weighed in with a book on Andrew Jackson that Hofstadter described as the final important
work of the Progressive tradition. Its portrayal of Jackson's administration as a forerunner to the New Deal was perhaps as clear a
case as one might find of a reform-minded historian reading the
assumptions of the present into the past.[28] Jackson, though certainly a populist reformer, was also a representative of the Southern slave interest, an advocate of states' rights and laissez-faire, and
a foe of Henry Clay's American System—and thus an unsuitable

model for Roosevelt's New Deal. Schlesinger's main purpose in this volume, and indeed in much of the rest of his historical portfolio, was to make a case for the Democratic Party as the instrument of popular reform in America dating back to its origins in the time of Jefferson and Madison. Republicans and the Whigs before them were seen as representatives of business interests and the status quo. Schlesinger's view of Democrats and Republicans was not far removed from the perspective of the Whig historians on Whigs and Tories.

Postwar liberalism was similarly represented by eminent historians, among them Hofstadter, Hartz, and Schlesinger, to name just a few. Hofstadter understood the link between historical scholarship and reform better than most, for one of his finest books was *The Progressive Historians,* a critical appraisal of the historical writings of Beard, Turner, and Parrington, and more generally a reflection on the relationship between politics and the writing of history. Hofstadter later acknowledged, both in *The Age of Reform* and in *Anti-Intellectualism in American Life*, that his interpretations of the American past were tinctured by the preoccupations of the 1950s—in particular, the threat from the radical right. Given his description of Goldwater as a manifestation of the paranoid style in American politics, Hofstadter was every bit as committed as Schlesinger to the view that the Democrats are the party of progress in American life and the Republicans the party of reaction. On this point, Hofstadter and Schlesinger spoke for many historians, as well as for postwar liberals in general.

It is an irony that such a forward-looking movement as modern liberalism should have been so preoccupied with the past, and not a little surprising that its most articulate proponents should have been historians. Their writings reinforced the sense that liberalism was the party of ideas while conservatism was, in the famous words of John Stuart Mill, "the stupid party," or at least, as Hofstadter suggested, the anti-intellectual party. The identification of liberalism with intellect reached a culmination following the election of John F. Kennedy to the presidency, for it now seemed that at last a genuine intellectual occupied the White House.

The liberal thinkers of the 1950s and early 1960s tried to establish their outlook as at once the authoritative liberal *and* conservative position in national politics. This was done, admittedly, through a certain amount of scholarly legerdemain that ignored real conservative arguments from the likes of Russell Kirk and William F. Buckley Jr., or by interpreting opposing viewpoints in sociological or psychological terms so as to discredit them. There was also a certain irony in their position, as Peter Viereck, the conservative writer and poet, pointed out in a 1955 essay: "The intellectual liberals who twenty years ago wanted to pack the Supreme Court as frustrating the will of the masses and who were quoting Charles Beard to show that the Constitution is a mere rationalization of economic loot—these same liberals are today hugging for dear life that same court and that same Constitution."[29]

The attempted merger of liberal ideals with conservative methods represented a novel synthesis in American political thinking. Also new was the idea that the challenge to liberalism came from irrational elements in society, as opposed to capitalists or "special interests." If the postwar liberals did not entirely succeed in the combative world of electoral politics, they did very well in the intellectual arena, where their writings were greatly influential among academics and journalists.

* * *

Accompanying the rise of liberalism over the first six decades of the twentieth century was a countermovement of social radicalism that had little resonance among the broad public but found adherents among the intellectual and academic classes, and in many instances among the idle rich. Christopher Lasch called this the "new radicalism" to distinguish it from the "old" radicalisms of socialism, anarchism, or extreme individualism.[30] The new radicals owed their intellectual debt more to Freud and Jung than to nineteenth-century radicals like Marx or Mill, and they identified the main source of human oppression as lying neither in capitalism nor in any specific acts of tyranny, but rather in the human psyche as it was shaped or "socialized" by the wider culture. According to Lasch,

> The new radicalism differed from the old in its interest in questions which lay outside the realm of conventional politics. It was no longer his political allegiance alone that distinguished the radical from the conservative. What characterized the person of advanced opinions in the first two decades of the twentieth century—and what by and large continues to characterize him at the present time—was his position with regard to such issues as childhood, education, and sex; sex above all.[31]

The new radicals, from their first appearance early in the last century down to the present time, were preoccupied with liberation—liberation of the child from the restraints of family and conventional schooling, liberation of women from the demands of family and conventional living, liberation of sexual impulses from old-fashioned morality, liberation of the human unconscious from the oppressive demands of modern civilization. Among the key figures in this movement were men and women like Randolph Bourne, John Dewey, and Jane Addams from the early part of the century, along with writers like Norman Mailer, Allen Ginsberg, and the Beat poets in the 1950s and 1960s. The new radicals cared nothing at all for run-of-the-mill political issues such as tariffs, taxes, and old-age pensions; they moved into politics in order to transform education, the family, religion, relations between the sexes, and attitudes toward life generally. They were preoccupied with what today we call "cultural politics."

These were the people whom Schlesinger dismissed because they were sentimental and ineffective, and whom other liberals (like Hofstadter) criticized as utopian and contemptuous of the beliefs and attitudes of the common man—all of which was undoubtedly true. The new radicals, for their part, attacked liberalism as lacking vision, as shoring up the status quo through incremental reforms, as too pragmatic to effect far-reaching change, as too boring to command the interest of creative men and women. If liberals like Hofstadter sought to contain or suppress the irrational element in politics, the radicals were eager to liberate it for the greater good of human happiness. The liberals held the upper hand over the radicals until the 1960s, when President Kennedy's assassination gave the radicals—who did not actually like the Kennedys—an instrument for discrediting the liberals.

The assassination of a liberal president, combined with the circumstances surrounding his death, challenged the assumptions of postwar liberalism as no other event could have done. It brought up, for example, the disquieting political question (raised just a few years earlier by Daniel Bell) as to whether the conventional reform agenda—of either the Progressive or the New Deal variety—was sufficiently compelling to give meaning to liberal politics or to public life generally. Conventional reform appears prosaic unless joined with a sense of historical movement that gives it broader meaning and purpose. It was often said, for example, that reform was a means of perfecting our democratic heritage or of delivering to everyone the promise of American life. Yet Kennedy's death severed the connection between the reform ideal and the notion of historical progress. Reform pointed toward more hope, more democracy, and more justice and equality in American life, but Kennedy's death pointed in quite another direction: toward a sense that public life is out of control or subject to direction by conspiracies or crazed individuals. The assassination was so shocking and unexpected that to many it made the reform agenda seem insignificant and meaningless.

Postwar liberalism had supplied the script, as it were, for the interpretation of Kennedy's presidency and his untimely death, but it led to a sense of confusion. Liberal Americans and especially liberal intellectuals were wholly unprepared to understand or to interpret the assassination of a liberal president on the basis of the doctrines and ideas they had absorbed. Thus the liberal reform doctrine came to be displaced by a new narrative of American life that supplied its own interpretation of that shattering event.

* * *

Lionel Trilling, the great literary critic and contemporary of Hofstadter, Bell, and Schlesinger, articulated a thoughtful critique of liberalism from the standpoint of one who was himself a liberal. In his introduction to *The Liberal Imagination* (1950), Trilling wrote that liberalism in America was prone to brittleness both because of its universality and because of its programmatic emphasis. There was no genuine opposition to liberal assumptions in America such as in other countries gave toughness and determination to liberal doctrine as a consequence of disappointment and occasional defeat. Moreover, because of its programmatic focus and an almost exclusive emphasis on politics, liberalism lacked an imaginative dimension that might have given it a better sense of the richness and complexity of life.

Trilling called attention to an epigraph used by Coleridge as an introduction to *The Rime of the Ancient Mariner*, which suggested that it is good that human beings contemplate invisible beings in the universe "lest the intellect, habituated to the trivia of daily life, may contract itself too much and wholly sink into trifles." His point was not that we should believe in demons, spirits, and fairytales, but that, as Trilling explained, "the world is a complex and unexpected and terrible place which is not always to be understood by the mind as we use it in our everyday tasks." Liberalism rejects as false and irrational the old myths and fairytales that in traditional societies spurred the imagination and supplied meaning and perspective to an unpredictable world. But because liberalism is committed to a rational view of the world, it does not follow that the world must always cooperate.[32]

Trilling's criticism of liberalism was far different in implication from that lodged against it by the various spokesmen for the new radicalism who dreamed of using the imagination as a tool for expanding the scope of political life beyond the confines of reformist liberalism. Trilling, who had little sympathy with the ambitious cultural agenda of the new radicals, saw in the imagination a means of bringing perspective to political liberalism by encouraging an appreciation of the complexity of life and the genuine difficulty of changing its terms by political means. He hoped that this imaginative dimension formerly encouraged by myth might now be supplied through art and literature, particularly the novel, which in contrast to political manifestos can portray life in its richness and variety. The essential task of literature is to serve as a corrective to liberal aspirations rather than as an expression of them. The task of the writer and critic, Trilling argued, is "to recall liberalism to its first essential imagination of variousness and possibility, which implies the awareness of complexity and difficulty."[33]

Liberalism, he observed, had become too formulaic, perhaps too worldly and too powerful, and rather more optimistic about the future than was justified by the real conditions of life. Because of their optimism and the complacency induced by the absence of any genuine opposition to their intellectual assumptions, liberals lacked a sense of tragedy that might help see them through times of difficulty. Trilling suggested, with an unusual degree of prescience, that liberalism was not immune to human tragedy, and he feared that its assumptions might prove too brittle to survive it.

CHAPTER SEVEN

Conservative Nation

Liberals in the 1950s and 1960s were confident that they owned the future. They believed liberalism to be the defining American creed and regarded conservatism as foreign to the nation's fundamental character. Clinton Rossiter spoke for many liberals when he wrote in *Conservatism in America* (1955), "Our commitment to democracy means that Liberalism will maintain its historic dominance over our minds, and that conservative thinkers will continue as well-kept but increasingly restless hostages to the American tradition."[1] According to Rossiter and other liberal thinkers, conservatism as a political philosophy ran against the American grain and thus could only play an incongruous and subordinate role in a revolutionary nation dedicated to equality, democracy, and restless change. While the conservative case for order, tradition, and authority may be useful as a corrective to the excesses of democracy, it could never hope to supplant liberalism as the nation's official governing philosophy. Liberals would always set the tone for public life, Rossiter argued. Conservatives might put up resistance to liberal reforms but then must adjust to them after they have been adopted. Accordingly, the revised edition of *Conservatism in America*, published in 1962, was subtitled "The Thankless Persuasion."

Along the same lines, in an article published in *The American Scholar* a decade earlier, Raymond English described conservatism as "The Forbidden Faith."[2] In fact, liberal observers of the postwar scene—most prominently Richard Hofstadter, Lionel Trilling, Louis Hartz, and Daniel Bell, along with Rossiter—remarked that an authentic conservative movement was difficult to locate in the United States. To be sure, there were some thoughtful conservatives to be found, such as Russell Kirk and Senator Robert Taft, but they had little in the way of a popular following, and their views on policy were hardly distinguishable from those of the business community. On the other hand, the new American right that arose in the 1950s to challenge the New Deal and the Cold War policies of the Truman and Eisenhower administrations did not seem to fit into the conservative tradition at all. Populist in tone and suspicious of leaders from both parties, the new right seemed to have more in common with extremist movements than with European-style conservative parties that distrusted democracy and defended traditional elites.

The radical right, as the liberals called it, was especially frightening because it mobilized huge popular followings behind figures like Joseph McCarthy, Richard Nixon, and the various fundamentalist ministers who spread their messages through the radio waves. The very idea of a President McCarthy or, more realistically, a President Nixon was enough to send chills down the spine of any right-thinking liberal. Naturally, those liberals preferred to deal with "real" conservatives like Senator Taft than with populist figures like McCarthy and Nixon who, because of their wide appeal, actually threatened to topple them from power.

The liberal analysis of conservatism that was passed down from the 1950s and 1960s has caused endless confusion about what conservatism in America is and is not. It is never a good thing for any philosophical movement to permit itself to be defined by its adversaries, but this is more or less what happened to conservatism in the postwar period, as liberals sought to define it in such a way as to guarantee its failure or ineffectiveness. For one thing, they created a combination of traps and paradoxes for conservatives that gave added meaning to Rossiter's concept of "the thankless persuasion." Conservatives, if they wished to maintain that designation (at least in the eyes of liberals), were obliged to endorse the status quo, which meant accepting all manner of liberal reforms once they were in place. Thus, the self-styled conservatives who attacked the New Deal were not acting like conservatives because they were, in effect, attacking the established order—and, of course, "real" conservatives would never do that. So it was that conservatives who wished to reverse liberal victories became radicals or extremists. Moreover, conservatives could have no program of their own, or at least no program that had a reasonable chance of succeeding, because any successful appeal to the wider public would turn them into populists, and thereby into extremists and radicals.

Conservatives, in short, could win power and influence only by betraying their principles, and could maintain those principles only by accepting their own subordinate position in the American political landscape. In the eyes of the liberal historians, therefore, conservatism could never prosper in America because if it did, it could no longer be called conservatism.

* * *

Rossiter published the first edition of *Conservatism in America* about a year after William F. Buckley Jr. launched *National Review*, and with it the modern conservative movement. A supporter of Senator McCarthy, ardent foe of the New Deal, and critic of Ivy League colleges, Buckley did not meet the requirements for conservatism as had been laid down by the liberal historians. In their eyes, Buckley was an extremist, as were most of the writers (like James Burnham, Max Eastman, and Frank Meyer) whom he recruited to his new fortnightly magazine. Buckley's quixotic project to build a conservative intellectual movement was not supposed to succeed, and even less was it expected to grow to a point where conservatives might be in a position to challenge liberals for intellectual and political influence.

As we know, it did exactly that. Surely one of the more significant political developments in the United States over the last half of the twentieth century was the rise of conservatism from its designated status as "the thankless persuasion" to become a rival to liberalism as the nation's most influential public doctrine. There are now more self-described conservatives in America than there are liberals, which was not the case in 1933 when Franklin Roosevelt launched the New Deal or in 1965 when Lyndon Johnson embarked on his Great Society. A Gallup poll conducted in 2013 found that about 38 percent of Americans classified themselves as "conservative" while only 23 percent identified as "liberal." Though not a majority, conservatives make up a highly significant minority of American voters. This reversal of fortune did not happen by accident, but through a long process by which conservative ideas and critiques of liberalism were developed well in advance of the popular support they eventually earned.

American conservatism began decades ago as a movement of ideas and has managed to maintain its original character even while gaining popular appeal. Thus David Brooks has observed that conservatives differ from followers of other political movements in their apparent preoccupation with a handful of influential authors and canonical books. It is rare to hear of liberal groups discussing major works written by the intellectual architects of the welfare state, such as John Dewey, Herbert Croly, or John Rawls; or sponsoring programs in honor of influential economists like John Maynard Keynes or John Kenneth Galbraith. One would be hard-pressed to identify an influential book or essay that sets out the principles of contemporary liberalism as they relate to feminism, multiculturalism, diversity, or economic planning.

Conservative organizations, on the other hand, regularly pay tribute in their programs to the founding fathers of conservative thought: the American Enterprise Institute sponsors an annual Irving Kristol Lecture, the Manhattan Institute bestows an annual Hayek Book Prize, and the Cato Institute awards a biennial Milton Friedman Prize. There are numerous programs and societies across the country named for conservative intellectual and political heroes, including (especially) James Madison, Alexis de Tocqueville, Abraham Lincoln, Winston Churchill, and William F. Buckley Jr. A handful of books sowed the intellectual seeds for the American conservative movement and remain influential to this day. One is Hayek's *The Road to Serfdom*, published in London in 1944 and in the United States in 1945, which made the case against central planning and called for a revival of classical liberalism and limited government. A second is Whittaker Chambers's *Witness*, published in 1952, which elaborated the religious and spiritual ideals at stake in the Cold War. *The Conservative Mind*, written by Russell Kirk and published in 1953, documented a continuous tradition of conservative thinking that goes back to Edmund Burke's writing on the French Revolution, and called for a renewal of Burkean conservatism. Kirk's book led in turn to the founding of *National Review* in 1954.

To a great extent, conservative thought evolved in the postwar period as these writers responded to unfolding events and to each other's arguments. The centrality of books and ideas in the formation of the modern conservative movement is surprising given the emphasis that conservatives have always placed on prudence, tradition, and experience—as against the application of abstract theories to politics, which has historically been the province of liberals and radicals. The emphasis on principles is a strength of the conservative movement, though it may have drawbacks (as we shall see) in the world of political practice.

Conservatives in America worked out their ideas partly in response to Hayek's critique of central planning, *The Road to Serfdom*, written during the war as momentum gathered for socialism in Great Britain. Hayek's answer to the lure of socialism and economic planning was found in the recovery of classical liberalism, which had given birth to the institutions of liberty and limited government in both Britain and America. Though Hayek claimed to be a liberal in the nineteenth-century sense, he made common cause with conservatives in the United States because he celebrated the wisdom of the Founding Fathers in creating a constitution designed to preserve liberty and limited government. As a consequence, Hayek enjoyed a far larger and more influential following in the United States than he was able to muster on the other side of the Atlantic.

In the view of traditional conservatives, Hayek's arguments were correct as far as they went, but his free-market liberalism was inadequate to the challenges posed by communism and the Soviet Union. Buckley, Kirk, and Chambers argued that the Cold War was not solely about preserving liberty; it was also about conserving the religious and moral tradition of the West. Thus they found Hayek's approach too narrow. Because of their efforts to mount a more comprehensive defense of Western civilization, the postwar confrontation with socialism was framed more in terms of "conservatism" than in terms of Hayek's vision of liberty and individualism. This response to Hayek would open up a schism between free-market liberals and traditional conservatives.

In the 1960s, the problems that attended the expanding wel-

fare state—along with the disturbing rise of anti-American sentiment on the left—prompted a different kind of synthesis among
those who came to be called neoconservatives, led by Irving Kristol and Norman Podhoretz, editor of *Commentary* magazine. Unlike classical liberals and traditional conservatives, the neoconservatives were not in principle opposed to the welfare state as long
as it upheld the ideals of family, order, and community. From their
point of view, the problem with the expanding social safety net
was not that it threatened liberty but that it promoted disorder,
crime, broken or unformed families, poor schools, and a general
loss of authority in society. The problem, in other words, was not
that the welfare state led to collectivism but that it undermined
the middle-class values upon which a successful commercial civilization must be based.

All of these writers were conservatives in one or another fundamental sense. An essential aspect of modern conservatism is the
conviction that liberal institutions cannot prosper or even survive
on the basis of their own internal resources and are vulnerable to
attempts to push one or another liberal theme—equality, democracy, or freedom—to a point of no return. According to the Whig
tradition of liberty, republics follow a cycle of rise and inevitable
decline as citizens and their representatives gradually sacrifice
their principles in the pursuit of money, security, or power. Conservatives, most of whom respect this tradition of thought, are thus
skeptical of liberal notions of inevitable historical progress that do
not take into account the ever-present possibilities of corruption
and decline. This is one reason why conservatives have always
sought external supports for representative institutions, whether
in nationalism and patriotism, in religion, family and community, or in the various "little platoons" of society, as Edmund Burke
called them, which provide direction and discipline for liberty and
self-interest. Conservatives thus oppose the liberal welfare state

not primarily because it is expensive, but more critically because they fear that it is eroding the network of private associations that support citizenship and sustain representative institutions.

For these reasons, conservatives look to authors and statesmen like Tocqueville, James Madison, Joseph Schumpeter, and of course Burke as important sources for their ideas. Tocqueville wrote that American democracy needed to maintain an appreciation for aristocratic excellence in order to balance the democratic passion for equality. Schumpeter, an economic historian, argued that capitalism needed support from precapitalist institutions like the family and the church to uphold the moral values that allowed it to thrive. Even Madison, who hoped that the Constitution contained sufficient internal protections to maintain itself, acknowledged that an element of virtue in the public was necessary to the success of the republican experiment. The seminal conservative thinkers of our day are in agreement on this larger principle, though they find these external supports for liberty and democracy in different places: Hayek in the heritage of constitutionalism; Buckley and his colleagues in religion, family and tradition; Kristol and the neoconservatives in bourgeois virtues and patriotism.

Despite the passage of time and the accumulation of events, the classical liberals, traditional conservatives, and neoconservatives still represent the main lines of conservative thought. Much to the surprise of critics, none of these lines of thinking has been discredited among conservatives by recent events or trends—not classical liberalism by the financial crash, not traditional conservatism by the libertarian cultural politics of our day, and not neoconservatism by the war in Iraq. At the same time, little that is new or fundamental has been added to the conservative movement since the neoconservatives emerged in the 1960s and 1970s. The conservative movement still operates by and large on the set of ideas developed in the postwar period in response to socialism, totalitarianism, and the expanding welfare state. It remains to be seen if these public doctrines will be adequate to the challenges of the twenty-first century.

Certainly there have been arguments among proponents of these three doctrines over the years. Traditional conservatives like Russell Kirk attacked classical liberals for their libertarian take on moral issues. During the 1980s, some traditionalists complained about the influence of neoconservatives in the Reagan administration. During the presidency of George W. Bush, Buckley and others challenged the neoconservative campaign to export democracy to the Middle East. Today, with a liberal administration in power, these differences are muted, and it is hard to find signs of impending internecine warfare among conservatives in the pages of the various intellectual beachheads of neoconservatism and traditional conservatism.

The most evident trend today is the revival of Hayek as a basic source of criticism of the left-liberal policies coming out of Washington. While criticism of Obama's agenda has come from all three branches of conservative thought, in popular circles it is increasingly framed in terms of "big government" as a threat to liberty and the constitutional order. *The Road to Serfdom* rose to the top of bestseller lists after a popular television host urged his viewers to read it as the clearest diagnosis of the challenges posed by left-liberal policies. Arthur Brooks, president of the American Enterprise Institute, has similarly framed the central political debate of our time as one between "free enterprise" and "big government." A few decades ago, classical liberalism was widely thought to be out-of-date and insufficient for contemporary needs, but it is now regularly presented as an alternative to the Democratic Party's left-liberal agenda. No doubt the end of the Cold War and the disappearance of the communist threat had something to do with this development, as a comprehensive civilizational defense seemed less urgent. Classical liberalism, with its emphasis on the individual, fits in comfortably with the libertarian cultural ethos of the present historical moment.

The Road to Serfdom offers a penetrating diagnosis of the corruptions of the welfare state but few prescriptions for unwinding it. Hayek warned against going down that road in the first place; he did not explain what should be done once we have traveled along it a considerable distance. In an ideal world, the massive social programs that strain the nation's resources and fray its social fabric would be eliminated, but that is easier said than done. So long as these programs are embedded within the established structure of politics and policy, conservatives will be forced to deal with them in ways that at least appear to be positive and constructive. This is the challenge to conservative governance in an age of "big government."

* * *

The widespread interest in Hayek today illustrates how conservatives have managed to turn their enterprise into a popular or even a populist movement without losing its intellectual core— something that few people thought possible when conservatism first took shape in the 1940s and 1950s. Indeed, popular conservatism still seems almost a contradiction in terms for those who take their bearings from abstract theories as to what conservatism should be: a force for order, continuity, and rule by traditional elites. Yet in a democratic polity, conservatism could not have thrived as an intellectual movement without also turning its ideas into a popular force.

Critics from Richard Hofstadter in the 1950s to Sam Tanenhaus more recently have denied that a popular conservatism is possible at all because, in their view, conservatives can win a mass following only by sacrificing their distinctive principles. Hofstadter and Tanenhaus have found American conservatism wanting in comparison with the model derived from Edmund Burke's writings on the French Revolution. After all, Burke endorsed governance by the most talented; he supported the status quo (with gradual reform); and he preferred prudence and realism over abstract theories as guides to political action. American conservatism, on the other hand, has sometimes played to popular prejudices, attacked the status quo and "the establishment," used terms like "the conservative revolution," and proposed an idealistic rather than a realistic approach to dealing with foreign threats, as in "rolling back" communism in the 1950s and exporting democracy to the Middle East in the 2000s. Thus, it is easy to see why some critics claim that American conservatism is not an authentically "conservative" movement but a radical or populist one.

This line of criticism is valid only if we concede that the Burkean ideal is the standard by which modern conservatism should be judged, and, indeed, that Burke's principles can be extracted from the context in which they were formed and easily applied to contemporary politics. The conservative movement is better understood as a mixture of Burkean and non-Burkean elements that developed out of factors unique to the American scene. If we make appropriate allowances for such factors, we see that American conservatives are undoubtedly "conservative," albeit in ways unique to the American experience.

American conservatism has taken on its peculiar aspect mainly because it originated outside the political mainstream. From the beginning, it was a movement of outsiders, critics, and those disaffected with contemporary political realities. Here there is a stark contrast with the European variety of conservatism. In Europe, especially in Great Britain, conservatism arose from inside governmental circles and in close proximity to power, as a defense of established interests or patterns of politics against challenges from radicals, egalitarians, and democrats. Burke's thinking was very much of this kind. European conservatives were always distrustful of mass or popular movements and they operated as defenders of established arrangements.

Conservatism in America, on the other hand, began as an opposition movement in a fully democratic system. Conservatives had to take their case to the public and employ populist rhetoric in order to win converts and supporters; they had little choice but to try to discredit the status quo while offering alternatives to it. Nor did conservatives operate from a strong party base; in the early years they operated as insurgents within the Republican Party, which in the 1950s had a powerful liberal or progressive wing. Because it developed as a challenge to business as usual, and particularly to the New Deal and its successive iterations, American conservatism came to embody some of the features of an insurgent or oppositional movement. Conservatives, for example, have from the beginning described their enterprise as a "movement," which suggests an image of an active and dedicated membership moving toward some definite destination. They continue to use that designation even as conservatism has grown into a large and diverse enterprise.

Conservatives have had significant victories over the years beginning with the presidency of Ronald Reagan, which brought a renewed patriotism and self-confidence to Washington after a period of pessimism and "malaise." His pragmatic proposals for tax cuts, deregulation, and defense spending were accompanied with inspiring rhetoric about national pride and a hopeful future. Conservatives solved a series of public challenges that liberals could not or at least did not address: ending the Cold War, rejuvenating the American economy from the "stagflation" of the 1970s, and restoring order and fiscal health to the nation's states and cities. Such achievements should have refuted the claims that there is something "un-American" about conservatism and that it must always play second fiddle to liberalism. Conservative victories in Congress in 1994 contributed greatly to the success of Bill Clinton's presidency. After major electoral successes in 2010 and 2014, conservatives now have strong representation in Congress, state legislatures and governorships, and in public opinion, though they are far outnumbered in the organs of bureaucracy.

* * *

Even with their many successes and the growth of their cause, conservatives have never really functioned comfortably within mainstream politics, in part because they are more concerned with ideas and principles than with programs and the day-to-day administration of government. Most conservatives still think of themselves as an embattled minority fighting a proud and insulated establishment, including powerful elements of the Republican Party. Shut out of liberal institutions, such as elite college faculties and the national press, along with mainline churches and even government itself, conservatives have set up their own counterinstitutions: think tanks, radio and television networks, magazines, book publishers, citizen associations, charitable foundations, newspapers, and even a few colleges with conservative faculty and curricula. Within this framework, conservatives attend meetings and conferences, form friendships and associations, and develop and exchange ideas without ever having to come in contact with liberals; in this respect, they have emulated the practices of liberal and left-wing college faculties and journalistic associations. From their own secure redoubts, conservatives rally the public against the liberal establishment, often with surprising success. It is understandable that liberal critics are prone to see them as dangerous radicals.

Conservatives have in this way created their own "nation" within the nation, complete with its own culture, institutions, canonical texts, and prominent personalities. In past generations, class, ethnic, religious and regional cultures have placed their stamps on parties and cause-oriented movements. Rarely has a philosophical orientation in politics been able to build such a multifaceted and politically influential culture. It is impossible to view American conservatism as an instrument of any particular class, or any religious, ethnic, or occupational group. This is what allows conservatives to make broad philosophical appeals. It is also why their leaders are susceptible to being bogged down by procedural details or ground up in the complex machinery of government.

As a political insurgency, American conservatives have naturally adopted the language of opposition. Some of this, admittedly, is exaggerated and overwrought, as when they denounce "the establishment" or call for "revolution," although they usually have something more modest in mind. Unlike a political party, which is a collection or coalition of interests, American conservatism is a movement of principles and philosophy. It focuses on large goals rather than incremental changes in policy, and it is interested in recruiting only likeminded members. Because of this character, the conservative movement is not much interested in "the politics of compromise" or in accommodations with liberalism and liberal politics.

As a separate culture, conservatism has a built-in resistance to being killed off: even if the voters should abandon it temporarily, its institutions will persist and prepare the ground for a revival. Political parties die when they lose too many elections, but movements can continue intact in the face of repeated defeats until their goals have been reached or they have been absorbed into the mainstream operations of government. In fact, the conservative movement may be more in its element in opposition, when principles can be advocated in pure form, rather than in power, when those principles are inevitably adulterated by compromise. Recent setbacks and a renewed challenge from liberalism may actually have reinvigorated the movement after the Bush years and brought new recruits into the ranks. Instead of killing off conservatism, the last two presidential elections may have created the conditions for its renewal.

* * *

In an excellent history of the movement, John Micklethwait and Adrian Wooldridge, both writers for the *Economist*, point out that the influence of American conservatism is one of the features that give the United States its unique identity in the world.[3] Indeed, the UK edition of their book, *The Right Nation*, is subtitled "Why America Is Different." To the extent their thesis is true (and there is much to be said in its favor), it is American conservatism that has opened up a chasm between the politics of the United States and that of other industrial nations.

The American left—with its industrial unions, government workers and public employee unions, college and university supporters, and liberal intellectuals—has its obvious equivalents in Great Britain, France, Germany, and much of the rest of Europe. The Democratic Party, though not as far to the left as its continental counterparts, would not be out of place within the European context. It is definitely not the American left or the Democratic Party that makes the United States an unusual or exceptional nation.

American conservatism, on the other hand, is an unusual movement in the modern world. Its various affiliated groups promoting liberty and free markets, lower tax rates, religion, traditional morality, patriotism, and national strength are largely unknown elsewhere. There are no political organizations in Europe that resemble the various components of American conservatism, such as the Christian Coalition, the Family Research Council, the National Rifle Association, the Tea Party movement, or the various other tax-limitation and patriotic groups now active. The prominent representatives of American conservatism, from Newt Gingrich to Sarah Palin to Rand Paul and Ted Cruz, would be far outside the mainstream in Great Britain, France, or Germany. While conservatism exists elsewhere as a philosophy of government, it nowhere else takes the form it has assumed in the United States.

The conservative movement thus increasingly defines American exceptionalism in the contemporary world. It is unlikely to die anytime soon, but if it did, much that is exceptional about America would expire with it.

≪

Adapted from an essay that appeared in *The National Interest*,
November/December 2010.

CHAPTER EIGHT

Is Conservatism Dead?

When Barack Obama moved into the White House in early 2009, the conservative movement in the United States was in disarray, at war with itself, uncertain about its future, and badly damaged by events it did not foresee and could not explain. An unpopular war in Iraq and a financial crisis coming to a head in the middle of the presidential campaign seemed to undermine two pillars of postwar conservatism: a nationalistic foreign policy and a reliance on free markets to spur and sustain economic growth. Naturally, some liberals were eager to overinterpret the results of the 2008 election and declare the death of conservatism as an influential movement in American politics. Among others, George Packer (in the *New Yorker*), E. J. Dionne (in the *Washington Post*), and Sam Tanenhaus (first in the *New Republic*, later in a book) asserted that the conservative era that began with the election of Ronald Reagan in 1980 had now come to an end with the failed administration of George W. Bush. Obama's victory, they believed, marked the beginning of a new liberal era in American politics.

Several years into this new age, those forecasts now appear to have been premature and based more on wishful thinking than on careful analysis. Going back at least as far as Theodore H. White's award-winning chronicle of the 1960 campaign, journalists have been tempted to turn every presidential election into a historic turning point of some kind. Obama's triumph may yet turn out to have marked such a crossroad, but probably not of the sort these liberal writers imagined.

Liberal critics have tended to endow conservatives and the conservative movement with Wizard of Oz–like characteristics, as being possessed of the power to manipulate events but also ever susceptible to exposure and well-deserved exile. While conservatives have never had the ability to control political events in the United States, they have built a large and varied movement that is not going to disappear anytime soon. They have done so not through a cynical political strategy concocted by Richard Nixon, Patrick Buchanan, or Karl Rove, as some liberals have misled themselves into believing, but by building an intellectual case (as Chapter 7 argued) and by solving a series of public challenges—from crime to the Cold War—that liberals could not or did not address. Any movement with that kind of political momentum behind it was never likely to evaporate as a consequence of a single lost election. Nevertheless, despite everything that has happened since William F. Buckley launched *National Review* in 1954, or since Ronald Reagan was elected president and reversed the Carter-era malaise, there are many who still hold fast to the old myths.

* * *

Sam Tanenhaus, the editor of the *New York Times Book Review* at the time, first declared that "Conservatism Is Dead" in a long article in the *New Republic* published on February 18, 2009, amid the breathless excitement surrounding Obama's inauguration. It was easy then to imagine that liberals had scored a knockout over their conservative adversaries. Many entertained hopes that the new president might bring about a wholesale transformation in the conduct of public affairs—a "revolution in the consciousness of our time," as Norman Mailer had put it in describing the hoped-for consequences of John F. Kennedy's victory in 1960.

The enthusiastic reception of Tanenhaus's message justified a rapidly written expansion of the essay into a short book, titled *The Death of Conservatism*,* in which he reprises old arguments about conservatism and tries to bring them up to date. Tanenhaus asserts that the conservative movement collapsed under the presidency of George W. Bush. He is not altogether certain as to the causes of this collapse, alternatively suggesting that conservatives undid themselves because they were corrupt and unprincipled in their pursuit of power, and that they lost the support of the American people because of their rigid devotion to right-wing "orthodoxy."

The one thing about which he is certain is that he dislikes conservatives—intensely and unremittingly, judging by the rhetoric in this book. Tanenhaus says at various points that conservatives are out to destroy the country, that they are driven by revenge and resentment, that they dislike America, and that they behave more like extremists and revolutionaries ("Jacobins") than like genuine conservatives. In effect, he has resurrected the liberal literature about Senator Joseph McCarthy and the "radical right," and sought to apply it to contemporary conservatism as if nothing of importance had happened in the meantime. All of this is nonsense, of course. Given some of the author's previous writings, particularly his balanced biography of Whittaker Chambers, one might have hoped that he would produce something more elevated than the partisan screed that he has packaged in this book.

Tanenhaus argues that American conservatives failed because they did not act like conservatives at all, but instead like radicals who aim to demolish everything associated with modern liberalism.

---

* New York: Random House, 2009.

The paradox of the modern right, he says, is that "Its drive for power has steered it onto a path that has become profoundly and defiantly *un*-conservative." According to Tanenhaus, conservatives have been divided since the 1950s between a Burkean inclination to preserve the constitutional order, and a reactionary or "revanchist" impulse to tear up every liberal accommodation to modern life. "On the one side," he writes, "are those who have upheld the Burkean ideal of replenishing civil society by adjusting to changing conditions. On the other are those committed to a revanchist counterrevolution, whether the restoration of America's pre–New Deal ancient regime, a return to Cold War–style Manichaeanism, or the revival of pre-modern family values." In recent years, he concludes, the "revanchists" have gotten the upper hand over the Burkeans and have run the conservative juggernaut over a cliff and into irrelevance. In a passage that gives a flavor of the exaggerated rhetoric contained in the book, Tanenhaus writes that today's conservatives "resemble the exhumed figures of Pompeii, trapped in postures of frozen flight, clenched in the rigor mortis of a defunct ideology."

These "exhumed figures" are presumably free-market economists and conservatives like Jonah Goldberg and Amity Shlaes whose books have been critical of the New Deal, neoconservatives who supported the war in Iraq, and social conservatives who have opposed abortion, easy divorce, and gay marriage. In Tanenhaus's view, genuine conservatives would accept the New Deal and the welfare state as "Burkean corrections" that served to adapt the American economy to modern conditions. Nor would "real" conservatives have supported a war in Iraq that was based upon a utopian ideal of bringing democracy to the Middle East. Tanenhaus also thinks that conservatives should accept gay marriage as a logical extension of family values. The reason conservatives have not followed such advice, he says, is that their attachment to orthodox doctrine trumps the practical advantages of finding areas of accommodation with their adversaries; in a most un-Burkean way, they have allowed ideology to prevail over experience and common sense. For this reason, he suggests, the right is the main source of disorder and dissension in contemporary society and the instigators of the country's long-running culture war.

Deploying this framework, Tanenhaus arrives at surprising judgments about some prominent conservatives. For example, he identifies Ronald Reagan as a "real" conservative because he made no effort to repeal popular social programs but accepted them as an integral aspect of the American consensus. This is gracious on the author's part, though it is a judgment that few liberals endorsed during the years of the Reagan presidency. They are certain that the only reason President Reagan did not repeal many of those programs is because Congress would not permit it. After all, one of Ronald Reagan's favorite sayings was "Government is the problem, not the solution." Reagan, like every other major Republican officeholder of recent decades, including George W. Bush and Newt Gingrich, was constrained in this area by a mix of congressional politics, interest groups, and public opinion.

Tanenhaus also maintains that William F. Buckley, after starting out as a "revanchist" in the 1950s, changed into a Burkean in the 1960s by his acceptance of liberal reforms, especially in civil rights. This may turn out to be a theme in the authorized biography of Buckley that Tanenhaus has long planned to write, though there are some obvious problems with it. For one thing, Buckley never took back anything he said or wrote during the 1950s about McCarthy, communism, liberalism, or higher education; nor is it evident from anything he said or wrote that he regretted taking those positions. It is perhaps true that Buckley became somewhat less polemical in style with the passing decades, but it is difficult to discern any change in principles that would justify the conclusion that the Buckley of 1968 and thereafter was a different kind of conservative from the one who launched *National Review*.

Tanenhaus uses the terms *revanchist* and *revanchism* promiscuously throughout his book, plainly as instruments for tarring conservatives as destructive reactionaries, and their use in this context is irresponsible and inflammatory. *Revanchism*, drawn from the French word for "revenge," originated as a term to describe European nationalist movements of the nineteenth and twentieth centuries that sought to restore lost territory or prestige through new wars of conquest and occupation. Though originally applied to movements in France that aimed to recapture territory seized by Germany in the Franco-Prussian War, the term more accurately applies to the nationalist parties that arose in Germany in the 1920s, dedicated to the overthrow of the Weimar Republic and the Treaty of Versailles. Revanchists reject liberalism and democracy in favor of nationalism and strongman rule, and surely cannot be said to endorse the ideals of liberty, limited government, and the rule of law that form the core of American conservative thought. The repeated use of this term in the American context is thus hard to justify, as much so as McCarthy's charge that American liberals of the 1950s were "crypto-communists." Tanenhaus condemns conservative writers who draw parallels between the New Deal and fascism, but carelessly suggests parallels between American conservatives and European fascists. This is one of the more unsavory aspects of a book filled with unsavory allusions and implications.

The argument that contemporary conservatives are reactionaries or revanchists is wrong on its face. The market school of economics cannot be dismissed just because it is critical of the New Deal or of Keynesian policies, nor are free-market thinkers reactionary in any sense of the term. Tanenhaus does not inquire seriously into the reasons why conservatives are uneasy with the welfare state, why some see in it a threat to liberty and others an encouragement to the breakdown of the family and self-government. The market revolution of the last thirty years, moreover, contributed greatly to global prosperity, to the fall of communism, and to much else that has been beneficial to the United States and the world. It is true that the financial collapse of 2008 presented a challenge to market thinking, but it does not vindicate central planning or the welfare state, nor does it justify the conclusion that market economics is dead. In fact, the path back to prosperity will undoubtedly lead through a return to free and flexible markets.

The drawn-out war in Iraq was a key factor in the sweeping Democratic electoral victory in 2008, but this does not support Tanenhaus's case for the death of conservatism either. That intervention, after all, was endorsed not only by conservatives and neoconservatives but also by every Democratic candidate for president in 2008 save for Barack Obama (who was a member of the Illinois legislature when the war began). President Bush justified the war on liberal or Wilsonian grounds, so if the war discredited anything it was the liberal ideal of achieving collective security through the promotion of democracy. One may argue that such an agenda is misguided, or even that it is inconsistent with conservative principles, but it is not revanchist.

As for the culture war—well, most conservatives would be glad to have it over with, if only cultural liberals and radicals would call a halt to their provocations. The historical record is clear that the first shots fired in every engagement of the culture war came from the left: in school busing, in the abortion decision of the Supreme Court, in the Mapplethorpe exhibition, in political correctness on the campus, and recently in the push for gay marriage. Indeed, what is often called the "religious right" came into existence in the late 1970s in response to the Carter administration's effort to deny tax exemption to religious schools because, Carter claimed, they were segregated. Without all those liberal provocations, there would have been no culture war and probably no "religious right" to wage it.

Like the liberal writers of the 1950s, Tanenhaus wants to see a conservative movement that accommodates rather than opposes liberalism, and that accepts its subordinate place alongside the dominant liberal tradition in American life. He acknowledges that there is an important role for conservatism if it is genuinely conservative in the sense that it preserves liberal gains rather than seeking to overturn them. In any event, he says, conservatives will have little choice but to adapt to liberal leadership because the election of 2008 effectively ended the era of conservative dominance in American politics. Much as liberals had to accommodate to conservatives after Reagan's election in 1980, conservatives will now have to accept the renewed dominance of reform liberalism, or else accept the consequences of being turned into "the exhumed figures of Pompeii, trapped in postures of frozen flight."

* * *

While Tanenhaus greatly exaggerates the death of conservatism, his premise that the period from 1980 to 2008 was a "conservative era" in national politics is also somewhat overstated. It is true that conservatives achieved groundbreaking victories in the 1980s by restoring national confidence, reigniting a stalled economy, restructuring the tax system, and engineering a military buildup that played a large role in bringing down the Soviet Union. It is also true that conservative ideas had a greater influence in national affairs during this period than at any time in the nation's history—to the point where a Democratic president, having seen Republicans win control of the House of Representatives for the first time in forty years along with the Senate, declared in 1996 that "the era of big government is over." Compared with the period from 1930 to 1980, our national politics from Reagan up to the election of Obama were generally conservative, and certainly so in foreign and economic policy.

Nevertheless, even during the conservative ascendancy, the

federal government's share of GDP was not reduced but merely stabilized; no major domestic social or educational program was terminated, and only one (welfare for the poor) was substantially reformed. Meanwhile, the libertarian revolution in cultural affairs launched in the 1960s continued apace and even gained speed through these decades. In the five presidential elections from 1992 to 2008, Republicans captured a popular majority exactly once, while the Democrats managed to turn several major states (California, Michigan, Illinois, and New York) into one-party jurisdictions. Indeed, from the late 1980s up to 2008, American politics resembled a stalemate more than anything else, as the two sides implicitly agreed to follow conservative policies to promote economic growth while allocating the proceeds to bolstering and expanding the welfare state. This particular era may have come to an end in the financial crash of 2008, but mainly because the engine of growth needed to sustain an expensive government establishment ran out of steam.

The election of 2008 was neither a repudiation of conservatism nor a public endorsement of liberalism. By the time Tanenhaus's book appeared in print, moreover, the extravagant hopes surrounding Obama's election were already giving way to more sober assessments of what is truly possible to achieve within the American system. President Obama—perhaps believing that the election gave him an ideological mandate, and blessed with liberal majorities in both houses of Congress—had decided early in his first term to govern from the left instead of trying to split his opposition by moving closer to the center. As a consequence, his approval ratings steadily fell back to earth, and a public wary of his agenda put Republicans back in control of the House of Representatives in 2010.

The two signal achievements of the Obama administration and the Democratic Congress, an $800 billion stimulus package and the health-care reform act, are so unpopular that Democrats who voted for them are now reluctant to bring them up. More significantly, popular doubts about growing federal deficits and looming tax increases operate as a check on ambitious new proposals. Today, more than half of all voters disapprove of Obama's policies. Many elected Democrats have refused to appear with him when he visits their districts. The mythical mandate of the 2008 election collapsed with surprising speed, as anyone with a basic grasp of political arithmetic could have predicted from the beginning, and Obama's reelection in 2012 did not revive it for long. Republicans solidified their hold on the House in the 2014 elections and won nine new seats in the Senate to gain control of that body as well. Nearly all of these successful candidates ran as outspoken conservatives, while many of their Democratic opponents distanced themselves from the liberal leader of their party.

In pronouncing the death of conservatism so quickly, Tanenhaus appears to have made the mistake of forecasting a trend on the basis of a single event. His obituary for conservatism seems less plausible with every passing month.

It is certainly true, as Tanenhaus says, that conservatism as a political doctrine has its flaws and weaknesses, which are magnified when it is judged in the immediate aftermath of a lost election or in isolation from alternative approaches to public life. When judged in relation to liberalism, however, modern conservatism takes on a more favorable outlook. Many of the sins that Tanenhaus attributes to conservatives—overly zealous attachment to principle or ideology, unwillingness to adapt to change, impatience with popular opinion—are on display as much or more among liberals. If Tanenhaus or anyone else wishes to see liberalism in action, he might venture onto an elite college campus where only liberal and leftist views are permitted peaceful expression, or out to Sacramento or Springfield, or up to Albany, or perhaps to Detroit or to Stockton, California— all places where liberal Democrats, long in control, have spent their states or cities into near bankruptcy. The liberal faculties and public employee unions that control those institutions and jurisdictions have not exactly distinguished themselves for their open-mindedness or farsighted leadership. In California and New York, the public employee unions that control the Democratic Party, and thereby the state governments, have exploited the prosperity of recent decades to build up huge government establishments that will no longer be affordable in an age of austerity, especially as taxpayers and businesses flee to other states like Texas and Florida that have followed more conservative paths.

As California, New York, and Illinois unravel, voters will have little choice but to turn to conservatives to restore levels of growth and prosperity sufficient to fund their social programs and educational systems. Liberals will come to understand that they will have to tolerate conservatives and conservative policies in order to fund their own programs. That will be a hard and painful lesson for liberals to learn. If conservatism is dead, in short, then so is liberalism and much else besides.

* * *

As previously noted, there are now more self-identified conservatives than liberals in America, by a margin of about 38 percent to 23 percent. This imbalance in public opinion, even allowing for the imprecision of the terms "liberal" and "conservative," is one of the cardinal facts of American politics that should make us wonder not about the death of conservatism, but rather how a new liberal era was ever going to be built upon such a meager public following. It suggests why liberals in power must tack to the center if they are to survive, while conservatives can govern more from the right; and it explains why Obama's attempt to reprise FDR or LBJ was likely to fail.

The financial crisis of 2008 and the war in Iraq undoubtedly damaged the Republican brand, but do not appear to have dampened in any significant measure the public's support for conservative ideas pertaining to free markets and limited government. The fact that conservatism continues to prosper while Republicanism falters is yet one more sign that conservatism is more of an independent movement than just an adjunct of the Republican Party. In the estimation of many conservatives, it is also a sign that the Republican Party would do better in elections by being more consistently conservative.

Conservatism is now a permanent aspect of American political life, supported by millions of Americans and defended by a large network of writers, journals, and think tanks. There is, however, a more important reason for its enduring appeal among Americans. Conservatism in America deploys the principles of tradition, reason, and orderly change in defense of fundamentally liberal institutions: the Constitution, representative government, liberty and equal rights, and the rule of law. It is generally the conservative, not the modern liberal, who emphasizes the inspired example of the Founding Fathers, the words of the Constitution, and the sacrifices made to build free institutions. Liberals want to overcome the past or to apologize for it—as in Obama's aim to "remake America" and his so-called "apology tour," in which he declared America's supposed sins on foreign stages. Conservatives, on the other hand, want us to remember, to learn, and to build constructively upon our past—as when President Reagan promoted national self-confidence and progress through an embrace of America's foundational principles. It is for this reason, and not because he accepted a liberal status quo, that the Reagan legacy continues to animate a distinctive brand of American conservatism that is very much alive.

❧

Adapted from an essay that appeared in *The New Criterion*,
September 2009.

CHAPTER NINE

Is Liberalism Dead?

Having established that conservatism in America is alive and well, I must now ask if liberalism is dead. The answer, despite some recent electoral setbacks, is no, and for some of the same reasons. Liberalism and conservatism are more or less permanent, antagonistic features of our system of state capitalism, such that neither is likely to disappear unless or until the whole system somehow blows up. If either liberalism or conservatism should expire, it will be through a crisis or cataclysm much in the way that secessionism disappeared with the Civil War and laissez-faire capitalism with the Great Depression.

Such an upheaval is not entirely out of the question, as the long recession that began in 2007 continues to strain public and private budgets and to undermine the legitimacy of market capitalism. Yet there are reasons to believe that this trend poses a greater threat to liberalism than to conservatism. If we are now in the midst of an extended period of stagnation, it is possible that liberalism in the form we know it today will not survive as a vigorous political movement.

For the greater part of the twentieth century, liberalism rode an ascending arc of influence before reaching a peak in the 1960s, and it has been on a more or less steady downward path since then. It is no longer the nation's dominant public doctrine as it was in the middle of the last century. The proportion of Americans willing to call themselves "liberal" is now far outweighed by those who describe themselves as "conservative." In popular circles—where liberalism is associated with high taxes, wild spending, and groups like the American Civil Liberties Union—the tag "liberal" is often thrown about as a term of abuse.

Liberalism has evolved from a popular philosophy at its high point into a "vanguard" movement with great support among experts, academics, journalists, and government workers, but far less among voters whom these elites purport to serve. At the same time, it has lodged itself more firmly within the structure of government and taken on the form of public sector liberalism, which brings advantages but also serious liabilities in the long term. Liberalism is not dead, but it may be under siege. It is likely to change its appearance once again, as it has several times in the past.

* * *

Liberalism became a force in U.S. politics only late in the nineteenth century, after extended conflicts over slavery and secession were resolved and industrial capitalism had introduced a new set of issues into the system. Up until that time, parties and interests framed their arguments in terms of the Constitution and the nature of the system it had created. Liberalism injected the element of abstract philosophy into these arguments. More importantly, it set them off in a new direction by asserting that the eighteenth-century Constitution was inadequate to the challenges of an industrial society. Instead of debating over what the founders intended, liberals argued about how the founders' Constitution should be reinterpreted and reformed to suit new economic conditions. Thus, American liberalism emerged as an aspect of modern capitalism and should be viewed as an enduring element of a democratic capitalist system.

Subsequently, liberalism has passed through at least four separate stages and is now well into a fifth. It first appeared under the banner of progressivism, which held that new political institutions had to be established to regulate industrial concentrations and to mediate conflicts between business and labor. Progressivism flamed out during World War I and seemed to have disappeared for good in the 1920s, but liberalism revived itself during the 1930s in a New Deal variation, which preserved some themes of progressivism. When New Deal liberalism ran out of steam because of World War II and the prosperity of the postwar period, liberalism transformed into a Cold War version, which was more technocratic than its predecessor but also staunchly anticommunist in foreign policy. It was in this form that liberalism achieved new peaks of popularity and influence during the Kennedy-Johnson years.

The rebels and protesters of the 1960s authored a fourth chapter by introducing the theme of liberation on various cultural fronts. In this phase, cultural radicals elbowed their way into the liberal mainstream and politicized matters relating to family life, sexual mores, and religion. Their agenda to remake and even rend the inherited fabric of society displaced the traditional liberal objective of providing economic security for the working man. As liberalism morphed into leftism, it strengthened its appeal to the educated classes but lost its broad support among middle- and working-class voters—the "Archie Bunkers" of America. This trend continued when, somewhat surprisingly, the theme of liberation from social conventions and moral strictures yielded ground to an angrier agenda of punishing a society seen as hypocritical and corrupt.

The shocking and disquieting events of the 1960s—the assassinations of President Kennedy and Robert F. Kennedy and Martin Luther King Jr., the urban riots, the war in Vietnam—produced a change of attitude among liberals and leftists toward American society and traditional concepts of reform. From the Progressive

Era until the 1960s, liberals had viewed reform as an instrument of progress through which the ideals of liberty and justice might be more perfectly realized. Liberal reformers such as FDR, JFK, and Lyndon Johnson aimed to bring the promise of American life within the reach of more people; they acted out of a conviction that the American experiment in self-government was inherently good and that the task of policy was to improve or even perfect it. By the end of the 1960s, however, the reform tradition took on an angry visage.*

When they looked around, liberals in the 1960s did not see progress; instead they saw blighted cities and ghettoes, a despoiled environment, and rampant bigotry and discrimination. White Americans had enslaved blacks and committed genocide against Native Americans; they had oppressed women and tyrannized minority groups, including Japanese Americans who were interned in camps during World War II. Americans had been harsh and unfeeling toward the poor. In our greed, we had ravaged the earth and were consuming a disproportionate share of the world's resources. The United States government coddled dictators and violated human rights out of an irrational fear of communism.

With this bill of indictment in hand, liberals began to recast the reform ideal, turning it from an instrument of progress into one of punishment. The "punitive liberals" held that Americans had no right at all to feel pride in their country's history or optimism about its future. They believed that the purpose of national policy should be to punish the nation for its past crimes rather than to build a stronger America and a brighter future for all. In particular, they sought to punish the wealthy and the middle class for winning

---

* I have made this case at greater length in *Camelot and the Cultural Revolution: How the Assassination of John F. Kennedy Shattered American Liberalism* (New York: Encounter Books, 2007).

success at the expense of higher ideals or designated victim groups. From this idea flowed compulsory school busing, race and gender preferences, the cosseting of criminals who were painted as "victims of society," and a legal culture based upon the idea that every wrong can be remedied by a lawsuit.

The punitive aspects of this doctrine were made plain in debates over its favored policies. If one asked whether it was really fair to impose employment quotas for women and minorities, the answer might be: "White men imposed quotas on us, and now we're going to do the same to them!" Was busing of school children really an effective means of improving educational opportunities for blacks? A similar answer was often given: "Whites bused blacks to enforce segregation, and now they deserve to get a taste of their own medicine!" Do we really strengthen our own security by undercutting allied governments in the name of human rights, particularly when they are replaced by openly hostile regimes (as in Iran and Nicaragua)? Answer: "That is the price we have to pay for coddling dictators." And so it went. Whenever the arguments were pressed, a punitive motive could be discovered behind most reform policies.

During the 1970s, punitive liberals built an impressive network of interest groups to promote and take advantage of a sense of historical guilt. These included the feminist and civil rights groups that pressed for affirmative action, quotas, and other policies to compensate women and minorities for past mistreatment; the welfare rights organizations that characterized welfare and various poverty programs as entitlements or, even better, as reparations owed to the poor in compensation for similar mistreatment; the environmental groups that pressed for ever more stringent regulations on business; and the human rights and disarmament groups that lobbied the government to punish or disassociate the United States from allies who were said to violate human rights. These groups ensconced themselves in university departments and advocacy organizations, and took up influential roles in the Democratic Party and in Congress.

Naturally, it was somewhat tricky to advance the tenets of punitive liberalism in the public arena, especially in electoral contests. The voters, after all, are unlikely to take kindly to the idea that they must be punished for the sins, real or imagined, of earlier generations. In many ways, Jimmy Carter and his leading appointees were exemplars of punitive liberalism, so it is no wonder that their leadership generated a sense of "malaise" among the American people. Even Carter's vice president, Walter Mondale, felt that Carter had made a serious mistake in seeming to attack the voters. Mondale later wrote, "I argued that if, having gotten elected on the grounds that we needed a government as good as the people, we now were heard to argue that we needed a people as good as the government, that we would be destroyed." That is pretty much what happened to the Carter-Mondale ticket in 1980.

Given the difficulties of advancing their cause in the electoral arena, the punitive liberals instead worked through the regulatory bodies and the federal courts—these being the more appropriate venues for leveling blame, exacting punishment, and collecting rewards. And they did so with considerable success, winning a series of court cases and regulatory decisions upholding employment quotas, school busing, and environmental and labor policies. Many civil judgments were also won in these areas against corporations, school districts, colleges and universities, and state and local governments.

These successes have played a large role in fraying the national consensus about the role of the federal government that developed in the 1940s and 1950s. Because they sought to cultivate guilt in order to leverage policy, the punitive liberals proved incapable of adopting practical measures to strengthen the economy or to advance American power in the world. Such goals, in any case, would have been contrary to their deeper longings, which were to dispel American pride and to shrink American ambitions at home and abroad. The Cold War in particular seemed to them a pointless struggle between two flawed empires, "two scorpions in a bottle." While they did not wish to see the communists win, neither were they prepared to swallow the triumphalism that would accompany a victory by the West. A strong economy, meanwhile, would disproportionately reward the rich and the self-satisfied middle classes— the very groups that the punitive liberals wished to chastise.

And thus it was perhaps inevitable that the policies of the punitive liberals would give us the worst of all worlds: weakness and embarrassment abroad, inflation and unemployment at home, and a public that was beginning to lose hope in its future. The manifest failure of liberal policies during the 1960s and 1970s—in escalating crime, soaring illegitimate birth rates, exploding welfare rolls, and the collapse of standards in education—were linked to the liberal and leftist attacks on conventional morals that doubly alienated middle-class voters. By 1980, the public had seen the results of its experiment with punitive liberalism and was looking for an alternative vision, so it elected Ronald Reagan, with his optimistic vision of progress rooted in the essential goodness of the American system and its people. The successes of conservatives during the 1980s would set liberal failures in stark relief.

Even so, punitive liberalism has not gone away. Grievance-based politics are flourishing in advocacy organizations and on college campuses, where the "diversity" agenda serves primarily to foster a sense of white guilt and to exact payback. Many Americans expected in 2008 that electing a black president would finally absolve the nation of its past racial sins, but instead today's punitive liberals have wielded racial guilt as a weapon against dissent. Meanwhile, the "climate justice" agenda aims to punish advanced industrial societies for their prosperity. Because it brings demands that various designated victim groups be compensated for the alleged injustices of society, punitive liberalism has fed the proliferation of distributional coalitions that make claims on public resources.

Liberalism today is thus a vanguard movement increasingly at odds with the voters who must pay for its agenda. It is true that liberalism has always relied upon its vanguard classes to supply it with new problems to solve and new programs for doing so. The Progressives had their academic experts and muckraking journalists, the New Deal had its Brains Trust, and the postwar liberals depended on the federal courts. What is different today is the extent to which the new agendas of liberalism—environmentalism, feminism, homosexual marriage, income redistribution—are dissociated from the practical aspirations of average Americans. The liberal vanguard once claimed to speak for the middle classes but now it seldom even pretends to do so.

At the same time, however, liberals and leftists have gained control of the Democratic Party. Up until the 1970s and 1980s, the party had also provided a home for southern conservatives, national security "hawks," conservative Catholics, and moderates of various kinds. These groups have by now left or been expelled from the party, which has turned into a coalition of ideological liberals, ethnic interest groups, public sector unions, and beneficiaries of public programs.

* * *

A common denominator through all the stages in the history of liberalism is the expansion of the national government's power. Every phase has brought forth a growing list of demands for government action to address one or another national challenge, or the needs of particular interest groups. This is true even of the cultural liberals of the 1960s (like Hillary Rodham Clinton) who sought liberation from just about every institution in American society except for the national state. The two themes of liberation and statism might seem contradictory, but in effect they are connected: as people free themselves from religion, family obligations, and community norms, they have nowhere else to turn for protection but to the state. This is why conservatives saw very quickly in the 1960s that "liberation" was a challenge to "liberty." Liberation from social norms and moral restraints leads to family breakdown, drug dependency and crime—and thus to demands for a bigger welfare state as well as more vigorous policing.

Liberalism in its successive incarnations represents an American version of the twentieth-century romance with the state. The disasters that befell other countries as a consequence of this infatuation did not happen here because our Constitution and the acquired political habits of the American people did not permit it. Instead there has been a more incremental process of state expansion over a period of nearly a century. But make no mistake: this slow revolution engineered by liberalism has succeeded in overturning the institutional prescriptions of the eighteenth-century Constitution. A charter designed to limit the central government has now been turned into one that empowers it to act in just about every area of life. Liberalism has by stages taken aim at one or another of the institutional pillars of limited government—federalism, strict construction, separation of powers, public thrift—until few are now left standing. Madison's "parchment barriers" have been blurred or obliterated to such an extent that today the only genuine limitation on national power is to be found in public opinion.

The statist agenda of liberalism, though it is usually framed in idealistic terms, serves a hardnosed political purpose. If there is a single lesson that liberals have learned through the decades, it is that the power and resources of the state can be used to build winning political coalitions and to put ideological opponents at a disadvantage. After nearly a century of this process, liberalism and the groups associated with it have entwined themselves in the day-to-day operations of government, implementing the programs they have managed to pass into law and organizing new voting groups around them. Liberalism is no longer merely a philosophy of government, as it was in the Progressive Era, but rather an integral part of modern government itself, which is why it cannot be killed by its policy failures, lost arguments, or even lost elections.

Liberalism has thus exchanged its broad support among the middle classes for the security and political leverage it finds in highly institutionalized sectors of American life. While conservatives now command broad support in public opinion, liberals can claim influence over leading colleges and universities, major newspapers and broadcast outlets, public sector spokesmen, and public employee unions, which in combination can shape—or go a long way toward shaping—the national political debate in the space between elections. Conservatives have learned to fight on this terrain as well, but they are still outflanked by liberals who occupy strategic positions in much closer proximity to government. As the party of "limited government," conservatism has gradually mobilized its forces at some remove from the state, while liberalism, as the "party of government," has by degrees attached itself to the state such that in many arenas (education, welfare, the arts) and locations (Sacramento, Albany, Washington, D.C.) it can be difficult to distinguish between them.

Much as liberalism has been absorbed into the state, so has the Democratic Party, even to the point where we may cease to regard it as an independent institution and view it instead as an instrument of the state (and vice versa, to some degree). No one should have been surprised to learn a few years ago that even the Internal Revenue Service is controlled by a labor union that endorses Democratic candidates. The latest transformation of liberalism has generated an unprecedented conflict between Democrats and Republicans, setting public sector unions and beneficiaries of public programs against the middle-class taxpayers and businesses that foot the bill. In states where public spending is high and public sector unions are strong—as in California, New York, and Illinois—Democrats have seized control; where the public sector is weak or not politically organized—as is the case across the South and Southwest—Republicans have greater strength. This configuration has resulted in electoral standoffs that are decided by a handful of swing states that do not fit readily into either camp.

Public sector liberalism represents the logical terminus for a movement that began in an effort to redraw the boundaries of government action in order to bring industrial capitalism to heel and that grew in tandem with the expansion of government. Over the course of the twentieth century, liberalism succeeded in rewriting the Constitution, building political coalitions around public spending, insinuating itself within the interstices of government, and gaining control of key institutions that manufacture and legitimize political opinion. From its impregnable redoubts, it fights a defensive struggle against voter sentiment that is growing more skeptical of its programs of high taxes and lavish public spending.

* * *

It is obvious that liberalism today can prosper only if it continues to build coalitions through public spending, public borrowing, and publicly guaranteed credit. These are the resources that underwrite their institutional advantages. Liberalism in its present form will recede as a political force when those resources dry up, public programs are cut, public employees are let go, and retirement arrangements with public sector unions are renegotiated. In some state public sectors, such outcomes now appear inevitable.

Conservatives are in a position to hasten this process along by refusing to approve the spending, borrowing, and federal bailouts that will be required to keep public sector liberalism afloat, though at the price of being blamed for the pain and suffering associated with its collapse. But this is undoubtedly a price worth paying to guide the nation through an adjustment that would otherwise take place later and under circumstances far less to anyone's liking.

※

Adapted from an essay that appeared in *The American Spectator*, January 2011.

CHAPTER TEN

Investing in Conservative Ideas

In the mid-1960s, liberalism was at high tide in the United States. "These are without doubt the years of the liberal," remarked John Kenneth Galbraith in 1964. "Almost everyone so describes himself." Liberalism was then a tough-minded doctrine that stood boldly for the working man at home and against tyranny abroad, while conservative thought was derided by Galbraith and other liberals as lacking intellectual substance. The long descent of liberalism from the late 1960s into the new century has thus been a perplexing development for thoughtful advocates of that faith who once believed that the future belonged to them. The corresponding rise of conservatism must seem doubly perplexing. Today, not only has conservatism gained prominence in the electoral sphere, but conservative thought has acquired a strong foothold in the intellectual sphere as well. For conservatives, a standoff in the world of ideas counts as a significant achievement.

Liberals have attempted to account for this reversal of fortune, but few of their explanations have been accurate, thoughtful, or constructive. Addressing the rise of conservatism, liberals often fall back on explanations that stress manipulation and trickery, with corporate payoffs to politicians looming large in the story. Conservative ideas play only a minor role in the account and are generally characterized as mere stalking horses for corporate interests. A particularly sinister role is ascribed to those conservative philanthropies that have helped fund thinkers, magazines, and research institutions—on the assumption that no one would advance such self-evidently meretricious ideas unless paid to do so.

Indeed, the left has displayed a near-obsessive interest in conservative philanthropies. A number of websites today are devoted entirely to charting the activities of the "right-wing foundations established by major corporate polluters," as the environmental activist Robert F. Kennedy Jr. described them in his book *Crimes against Nature*. Similarly, the journalists David Brock and Eric Alterman have devoted much energy to "exposing" the projects supported by these institutions as well as their links to other organizations and their place in the broader constellation of conservative activism. Reports by People for the American Way and the National Committee for Responsive Philanthropy dwell with heavy emphasis on the supposedly underhanded strategies and tactics employed by the foundations to advance their dubious causes.

These broadsides ignore the substance of the ideas themselves, quite as if John Stuart Mill's famous characterization of conservatives as "the stupid party" were still the rule in the early twenty-first century. But the plain fact is that modern conservatives have been engaged with the world of ideas to a far greater extent than most modern liberals. David Brooks observed that most conservatives can list a number of books or authors that influenced their political thinking, while liberals have difficulty identifying any. This lively engagement with a coherent body of ideas is a crucial if much-overlooked aspect of the rise of conservatism, and one in which conservative foundations have played a central role.

* * *

During the six or seven decades running from the end of World War

II down to the present, conservative philanthropy has gone through at least two distinct phases and is now entering a third. Surprising though it may seem to liberal critics, both of these phases were guided far more by ideas than by narrow business or corporate interests.

The first phase, which began in the mid-1940s and ran well into the 1970s, was guided primarily by the doctrine of classical liberalism. The main donors were the Volker Fund, the Relm and Earhart foundations, the Liberty Fund, and business leaders like Jasper Crane of DuPont, Henry Weaver of General Motors, B. E. Hutchinson of Chrysler, and the British entrepreneur Anthony Fisher. (The Liberty Fund and the Earhart Foundation live on today, though the latter will spend its remaining funds and close its doors in 2015. The Charles Koch Foundation and the Searle Freedom Trust, with combined assets of around $500 million, are contemporary successors to this tradition of classical liberal philanthropy.) These donors had only modest sums at their disposal, giving away around $3 million per year all together, as compared with the $300 million that the Ford Foundation alone allocated annually in the mid-1960s.

There were, to be sure, important differences among these donors. The Volker Fund was generally libertarian in its outlook, while the Earhart Foundation bridged the divide between classical liberalism, with its emphasis on liberty, and modern conservatism, with its emphasis on tradition and order. But the interests of all were, by design, intellectual and theoretical.

The seminal influence on these funders was Friedrich Hayek's *The Road to Serfdom*, published in London in 1944 and in the United States the following year. This slender volume, an articulate call to battle against socialism, turned its author, then an obscure professor at the London School of Economics, into an enduring hero among conservatives and classical liberals on both sides of the Atlantic. No other writer at the time had made the case against collectivist ideas and policies with such audacity and clarity. For this reason alone, *The Road to Serfdom* quickly became a reference point for those with misgivings about the expanding welfare state.

Named in many surveys as one of the most influential books of the twentieth century, *The Road to Serfdom* caused something of a sensation when first published, provoking reviews and comment from such leading figures as John Maynard Keynes and George Orwell, and scathing rebukes and rebuttals from scores of lesser lights. A condensed version, brought out in 1945 by *Reader's Digest*, reached over two million of the magazine's subscribers and aroused enough interest to bring Hayek to the United States for a national lecture tour.

The Road to Serfdom advanced two broad themes, one negative and the other positive. The first was that socialism leads almost inevitably to tyranny and the loss of liberty in all its forms. The second was that the antidote to socialism is to be found in the revival of classical liberalism as articulated by British Enlightenment thinkers like Adam Smith, David Hume, and Edmund Burke. The book was in some ways quite pessimistic: socialism was advancing everywhere and appeared irresistible. (As if to confirm Hayek's analysis, the UK parliamentary election of 1945 saw the Labor Party winning on a platform that called explicitly for the nationalization of British industry, and the victorious party proceeded to make good on its promise.) At the same time, Hayek saw a way out through the revival of a tradition of thought that was in the process of being lost.

As for the conservatism of his day, Hayek believed it suffered from a fatal weakness. Because it relied on tradition rather than principle, it could slow down or resist but never fundamentally alter the direction in which events were moving. That is why he took pains to emphasize that he himself was not a conservative at all, but rather a liberal in the Whig tradition. (A later essay of his was titled, simply, "Why I Am Not a Conservative.") This, as it happened, was one feature of Hayek's thinking that appealed in particular to Americans.

The American polity, as Hayek understood, was originally built

on the principle of liberty, and its political tradition was greatly influenced by the Whig ideals of limited government and the rule of law.
As a consequence, defenders of the American tradition were themselves frequently "liberals" in the European sense. For Americans
concerned about the expansion of government, the alternative to socialism and the welfare state was not conservatism but individualism.

Another enduring contribution of *The Road to Serfdom*, perhaps
more influential in the long run than Hayek's critique of socialism, was its emphasis on the importance of ideas in the growth
of political movements. Challenging the claims of historicists of
different stripes, Hayek insisted that socialism, collectivism, and
worship of the state were products not of economic forces beyond
anyone's control but of erroneous and destructive *ideas*. The Whig
principles that had been influential in Great Britain and continental Europe during the eighteenth and nineteenth centuries had
been displaced by collectivist and nationalistic ideas coming out of
Germany. Hegel and Marx led the attack on Whig ideals of liberty
and limited government; Sombart, Mannheim, and others continued the campaign in the twentieth century. Their ideas of class
struggle, capitalist exploitation, revolution, and socialism captured
the imagination of intellectuals in Europe and across the world.
Once the intellectuals were converted, they spread the message of
socialism through books, newspapers, and the schools.

In another essay, "The Intellectuals and Socialism" (1949),
Hayek mapped out a broad, long-term strategy for meeting this
challenge. Practical men of business, Hayek wrote, were at a decided disadvantage in the war of ideas because of their deep distrust of theoretical speculation and their "tendency to orthodoxy."
Businessmen, moreover, did not understand the link between ideas
and political movements, and therefore did not see the need to
mount a sustained intellectual defense of their own interests. He
urged his followers to learn from the success of socialism, which had

originated as a construction of theorists and philosophers and only later emerged as a political movement fielding candidates for office and appealing to voters.

"What we lack," Hayek wrote, "is a liberal Utopia, a program which seems neither a defense of things as they are nor a diluted kind of socialism, but a truly liberal radicalism...which does not confine itself to what appears today as politically possible." The positive content of such a program was necessarily vague, but it was plain that Hayek envisioned a movement operating at the level of principles and theory and aloof from electoral and legislative agendas or the immediate controversies of political life. He proposed, in other words, a true war of ideas that could appeal to the best and most adventuresome minds of the age but might take a generation or more to bear fruit.

Hayek's platform—theoretical, abstract, and utopian—might appear to be an impractical basis on which to build a philanthropic program. There was no pretense here of promoting piecemeal reforms, of helping a party or a candidate, of passing a piece of legislation, or, indeed, of producing immediate consequences of any kind. Yet the philanthropists mentioned earlier responded enthusiastically to his call.*

Hayek's writings had a direct impact in Great Britain, where

---

* Because of their theoretical approach, these donors were not necessarily involved in some of the other key intellectual events of the period, among them the founding of *National Review* in 1955. In launching this magazine, which was to play so great a role in the rise of modern conservatism, William F. Buckley Jr. aimed to create a forum of ideas that would at the same time address the controversial issues of the day; he also intended it as a for-profit enterprise, legally free to support and oppose candidates for public office. Both factors made the participation of these particular donors unlikely; in addition, their commitment to classical liberalism did not fit neatly with Buckley's own economic views.

Anthony Fisher (with Hayek's encouragement) established the Institute for Economic Affairs (IEA) in London in 1955. Led by the economist Ralph Harris, the IEA was the original free-market think tank, publishing books and pamphlets that documented the inefficiencies of socialism and state-run enterprises. True to Hayek's prediction, it would spend more than two decades advancing these ideas and gradually winning converts until a sympathetic friend, Margaret Thatcher, was elected prime minister and began to implement reforms that were much influenced by its work.

In 1947, the Volker Fund sent a group of Americans to Switzerland for the organizing meeting of the Mont Pelerin Society, founded by Hayek to promote the free market in economics and the broad ideals of classical liberalism. In conformity with Hayek's vision, Mont Pelerin functioned as an exclusively scholarly enterprise, avoiding political debate in favor of in-depth theorizing about the foundations of a free society. A short time later, Volker underwrote Hayek's appointment as professor of moral science (which had been Adam Smith's title at the University of Edinburgh) in the Committee on Social Thought at the University of Chicago, and also provided funds for New York University to hire Ludwig von Mises, Hayek's Austrian mentor and friend.

In addition to these appointments, Volker and other donors lent assistance to the "Chicago school" of economics, led by Milton Friedman and George Stigler, and to the "Virginia school" of political economy, led by James Buchanan; all three economists would later win the Nobel Prize in economics. These donors supported hundreds or perhaps thousands of graduate students, mostly in economics but also in allied fields like government and history; many later became prominent scholars in their own right. And they subsidized a few institutions, generally libertarian in outlook, including the Foundation for Economic Education, the Institute for Humane Studies, and the Intercollegiate Society of Individualists, which helped circulate market-oriented ideas to professors, students, and even businessmen.

It is difficult to recall today how radical the ideas of a Friedman or a Hayek appeared in the 1950s and 1960s, when the future seemed to point in the direction of central planning, socialism, and the welfare state. In those decades, the aim of the philanthropists who promoted Friedman and Hayek was to maintain the vitality of a remnant of thought until it could again be presented as an alternative to doctrines that had failed. That the movement did not find its way into the wider world of policy and public debate was in part deliberate: aiming for influence beyond the daily headlines, Hayek and his followers eschewed a strategy that might have enabled them to reach a broader audience. But, working as they were against the intellectual grain of the time, they also had little success in breaking into the world of the universities—and without gaining a foothold in the academy there was little hope of converting the next generation of scholars.

By the early 1970s, Hayek himself had been dismissed as an extremist, even a reactionary. After a quarter century of dedicated effort, the classical liberals had less influence in American life than they did when they launched their campaign in the 1940s.

* * *

While the right-of-center foundations in this period attracted little attention beyond their immediate circle—they are not mentioned at all in Waldemar Nielsen's standard histories, *The Big Foundations* and *The Golden Donors*—the leading liberal philanthropies were advancing their own agenda with vigor and to general applause. These foundations, Ford and Rockefeller along with the Carnegie Corporation, were guided by the view that social progress was to be achieved through expert knowledge and scientific research, by the expansion of government's role into new areas, and by the use of international organizations to promote cooperation among the major powers. Their funds went to well-entrenched and highly regarded institutions: universities, research centers, international organizations, and, occasionally, governmental bodies. In sum, the liberal foundations formed an integral part of the liberal establishment, a circumstance for which they were roundly criticized (to little effect) by both conservatives and left-wing radicals.

A significant shift in liberal philanthropy took place after McGeorge Bundy, a former dean at Harvard and national security adviser to the Kennedy and Johnson administrations, was appointed president of the Ford Foundation in 1966. Sharply preferring activism to research and expertise, Bundy pioneered a strategy of "advocacy philanthropy." Soon the Ford Foundation and other liberal donors were investing in a maze of activist groups promoting feminism, affirmative action, environmentalism, disarmament, and other cutting-edge causes. The Environmental Defense Fund, the Natural Resources Defense Council, the Women's Law Fund, and the Mexican American Legal Defense and Education Fund were among the products of this initiative.

These organizations claimed to be the legitimate representatives of their respective causes and interest groups. In that capacity, they promoted ideas that led to legislation, and then sought to influence the regulatory bodies and federal courts that implemented and interpreted the laws. They were particularly effective in exploiting the broad language of newly passed civil rights and environmental laws. Thus, Bundy and the Ford Foundation helped develop an institutional structure that, by means of litigation and the leverage it exercised over administrative agencies, could push its favored programs beyond any limits contemplated by the politicians who enacted those laws.

A strategy designed to bring about large change by circumventing the electoral process was well suited to philanthropic institutions with links to experts and advocates. And it led indisputably to results: employment quotas for women and minority groups, the expansion of welfare, new environmental regulations, court orders and favorable Supreme Court decisions, and the like. It also produced some spectacular blowouts, most notably the misguided effort led by the Ford Foundation in 1968 to decentralize the New York City public schools, which led to a series of citywide teachers' strikes and poisoned politics and race relations in the city for years thereafter. Nevertheless, over the long haul, the Bundy approach was instrumental in inventing what is by now a familiar phenomenon on the American political scene: the well-placed advocacy group nursing a grievance against American society and seeking compensation on behalf of its members.

Reinforcing this trend was the fact that the Democratic Party was simultaneously beginning to reform its internal operations along parallel lines. Following the tumult at their 1968 convention in Chicago, the Democrats established a commission, chaired by Senator George McGovern, whose mandate was to make the nominating process more representative of American society as a whole. Quickly captured by liberal activists, the commission pushed through new rules for delegate selection mandating the representation of women, blacks, and young people in line with their proportions in the population.

The effect was to displace the elected officeholders, party officials, and union leaders who had controlled Democratic conventions in the past and to replace them with activists speaking for designated groups. Under this approach, the groups that now found a home in the party began to look very much like the ones that Bundy had tried to organize through the Ford Foundation. In many cases, they were the same groups.

Consequently, liberalism itself came to be recast along interest-group lines, and the welfare state was redefined: rather than a package of programs through which Americans lent assistance to the poor, the sick, and the disabled, it came be regarded as a system through which certain defined groups could command government support as a matter of right and as compensation for past injustices. Society was cast as the guilty party, the recipients as its aggrieved victims. This sleight of hand in turn made it difficult for government to require the beneficiaries of its aid to adapt their behavior to the standards of middle-class life.

As liberalism gradually absorbed the adversarial assumptions of the day, group-based claims became ever more strident and accusations of discrimination and injustice multiplied. In time, the new order would erase those large-hearted features of liberal philosophy that had made it appealing to middle-class Americans from the 1930s through the 1960s.

These developments could not have been foreseen. They were not a consequence of broad social or economic factors or of public pressure, but were engineered by a narrow circle of activists with access to money and influence within the Democratic Party. Their success also contradicted Hayek's assessment that far-reaching changes take a generation or more to be put into place. Here, an established doctrine and a political party with a proud tradition were turned upside down within just a few years.

At the time, many observers took note of the role that charitable foundations had played in this upheaval. Inserting themselves into the political life of the nation, liberal philanthropists parlayed their ability to fund experts, research, and advocacy groups into a new potential for influence. With their inbuilt advantage over elected politicians and traditional business associations, they were a quintessential expression of what came to be known as the "new politics," a politics driven largely by ideas, advocacy, and confrontation. This was, without question, a crucial development in our political life—and in response to it, more than a few conservatives, joined by alarmed or disillusioned liberals, began to look for a different way.

* * *

The second phase of conservative philanthropy began to take shape in the mid-1970s through the work of a handful of donors, especially the John M. Olin and Smith Richardson foundations and, later, the Bradley Foundation. The Scaife Trusts of Pittsburgh were also involved to a certain degree. These funders were more self-consciously conservative than libertarian. While sympathetic to the writings of Hayek and the ideals of classical liberalism, they adopted a broader intellectual framework encompassing fields beyond economics, especially religion, foreign policy, and the traditional humanities. In contrast to Hayek and his followers, they were also prepared to engage the world of politics and policy and to wage the "war of ideas" in a direct and aggressive style to match the efforts of Bundy and his liberal allies.

These conservative foundations were endowed and funded by successful businessmen who wanted to preserve the system of private enterprise that had enabled the country to prosper and which they thought was very much under attack from an aggressive and energized left. In the mid-1970s, the outlook for any such program appeared especially bleak, but the sense of swimming against the tide gave their efforts an air of invigorating urgency. And they soon discovered, within the intellectual world, an unlikely group of allies inspired by parallel concerns and priorities.

Just as the earlier donors had looked to Hayek for guidance, these foundations looked to intellectuals, but of a different kind. They were guided by the so-called neoconservatives—writers and editors like Irving Kristol, Norman Podhoretz, Hilton Kramer, and Michael Novak who had for the most part spent their formative years on the left but were now tracking rightward as a consequence of the ideological excesses of the period. For intellectual mentors, the neoconservatives looked to thinkers like George Orwell, Lionel Trilling, and Raymond Aron—intellectuals of Hayek's generation who had written well on the evils of totalitarianism from a broad moral and political standpoint. Many of them, like Hayek, traced their intellectual lineage back to the eighteenth-century Whigs, but in so doing they once again emphasized the moral and cultural rather than the economic dimension, typically preferring Adam Smith's *Theory of Moral Sentiments* to his *Wealth of Nations*. In brief, they understood the moral foundations of a free society to be prior to and at least as important as its economic foundations.

The neoconservatives had an added advantage: having come from the left, they understood the thought and strategy of contemporary liberals and leftists. They also understood that the war of ideas had to be fought by engaging in real-world controversies, with stakes wagered on the outcome. While the neoconservatives were sympathetic to long-term strategies, they also thought that events were moving too quickly at that time for such approaches to be effective. Through their writings, and through the advice they offered, the neoconservatives helped to orient the conservative foundations to the ongoing contest over which set of ideas would govern the nation.

The political world that these writers saw in the 1970s looked much different from the one that had so troubled Hayek in London in 1944. Instead of leading down the path to collectivism, the welfare state had produced fragmentation, group conflict, disorder, and a general loss of authority in society. In the United States, moreover, the welfare state had advanced itself not through the nationalization of industry but through incremental expansions of social programs and accretions to federal regulatory power. It was the intersection of these programs with the cultural revolution of the 1960s and 1970s that gave rise, as the neoconservatives saw it, to urban crime, broken families, and educational failure. The contemporary problem was thus not so much collectivism or socialism as the loss of morale and self-confidence that was in some ways characteristic of all affluent societies—a problem to which classical liberalism did not promise any obvious solution.

In contrast to Hayekian liberalism, the neoconservatives never developed a full-blown theory of government, economics, or society. Instead of a movement, neoconservatism was more a "persuasion," as Kristol called it, or a "tendency," as Podhoretz described it. Rejecting orthodoxies and abstract theories alike, the neoconservatives tended to operate in close proximity to ongoing events. Kristol, though sympathetic to Hayek, once wrote that "He often gives the impression that he considers reality to be one immense deviation from true doctrine." Kristol saw Hayek's approach as utopian, and thus incapable of yielding practical results.

In keeping with their stress on real-world outcomes, neoconservatives drew upon social science to assess the practical consequences of the various programs and policies that made up the modern welfare state. Documenting the disturbing consequences of initiatives that had promised to end poverty or to transform the cities, analysts like James Q. Wilson and Charles Murray demonstrated that ideas adopted with the best of intentions were making matters worse by promoting crime, disorder, and economic failure. The effect of such studies was to throw cold water on the vast expectations that had been nourished by liberal theorists and activists. As promises were scaled back, so was the momentum behind the expansion of the welfare state.

The neoconservatives were not against a welfare state in principle, nor did they necessarily embrace the unfettered market either. They criticized the welfare state because it demoralized the poor and made them dependent on government, but they hardly objected to well-crafted measures to aid the unemployed. A conservative welfare state, one that encouraged work, family, and middle-class values, was something they could endorse. In foreign policy, they believed that the Cold War was a vital moral and political struggle, and they rejected efforts to conciliate the Soviet Union as naïve or worse. In another time, they might well have been called liberals; in the 1970s and beyond, they were most definitely conservatives.

Like Hayek, the neoconservatives envisioned an important role for intellectuals, but they were not prepared to wait a full generation for their efforts to yield results. It was plain that liberal and left-wing intellectuals had promoted ideas and programs that were far out of touch with the operating assumptions of the vast majority of Americans. This opened up a political opportunity. The task of conservatism, as Kristol said, was "to show the American people that they are right and the intellectuals are wrong." Over time, that is more or less what happened.

The neoconservatives understood that the intellectuals' dislike for capitalism and their faith in socialism could not be explained on the basis of economic analysis. By the mid-1970s, the economic promise of socialism was dead; it was obvious to everyone that socialist economies could not even feed their own people. Everywhere one looked, socialist governments were presiding over failed economies and starving people. What attracted intellectuals to socialism was something else: mainly, the ideal of community, which they contrasted invidiously to the individualism and competition found in a market society. Thus, as Kristol and others argued, an effective defense of capitalism required a defense of the cultural assumptions on which a commercial civilization is based. It had to be shown that free societies encouraged values far superior to anything that socialism could deliver.

The conservative foundations followed this lead. Though they continued to fund programs in free-market economics, they also made gifts in the fields of history, philosophy, government, even art and literature. They came to consider religion, morals, and marriage to be as important as economics and markets—and closely bound up with them. The foundations strove to move into every major area of debate and controversy. They allocated funds to prominent institutions, including Ivy League universities where conservative ideas were decidedly marginalized, and they proved ready and willing to support magazines and journals addressing a spectrum of controversial issues.

Such magazines, they understood, were not simply products for sale in the marketplace, as businessmen were prone to see them, but institutions in their own right, with ongoing responsibilities, reputations to be built and preserved, and networks of authors and supporters. Above all, they were seedbeds of ideas, nurseries of new talent. Not only was their cumulative effect large, but individual articles published in any one of the major conservative journals could have far-reaching consequences.

The neoconservative magazines, *Commentary* and the *Public Interest* in particular, routinely published authors whose critiques of liberal ideas and policies were factual, pointed, and ruthlessly logical, and whose analyses pointed the way to everything from the welfare reform of the late 1990s to the paradigm shift in American global policy that was being carried out by the Bush administration. There were also the *New Criterion*, a journal of literature and the arts edited by Hilton Kramer, and the *National Interest*, a foreign policy quarterly established by Kristol and edited for many years by Owen Harries.

In bringing a different approach and emphasis to modern conservatism, the neoconservatives enlarged its appeal, made it more effective in the political world, and helped it adapt to the challenges of the time. The advance of conservatism in recent decades owes much to them, and to their partnership with the conservative foundations.

* * *

When Ronald Reagan was elected to the presidency in 1980, there were but few organizations that he could look to for research, information, and personnel. The Heritage Foundation and the American Enterprise Institute were available to help, but there was not much beyond them. President Reagan had considerable difficulty finding enough principled conservatives to staff his administration. By the time George W. Bush was elected in 2000, there was a proliferation of such groups working actively in every area of public policy, from economics and law to foreign affairs and social policy. These organizations have developed ideas and nurtured talent that over time have helped change the balance of power between liberals and conservatives in America. They continue their work today.

All this was accomplished with modest financial resources—amazingly modest when compared with the spending of their liberal counterparts. In recent years, the five leading liberal philanthropic organizations—the Ford, Rockefeller, and MacArthur foundations, the Carnegie Corporation and George Soros's Open Society Foundation—reported combined assets in excess of $25 billion and annual expenditures of more than $1.2 billion. By contrast, the assets of the largest conservative foundations never exceeded $2 billion and their annual expenditures did not go much beyond $100 million. The John M. Olin Foundation, which was very influential but ceased operations several years ago, never had assets that exceeded $120 million and never spent more than $20 million in a single year. Yet these foundations were able to achieve a great deal with focus and discipline, and by allying themselves with an unusually talented generation of writers and scholars.

The network of publications, university programs, and research centers built from the 1970s onward will continue to wield influence in the years ahead. But this phase of conservative philanthropy has now run its course—in part because it has done its work, in part because conditions have changed, and in part because some key donors are leaving the scene or have already left. In addition, new technologies are changing the landscape in magazine publication, thereby challenging the continued survival of various magazines that have wielded influence in the past. In the decades ahead, new funders now entering the field and new approaches to the "war of ideas" will shape the next chapter of conservative philanthropy.

That next phase will necessarily be different from those that have gone before. For one thing, conservative philanthropy will likely be based more on individual donors and less on philanthropic institutions than has been the case up to now. The prosperity that began in the 1980s, especially the stock market boom, created a cohort of such individuals, few with enormous wealth but many prosperous enough to make significant gifts to conservative enterprises. At the same time, some conservative foundations—Olin preeminently among them—have spent themselves or intend to spend themselves out of business in accordance with their founders' wishes. Others have been shifting their priorities in new directions.

The reason for this change of course is connected with the fact that conservatism has moved from outside to inside the mainstream of political debate. As a consequence, conservative donors and policy groups are becoming more practical and specific in their objectives, and somewhat less general, intellectual, and adversarial. This is a natural evolution in a movement that has assumed national responsibility and now requires a practical policy agenda— school vouchers, charter schools, medical savings accounts, personal retirement accounts, legal reform, elimination of the estate tax, and so forth. In addition, various conservative donors have themselves become involved in promoting one or another specific policy, and they see the passing of legislation or the implementation of a reform as the most tangible measure of their success.

Does this mean that there is no longer a need to sustain and renew the intellectual basis of conservatism? The dynamism of American life, with relentless competition between the political parties and among interest groups, forces every movement of ideas to test those ideas on a more or less continuous basis if it means to survive and flourish. Conservatism has renewed itself more successfully than any of its competitors in the postwar period—not so much through an emphasis on policy as through broader arguments about where we have been, where we ought to go, and what threats and obstacles stand in our way.

"Who owns the future?" Orwell asked. It is the great question of political life. Few will be persuaded to embrace conservatism only on the grounds that it promotes private social-security accounts or caps on liability awards. In the end, the struggle to shape the future must be fought out on a wider front of culture and morals as well as politics. Any movement, if it is to maintain or augment its influence, will need to wage an ongoing battle of ideas, and it will need the help of sympathetic philanthropists.

A version of this chapter appeared in *Commentary*, May 2005.

PART THREE

The Kennedy Legend and the Liberal Ideal

CHAPTER ELEVEN

The Kennedy Legend

American liberals in the early 1960s espoused an optimistic creed with a muscular foreign policy and wide sympathy among the working and middle classes; but after John F. Kennedy's assassination, the foundations of liberalism began shifting under their feet. Somehow Kennedy managed to change the character of American liberalism: from a doctrine of programmatic reform with an emphasis on economic security and national defense, to one of cultural criticism with an emphasis on liberation from traditional mores. This transformation resulted in large measure from the myths that were spun around Kennedy after his tragic death, when he came to be viewed as a liberal visionary and path-breaker, but more of a revolutionary cultural figure than an architect of new policies like FDR.

Kennedy was certainly a popular president. In November 1963, as he prepared for the electoral campaign of 1964, his approval ratings hovered around 60 percent, an encouraging sign for his re-election.* At the same time, Victor Lasky's broadside against the president, *J.F.K.: The Man and the Myth*, reached the top of the

---

* Kennedy's approval rating was at 58 percent according to a Gallup poll taken November 8–10, 1963.

bestseller lists. This book contrasted the carefully crafted image of idealism and competence with the actual man, whom Lasky described as shallow, immature, and untrustworthy. Widely read though it was, Lasky's book failed to dent Kennedy's popularity and quickly disappeared from the bestseller lists after the assassination. Stories that came out later about Kennedy's conduct in the White House suggested that Lasky was more right than wrong in his assessment.[1] Nevertheless, the gulf between the man and the myth was magnified many times over following Kennedy's death.

Lasky was on target with his main point: John F. Kennedy, with the assistance of his family and loyal associates, paid careful attention to promoting an image of himself that did not necessarily accord with reality. He did so—and they did so—out of the conviction that the public mind attaches itself more readily to images and symbols than to facts. Numerous Kennedy biographers, following Lasky's lead, have documented the discrepancies between the popular imagery of John F. Kennedy and his actual behavior in public office. Yet President Kennedy remains popular with the American people even as scholars and historians increasingly discount his importance and influence as a political leader.* In recent opinion polls, Americans have ranked Kennedy as the "greatest president ever," or as second only to Abraham Lincoln.[2] Kennedy topped a poll taken in 2013 asking Americans to rate the presidents who have served in office since 1900.[3]

"Grief nourishes myth," as one of Kennedy's aides later wrote about the legends that quickly grew up around the assassinated president.[4] It has happened in the past: the death of a young and popular leader nourishes efforts to keep him alive as a cultural ideal. In this way he

---

* In 2006, the *Atlantic Monthly* commissioned a group of historians to rank the one hundred most influential Americans since 1776. Lincoln, Washington, Jefferson, and Franklin Roosevelt led the list. Among contemporaries of John F. Kennedy, Presidents Truman, Eisenhower, Johnson, Nixon, and Reagan made the list. Kennedy did not. See *Atlantic Monthly*, December 2006.

becomes an inspiration for others and a standard against which aspiring leaders are measured. At the same time, Kennedy's violent death was a potent reminder that "the world is a complex and unexpected and terrible place," as Lionel Trilling had said. Kennedy in life was held up as a standard of excellence and achievement, but no one could ignore the fact that his death demonstrated how ugly, unpredictable, and unfair the world could be. If some looked to Kennedy as a source of inspiration, others looked on his death as a reason for despair. Often these conflicting emotions were operative in the same people.

Following his death, Kennedy was portrayed by family loyalists as a liberal hero who, had he lived, might have led the nation into a new age of peace, justice, and understanding. This theme emerged in tributes and memorials inspired by Jacqueline Kennedy and friends and other family members of the slain president, and in numerous books published after the assassination, particularly those by the presidential aides Arthur Schlesinger Jr. and Theodore Sorensen, both of whom depicted the fallen president as the brightest star of the time and a leader impossible to replace. Sorensen wrote that Kennedy was the equal of any of our earlier presidents. Schlesinger went further to say that "He re-established the republic as the first generation of our founders saw it—young, brave, civilized, rational, gay, tough, questing, exultant in the excitement and potentiality of history."[5] There was a sense in these tributes that the loss of John F. Kennedy had deprived the nation and the world of a new beginning.

This sentimental image, an understandable byproduct of the grief felt by those close to Kennedy, gnawed at Lyndon Johnson, who thought with good reason that his own record of liberal legislative victories dwarfed anything that Kennedy might have achieved. Johnson believed that he had in fact earned the mantle that had been granted posthumously to JFK. His resentment merely demonstrated how far out of touch he was with the new liberal ethos after its redefinition in the 1960s both by Kennedy himself and by his shocking assassination. Johnson was a practitioner of the old liberalism at the moment it was being overtaken by the new. The rapidly shifting standards of American liberalism in the 1960s quickly turned Kennedy into a heroic figure at the same time that they made old-style reformers like Johnson and Hubert Humphrey look like boring and tiresome politicians. Kennedy became a liberal prophet because he changed the character of liberalism and helped create new standards according to which he and other leaders were subsequently judged.

* * *

Veteran politicians who knew Kennedy well and who had followed his career over the preceding two decades, including most especially his opponents like Johnson, Humphrey, and Richard Nixon, were taken aback by the postmortem tributes to President Kennedy as the inspirational symbol of American liberalism, since neither his career leading up to the presidency nor his conduct in office seemed to justify this designation. Kennedy was viewed during the 1950s, and even after he was elected to the presidency, as more of a pragmatic and moderate liberal who worked cautiously to extend the legacy of the New Deal without getting too far out in front of public opinion. He was, as he said at the time, "a liberal without illusions," a practical more than a sentimental liberal, whose thinking was very much in tune with the mood expressed by intellectuals like Hofstadter, Schlesinger, and other postwar liberals.

Liberal Democrats like Hubert Humphrey, Adlai Stevenson, Harry Truman, and Eleanor Roosevelt, along with liberal interest groups like the Americans for Democratic Action, were understandably skeptical about Kennedy's candidacy when the 1960 campaign began. Kennedy had not distinguished himself as a leader of any important liberal causes during his years in Congress, and indeed he usually went out of his way to avoid any such associations. He was known to be friendly to Joseph McCarthy and Richard Nixon, both hated foes in the eyes of liberals at the time. Liberals distrusted Kennedy's father, and with good reason. In his campaigns, Kennedy carefully positioned himself so as to make it difficult for anyone to pin him down as either a liberal or a conservative—a tactic designed to highlight his attractive looks and personality.

At times, Kennedy disdained the "liberal" label altogether, preferring to say that he was simply "a Democrat." In 1953, a *Saturday Evening Post* article quoted him as saying, in response to criticisms of his record, "I'd be very happy to tell them that I'm not a liberal at all.... I'm not comfortable with those people."[6] *Time* magazine in 1957 said that he was in many ways a conservative, while *Newsweek* reported that he was "an authentic moderate." Herbert Hoover called Kennedy his "favorite" senator.

During his tenure in the House of Representatives and the Senate, Kennedy failed to lead the charge for any important piece of reformist legislation. As a senator, he avoided taking strong positions on civil rights proposals for fear of antagonizing southern colleagues.[7] Lasky wrote that when in 1957 the liberal Americans for Democratic Action gave Kennedy a highly favorable rating on the votes he had cast in the Senate, he went well out of his way to explain that the ADA's ranking was inaccurate and that he was in truth one of the more moderate members of the Senate.[8] It was left to other political figures like Humphrey and (to a lesser extent) Stevenson to carry the banner of crusading liberalism during the 1950s. The transformation of Kennedy's reputation following his death was thus all the more remarkable because so many aspects of his career pointed in a different direction altogether.

An important sticking point for liberals, aside from his legislative record, was Kennedy's association with Senator McCarthy, who had been a friend of the Kennedy family since he and John F. Kennedy were elected to Congress together in 1946. The senator from Wisconsin was a frequent guest in Kennedy's Georgetown home during those early terms in Congress, and occasionally even dated one of the Kennedy sisters. When McCarthy emerged as the leader of the anti-communist cause a few years later, Kennedy flatly refused to criticize his methods. Kennedy's father, a devoted anticommunist himself, applauded McCarthy's efforts to remove communists and their sympathizers from government service. The elder Kennedy contributed financially to McCarthy's re-election campaign in 1952, perhaps (as Lasky and others have suggested) as a way to discourage the popular McCarthy from coming into Massachusetts to campaign on behalf of Senator Henry Cabot Lodge, who was his son's Republican opponent in the 1952 Senate race. Following that year's election, in which both Kennedy and McCarthy won their races, McCarthy hired Robert F. Kennedy as his staff counsel on the Senate Permanent Committee on Investigations. In 1954, when McCarthy faced censure from Senate colleagues, Kennedy was able to avoid the vote because at that time he was recovering from back surgery in a New York hospital.[9]

Kennedy was a target of criticism from liberals because of his apparent support for McCarthy, or at least for his reluctance to condemn McCarthy's methods and for ducking the vote on censure. A few years after the censure, Kennedy tried to explain his position in terms of his family's personal relationships with the Wisconsin senator. When pressed by a reporter on this point in 1956, Kennedy said, "You must remember that my father was a friend of Joe's, as was my sister, Eunice, and my brother Bobby worked for him."[10] What he did not say but many suspected was that these connections had been deliberately arranged by Kennedy's father.

Joseph P. Kennedy was even more of a liability for John F. Kennedy than was the association with McCarthy, at least in the eyes of the liberal wing of the Democratic Party. The elder Kennedy zealously deployed his wealth and vast influence in behalf of his son's political career, and as the 1960 campaign began, Truman was quoted as saying about the Catholic Kennedy that it was not the Pope he was worried about but rather "the Pop."[11] On this point, he expressed the worries of many in the Democratic Party.

Though today he is viewed as a footnote to history, Joseph Kennedy was widely known in the 1940s and 1950s for his investments in film studios and liquor interests and for his own aborted political career, in which he managed to place himself at odds with both Winston Churchill and Franklin Roosevelt. The patriarch of the Kennedy family earned his vast fortune from bootlegging and smuggling liquor during the Prohibition era—activities which brought him into partnership with organized crime and to the attention of federal authorities. He was shrewd enough to understand that in order to protect his illicit gains he had to deploy some of his money to establish friendships with gangsters, politicians, and journalists. So he put money into FDR's presidential campaign in 1932, and he formed a business association with James Roosevelt, FDR's oldest son, who helped him secure appointments in the Roosevelt administration. He nurtured friendships with the columnist Walter Winchell and with Arthur Krock, Washington bureau chief of the *New York Times*, to whom he provided information and money in exchange for favorable coverage in the paper. It was Kennedy's experience as a black-market businessman that made him such an effective behind-the-scenes promoter of his son's political career. As Lasky wrote, "the story of John Fitzgerald Kennedy is not wholly separable from the story of his father."[12]

By the time his son ran for president, Kennedy had earned a reputation not merely as a shady businessman but also as an archconservative and anticommunist. He was a Democrat not because he was liberal but because, as an Irish Catholic from Boston, he was culturally born into the party. Nevertheless, his business and personal affairs make for an inexhaustible reservoir of lurid tales.[13] His own aborted political career was perhaps even more important in establishing his later reputation as an untrustworthy character. It was also significant as a formative experience for his son's career in politics.

The elder Kennedy came to public attention during the New Deal when he was appointed as the first chairman of the new Securities and Exchange Commission, much to the dismay of liberals who thought it was akin to placing the fox in charge of the henhouse. He secured an even more important position in 1938 when he persuaded President Roosevelt to appoint him ambassador to the Court of St. James's. Kennedy was the first Irish Catholic to hold this prestigious post, a distinction of which he proudly boasted in Protestant Boston. As ambassador he turned in one of the most spectacularly incompetent performances in the history of American diplomacy.

He arrived in London at precisely the time when Hitler's challenge to France and Great Britain was reaching a point of crisis. Kennedy made it clear that he supported the British government's policy of appeasement toward Nazi Germany as the only means of avoiding war. He strongly endorsed Prime Minister Chamberlain's decision at Munich in September 1938 to allow Hitler to annex the Sudetenland in return for a promise of peace. Kennedy claimed, as did others in Britain at the time, that such a policy reflected the wishes of the British people to avoid another war. In any case, he said, Great Britain was far too weak militarily to oppose Hitler, who had deliberately cultivated an exaggerated estimate of Germany's military strength in order to deter a British military response. Kennedy believed that Hitler, if properly managed, might serve as a fortification in Europe against communism—a widely held view at that time. On all these points, Kennedy opposed Churchill, who denounced appeasement as a policy that was not only cowardly but also ineffective in deterring Hitler from future provocations. Churchill regarded Hitler as a more immediate threat to European civilization than Stalin.

Even after Britain declared war on Germany in 1939 following Hitler's invasion of Poland, Kennedy maintained his stance in favor of appeasement, and he advised Roosevelt to keep the United States out of the European conflict at all costs. The British position was hopeless, he said, and he judged it likely that the British would be "badly trashed" by the German military machine. Here Kennedy also proved an embarrassment to his own government because his position ran directly counter to Roosevelt's wish to assist the British. According to observers at the time, Kennedy harbored ambitions to succeed FDR in 1940 as the Democratic candidate for president, in which campaign he would highlight his role in keeping the United States out of the war. Word of such ambitions naturally got back to Roosevelt. Kennedy was bitterly disappointed—and made no secret of it—when Roosevelt announced his intention to run for a third term.

Kennedy's already tenuous position in Britain was further compromised when Churchill was appointed prime minister in 1940 after the fall of France. Churchill had little use for the appeasement-minded ambassador, a feeling that was fully reciprocated. Late that year, after Roosevelt was safely re-elected, Kennedy delivered his opinion to the American press that "democracy is finished in England" and that the British could not long hold out against the German bombing campaign. This tirade, which Kennedy claimed was supposed to be off the record, was also laced with indelicate comments about Churchill, the queen, and even the president's wife. Once his comments were published, Kennedy saw that he had little choice but to resign.[14]

The fiasco in London effectively ended the elder Kennedy's political career and closed the door on any possibility that he might run for public office on his own. In the span of a few years he managed to antagonize the two great democratic leaders of the time, while promoting a position that was soon discredited by events. A reputation for a loose tongue and poor judgment was further stained by insinuations of anti-Semitism because of his willingness to do business with Hitler.[15] Kennedy then retreated to his business interests, but after the war he remained politically active behind the scenes, promoting Jack Kennedy's budding career in national politics and befriending important national leaders, including Senator Joseph McCarthy. All this and much more were known about the elder Kennedy when his son began his run for the presidency in 1960.

* * *

John F. Kennedy appears to have been every bit as sure as his father was about the wisdom of the British government's policy of appeasement. The younger Kennedy had spent much of the period of his father's ambassadorship in London on leave from Harvard University on a travel-study fellowship, which gave him the opportunity to observe at close hand the historic debates between British leaders who sought to appease Hitler and those who thought it necessary to confront him. In late 1939, with the war now on and events moving quickly, he returned to Harvard to work on a senior thesis on the subject of British policy toward Germany from 1932 to the outbreak of war.

His thesis, completed in March 1940 under the title "Appeasement at Munich," was a defense of appeasement on the grounds that the British public was strongly opposed to rearmament and, indeed, to any confrontational policy against Hitler that might make war more likely. Since it is unrealistic, he argued, to ask political leaders to risk their offices by going against public opinion, Britain's leaders were bound by the canons of democratic politics to embrace any policy that might avert another war. The blame for Britain's failure to arm, he said, lay with the voters and the democratic system itself, not with Chamberlain or his predecessor, Stanley Baldwin.[16] This seemed such a transparent defense of his father's record that one of the Harvard professors who read the thesis said it should be titled "While Daddy Slept," a sarcastic takeoff on a (then) recently published collection of Churchill's speeches titled *While England Slept*.[17]

Kennedy received encouragement from his father and a few of his father's associates, especially Arthur Krock of the *New York Times*, to publish the thesis as a book. Before doing so, however, he saw the necessity of adjusting the main argument in response to withering criticism from friendly reviewers who pointed out that it was a counsel of cynicism to leaders to tell the voters whatever they want to hear.[18] From the vantage point of early 1940, the policy of appeasement looked much different, and far more dangerous to the security of Britain, than it had two years earlier when Chamberlain ventured to Munich. Kennedy recast his thesis to suggest that leaders should make the effort to educate the public and to shape public opinion when they believe the security of the nation is at stake, even if they risk defeat in the process. This barb was aimed less at Chamberlain than at his predecessor, Stanley Baldwin, who by failing to prepare for the threat from Hitler in the mid-1930s had limited Chamberlain's range of options in 1938. The revision nonetheless retained the general theme that the democratic system itself, combined with the peace-loving character of democratic peoples, was largely responsible for the failures of the 1930s. Though the revised version made a gesture in the direction of Churchill's position, which in any case was being vindicated by events, it also sought disingenuously to absolve Chamberlain (and Kennedy's father) of blame by suggesting that the appeasement of Hitler at Munich was made necessary by earlier decisions, and that it bought time for Britain to arm itself before war became unavoidable.[19]

Kennedy concluded his revised thesis with a coda directed to Americans, urging them to learn from the British the lesson that it is necessary to maintain military strength commensurate with the requirements of national security and threats from abroad. This conclusion was crafted to establish the book's importance for the American reading public. Realizing that events in Europe were moving so rapidly as to make the book seem dated, Kennedy quickly found a publisher (with his father's help) who brought it out in America in July 1940 under the title *Why England Slept*—another reference to Churchill's recently published collection of speeches. The book received generally positive reviews and, with the help of large purchases by Kennedy's father, even made a few bestseller lists.[20] In regard to his future career, the book gave young Kennedy favorable publicity as an author and intellectual.

It is worth dwelling on this episode because of the formative role it played in Kennedy's political career and the influence this chapter in history had on postwar political debates. Chamberlain's appeasement at Munich, observed at close hand and ably defended by Kennedy, later became the central object lesson for American statesmanship during the Cold War. Liberals and conservatives alike took to heart the lessons taught by Britain's failure to maintain its strength in the face of Hitler's challenge. The episode demonstrated the futility of giving in to aggression, and it seemed to prove to democratic leaders that the best way to avoid war is to make preparations for it. The "Munich analogy" became a touchstone of foreign policy doctrine in the postwar period; while Churchill was held up as the model of wise and courageous statesmanship. After the war, the lessons of Munich were redirected to the Cold War struggle against communism. Kennedy absorbed these lessons just as deeply as did others in the postwar period. After the war, Kennedy cited Churchill as his model of courageous statesmanship, thereby reversing the position he had earlier taken.[21]

This episode, far from marking just a youthful chapter in the life of a statesman in training, was in many ways representative of Kennedy's later career. It brought into play his loyalty to his father, the prominent role played behind the scenes by the elder Kennedy in arranging for the publication and promotion of his son's book, and Kennedy's own willingness later to reverse his position on Churchill and appeasement even as he adhered to the argument of his book. There was also a question as to whether Kennedy actually wrote the book himself or relied on the writing skills of others in his father's circle to form the final product—a controversy that would arise again a few years later on the publication of Kennedy's second book, *Profiles in Courage*.[22] There can be little doubt, however, that Kennedy's immersion in the appeasement controversy was invaluable preparation for a career in national politics. Here, as at other critical points in his career, John F. Kennedy proceeded under the careful tutelage of his father.

* * *

Profiles in Courage, published in 1956, is a good illustration of Kennedy's penchant for defying political labels and adopting views that are difficult to pigeonhole as either liberal or conservative. The subject of political courage might seem a strange subject for Kennedy's second book, given the position he took before the war and his father's antagonism toward Churchill for doing precisely what Senator Kennedy would go on to praise in his second book. It was also a somewhat risky topic for a young politician, as it would naturally establish a standard by which the author's own record would be judged.

This volume, as Kennedy wrote in the first chapter, was dedicated to United States senators who over the course of American history have gone against the particular interests of state or section or the views of their constituents to uphold the Constitution or the welfare of the nation. Risking one's political career or reputation for principle or the greater good was for Kennedy the definition of political courage. This was, as some said at the time, an expression of the Whig concept of representation under which the duty of the representative is to the public good, as opposed to the narrower interests of his constituents. *Profiles in Courage* won the Pulitzer Prize for nonfiction in 1956, albeit with some help from Kennedy's father and the timely intervention once more of Arthur Krock, who happened to be a member of the Pulitzer committee.[23]

In this exercise, Kennedy managed to praise political figures on all sides of the difficult issues that have divided the nation in the past. Both Democrats and Republicans came in for praise in nearly equal measure. Kennedy paid homage to Senators Daniel Webster, Henry Clay, and even John C. Calhoun for the various and conflicting positions they took on secession, sectionalism, and the Compromise of 1850. He commended the Unionist senator Edmund Ross of Kansas for casting the decisive vote against the impeachment of Andrew Johnson, but also the secessionist and former Confederate military officer Lucius Cincinnatus Lamar for his sympathetic eulogy in 1874 for Senator Charles Sumner, who had been the most radical of antislavery Republicans. More importantly for contemporary politics, he devoted a chapter to praising the late Senator Robert A. Taft of Ohio, the titular leader of the conservative wing of the Republican Party and briefly Kennedy's colleague in the Senate until he died of cancer in 1953. Taft was singled out for commendation because of his criticisms in 1946 of the Nuremburg war crimes tribunals. Taft characterized the verdicts at Nuremberg as a form of victor's justice. He further said that the trials violated our own Constitution's ban on ex post facto laws. Kennedy lauded Taft for speaking up for principle in defense of legal standards, unpopular though his position may have been at the time.

Kennedy thus touched nearly every political base during the course of his historical survey of political courage. As if to make his message more confusing still, he wrote also in support of moderation and compromise and against "fanatics and extremists" who think only of their own principles and points of view.[24] Though some might think of political courage as standing up for principle—and, indeed, this seemed to be the author's point in praising Taft—for Kennedy it also meant the courage to compromise in the fashion of Webster or Clay. By the end of the book, it was unclear whether Kennedy meant to encourage principled leadership or compromise, or perhaps a little of both, each at the proper time. The book, moreover, totally divorced political courage from any cause it may have advanced. Webster's courageous defense of the Union was placed on

the same footing as Calhoun's principled defense of slavery and secession. From the standpoint of philosophy or consistent principle,
Profiles in Courage was a muddled production.

⋆ ⋆ ⋆

The mixed message conveyed by *Profiles in Courage* did, however, reflect Kennedy's overall political strategy. In each of his two major
campaigns, for the Senate in 1952 and for the presidency in 1960, he
managed to outflank Republican opponents by adopting positions
to their right. Thus he presented to the voters an ideologically ambiguous image: neither liberal nor conservative, or perhaps a little of
both. Most importantly, Kennedy did not want anyone to tag him
as a liberal, which he (along with his father) regarded as the kiss of
death in electoral politics.

Kennedy's campaign for the Senate in 1952 pitted him against the
popular Republican incumbent Henry Cabot Lodge, himself a member of a prominent Massachusetts family, albeit one with Protestant
roots in contrast to Kennedy's Irish Catholic background. It was a
race that few thought Kennedy could win. Lodge, after all, had represented Massachusetts in the Senate since 1936, except for two years
of military service during the war. Moreover, he was an influential
national figure who took the lead in convincing Eisenhower to run for
president that year on the Republican ticket and in ensuring that he
received the nomination against a strong challenge from Senator Taft.

During the campaign, Kennedy sought to win votes from conservatives by claiming that his positions on foreign policy were
much more in keeping with Taft's positions, even though Kennedy
was a Democrat while Taft and Lodge were Republicans. Kennedy
claimed that between the two candidates he was the stronger critic
of Truman's foreign policy, which he said was soft on communism.
"In this respect," a campaign statement claimed, "he [Kennedy] is
much closer to the position of Taft than to Lodge."[25] Kennedy also

tried to exploit the resentment of conservatives against Lodge for assisting Eisenhower in elbowing aside Taft for the Republican nomination. When the Republican National Convention concluded with Eisenhower the nominee, Kennedy openly courted supporters of the Taft campaign in Massachusetts by setting up a group called "Independents for Kennedy," directed by one of the leaders of the Taft organization. In this way he gave disappointed Taft supporters a place to rally after the defeat of their candidate. He also gave them a means of getting even with Lodge—even though Taft himself would later endorse Lodge over Kennedy. Nevertheless, Kennedy's successful appeal to conservative Republicans played an important role in his narrow victory over Lodge in November.[26]

Kennedy replayed the same tactic in the 1960 presidential race against Richard Nixon when he accused the Eisenhower administration of jeopardizing the nation's security by allowing a "missile gap" to develop between the United States and the Soviet Union. Following the successful launch of the *Sputnik* satellite in 1957, Americans were panicked at the possibility that the Soviet Union had gotten the upper hand in the space race and in science generally. Speaking in the Senate in 1958, Kennedy expressed concern that the Soviet Union was gaining an advantage in long-range missiles.

This was a theme that he returned to frequently as he made preparations for a presidential race. Throughout the 1960 campaign, Kennedy stressed the idea that the Eisenhower administration had been asleep at the switch, thus allowing a communist tyranny to establish a base in Cuba and the Soviets to build a dangerous advantage in offensive missiles. Further emulating Churchill, Kennedy also called for a spirit of sacrifice among Americans so that they might begin to turn back the challenge of communism. Such charges and appeals were effective in placing Vice President Nixon on the defensive in the campaign. Both Eisenhower and Nixon, however, knew the "missile gap" to be a fabrication since they had secret intelligence from surveillance aircraft to show that the Soviets had no advantage of the kind Kennedy described. Yet they were unable publicly to reveal the sources of their information.[27]

Kennedy's charge was part of his overall campaign theme to "get the country moving again" following eight years of lethargic and unimaginative Republican leadership. It was also part of his design to run "on the Churchill ticket," as Harold MacMillan called Kennedy's tactic, meaning that Kennedy was now playing Churchill's role of bravely warning the people of dangers on the horizon. When the Soviet leader Nikita Khrushchev canceled a planned summit meeting in May 1960 after an American reconnaissance aircraft was shot down over Soviet territory, Kennedy said that it marked the end of an era—an "era of illusion."[28] From this point forward, Kennedy's campaign emphasized the international weakness and passivity of the Eisenhower administration, along with his own pledge to restore the nation's security. His emphasis on national security was especially helpful in the South, where it neutralized doubts about his stand on civil rights.

As many pointed out at the time, however, there was a great difference between Kennedy's use of the "missile gap" in the 1960 campaign and Churchill's warnings about Hitler in the 1930s—because while Churchill warned of a real danger to Great Britain, Kennedy exploited a nonexistent danger to the United States. Americans were well aware of the dangers they did face from the Soviet Union; indeed, in the eyes of many liberals they were excessively aware of the threat. But the missile gap never existed at all, a reality that Kennedy was forced to acknowledge soon after he became president. It was, as he admitted to associates, a fabrication designed for the immediate purposes of his campaign. Once he took office, he saw that it was risky to call attention to the issue because it might encourage Soviet leaders to act against the United States out of a false sense of advantage.[29]

The missile gap, like the appeal to Taft voters, was a shrewd effort on Kennedy's part to broaden his appeal to voters across the entire spectrum of opinion. His narrow victory in 1960 proved both the wisdom and the necessity of that strategy.

* * *

Kennedy assumed the presidency as a moderate representative of the postwar consensus: tough and aggressive on communism and national defense; confident of America's crucial role in the world as champion of liberty and democracy; devoted to economic growth as the surest and most direct path to national progress; a prudent supporter of civil rights and the welfare state. When Daniel Bell spoke of the consensus among intellectuals around the welfare state, political pluralism, and a mixed economy, he might just as easily have been speaking of Kennedy along with the advisers and officials who formed his inner circle. Indeed, in the sorrowful days after Kennedy's death, Richard Rovere would comment on the president and his circle of associates in tones reminiscent of Bell's thesis on the end of ideology: "There was not a reformer among them as far as anyone could tell," he wrote. "Pragmatism was rampant. 'Facts' were often valued beyond their worth. 'Ideology' was held in contempt and was described as a prime source of mischief in the world."[30] Kennedy and his men were pragmatists, at least so they thought, because they had witnessed the consequences of ideology in politics.

In view of his posthumous reputation as an idealistic liberal, it is curious that Kennedy's brief presidency is notable in retrospect as a time when Cold War tensions reached their most dangerous point—and, indeed, might easily have escalated into an all-out nuclear war during the Cuban missile crisis. Kennedy meant it when he said that he would challenge Soviet ambitions in Europe, Latin America, and the developing world. Cuba, as things turned out, was the flashpoint of the conflict between Soviet expansion and the Kennedy administration's aggressive resistance to it. Kennedy tried to overthrow

Castro by force in 1961, and then a year later threatened to use military power to remove Soviet-placed offensive missiles on the island. Throughout his tenure in office, Kennedy approved and encouraged assassination plots against the dictator, though these plans were not known to the public or to most officials in the government until more than a decade after his death.[31] These efforts eventually proved so dangerous and destabilizing that Lyndon Johnson and presidents who followed him decided that a better policy was simply to ignore and isolate Castro in the hope that his regime would collapse of its own ineffectiveness.

Looking back on Kennedy's actual record in office, one finds the same ideologically ambiguous mix of policies and appeals that was so evident in his major election campaigns. There were some progressive initiatives in the field of foreign policy—such as the Alliance for Progress, by which he tried to promote development and democracy in Latin America, and the American University speech in 1963, where he proposed a nuclear test ban treaty with the Soviet Union (following the dangerous confrontation over nuclear weapons in Cuba). There were also counterbalancing initiatives of a more conservative nature, such as Kennedy's military buildup in Vietnam, his support for counterinsurgency efforts, his harsh approach toward Castro, his vigorous anticommunist rhetoric, and, in the domestic arena, his 1963 tax-cut proposals.

Because of this ambiguous record, liberals and conservatives alike have exploited Kennedy's policies and rhetoric in order to advance their respective causes. Kennedy's anticommunism, for example, was shortly rejected and abandoned by liberal Democrats like George McGovern and Jimmy Carter, but was thereafter carried forward by conservative Republicans like Ronald Reagan. Kennedy's aim of spreading democracy abroad as an element of U.S. foreign policy was picked up in the 1980s by Reagan and later by George W. Bush, who made it a centerpiece of his foreign policy.

Kennedy's efforts to assassinate Castro, when they were eventually revealed, scandalized liberals far more than conservatives.

Kennedy's bold and patriotic rhetoric provides a more vivid illustration of this point. To the extent that anyone today hears the kinds of themes and concepts deployed by Kennedy, it is usually in speeches given by conservatives. In a speech to the Massachusetts legislature a week before his inauguration, Kennedy said (quoting the Puritan John Winthrop) that America is like a "city on a hill," an example of liberty and democracy looked up to by people around the world. This has since become a hackneyed reference, but it was not so when Kennedy cited it. A few decades later, the "city on a hill" would be a favorite image for President Reagan, who used it as a central theme in his farewell address (for which he was derided by liberals).

Kennedy, in his inaugural address, announced what was at stake in the Cold War and declared his intention to contest it with both arms and ideals: "Let every nation know, whether it wishes us well or ill, that we shall pay any price, bear any burden, meet any hardship, support any friend, and oppose any foe to assure the survival and the success of liberty." This was perhaps the most sweeping and ambitious statement of American aspirations in the world until George W. Bush announced in his 2005 inaugural address that the objective of U.S. policy would be to end tyranny in the world. To meet the challenges of world leadership, Kennedy called for a new spirit of patriotism that would guide Americans to think more of what they can do for their country than of what their country can do for them. He embraced Churchill's strategy of arming for peace (later phrased by Reagan as "peace through strength"), and asserted that "only when our arms are sufficient beyond doubt can we be certain beyond doubt that they will never be employed." Kennedy pointedly rejected the argument that armaments themselves are a cause of war.[32]

Kennedy's domestic agenda, though appropriately modest, was more consistently liberal in orientation than his foreign policy. He supported and favored labor unions in their conflicts with business and accepted the advice of Keynesian economists that the federal government could smooth out the business cycle with a carefully calibrated fiscal policy. He favored, but did not push hard for, a program of federally funded medical care for seniors. One of the major items on his agenda at the time of his death was a landmark civil rights bill, which (when it was passed in 1964) outlawed racial discrimination in interstate commerce, employment, and government operations.

Another important item, however, was a major tax cut to stimulate the economy. "The lesson of the last decade," he said in 1962, "is that budget deficits are not caused by wild-eyed spenders but by slow economic growth and periodic recessions. In short, it is a paradoxical truth that tax rates are too high today and tax revenues are too low and the soundest way to raise revenues in the long run is to cut rates now."[33] Kennedy proposed to cut marginal rates across the board by some 30 percent, with the highest rate to be reduced from 91 percent to 65 percent—the largest tax cut ever proposed. He pushed for this bill in the belief (later vindicated) that a cut in tax rates would stimulate economic activity to the point where tax revenues would actually increase. His tax bill was passed in 1964 with small adjustments, and it had impressively favorable results for the economy in the mid-1960s.

Kennedy's innovative tax policy was never again pursued by Democratic leaders or by post-Kennedy liberals, but was instead later picked up by Republicans who used the tax issue to restrain the growth of government. Ronald Reagan used Kennedy's tax cuts as political ammunition for his own proposals to cut taxes to reverse the "stagflation" of the Carter years. That policy had similarly favorable results in reversing an economic slide. From the late 1970s forward, tax cutting as a means of stimulating the economy has been orthodox Republican doctrine but anathema to Democrats.

From the standpoint of consistent principle, Kennedy was thus very much an ambiguous figure, with one foot each in the liberal and the conservative camp—a characteristic that helps account for his popularity with the public. Voters, before and after his death, never saw him as an ideological figure. It is impossible to rank Kennedy alongside figures like Woodrow Wilson or Franklin D. Roosevelt as a path-breaking liberal leader. Kennedy broke little new ground in the field of policy, no doubt because of his tragically abbreviated tenure in office. His best speeches, while memorable, did not introduce anything new or important into liberal thought, as Wilson did with his "Fourteen Points" or FDR with his "Four Freedoms."

Kennedy's legacy is further complicated by the fact that liberals would repudiate many of his central ideas within a few years of his death, thereby paving the way for conservatives to claim them. The liberalism of 1970 had only a tenuous connection to the liberalism that Kennedy stood for when he ran for president in 1960. Liberals admired Kennedy after his death and continue to do so, though their admiration is but loosely related to his actual program. Kennedy stood for something important in the evolution of American liberalism, but it is not to be found in anything so concrete as a program or a speech.

* * *

Arthur Schlesinger Jr. tried to get at Kennedy's unique contribution to American liberalism by suggesting that he communicated change and progress through the force of personality. Kennedy, he wrote, personified a series of qualities that he transmitted to the liberal cause via his presidential leadership. Such qualities were distinguishable from actual positions he may have taken on civil rights, communism, or taxes. In the first place, Kennedy encouraged a more critical and detached attitude toward American society than was the norm in the complacent 1950s. By his wit and good humor, he stood in marked contrast to bland Republican figures like Nixon and Eisenhower. Kennedy appreciated ideas, artists, and intellectuals, and thus cultivated channels of communication between the worlds of thought and of political power. Indeed, as a prize-winning author, Kennedy was something of an intellectual himself.

His appreciation for intellectuals and artists was reflected in Schlesinger's own presence on the White House staff, but more powerfully and publicly in Robert Frost's participation in the Kennedy inaugural ceremony. Frost prepared a poem for the occasion declaring that Kennedy's election marked the arrival of a new Augustan age, "A golden age of poetry and power of which this noonday's the beginning hour." Such grandiose expressions may have been appropriate for the occasion, so long as no one took them all that seriously. Yet it was still true that Kennedy kindled hopes in many for national renewal. His wit and humor, his detachment and penchant for self-criticism, his appreciation for ideas and artists—these qualities (according to Schlesinger) brought a new and creative dimension to American liberalism. This was the key to Kennedy's influence and popularity—and to his posthumous appeal.[34]

Schlesinger was on to something here, especially in his suggestion that such stylistic qualities were now central to the advancement of liberalism. Kennedy had managed to enlarge the boundaries of liberalism. No longer a purely programmatic doctrine, it would henceforth be a cultural creed as well and would have its own style, marked by elegance, wit, and intelligence.

The only difficulty with Schlesinger's analysis is that none of the attributes that he claimed for Kennedy was particularly characteristic of post-Kennedy liberalism. While it is true that liberal thinkers and activists began to focus on the cultural dimensions of politics after Kennedy's death, they did so in ways that were not entirely consistent with his ironic and detached demeanor. Indeed, liberal thought as it developed in the 1960s was notable for qualities directly opposite of those that Schlesinger admired in Kennedy. If post-Kennedy liberals and leftists were known for anything, it was for taking themselves and their causes far too seriously. Amid all their serious work, there was little place for wit and humor, even if Kennedy's death had not cast a pall over their political mood. Far from admiring detachment and self-criticism, they exalted unquestioning commitment to their cause. The work of artists and intellectuals came to be viewed as diversions from direct political action; in order to be worthwhile, such work had to be politically "relevant." By the end of the 1960s, authors like Robert Frost who celebrated America were now judged to be well outside the mainstream of liberal thought. Liberalism, long the party of ideas in American politics, began to abandon that terrain in favor of action, confrontation, and advocacy. Even more surprising was the fact that much of this was done in the name of John F. Kennedy.

While all this was so, Schlesinger may not have gone far enough in identifying the source of Kennedy's appeal and influence. For all his conventional political positions, Kennedy added something strikingly novel to the legacy of American liberalism: that is, he skillfully managed to transcend his role as a politician to become a cultural figure or, indeed, a celebrity. The historian Daniel Boorstin drew a distinction between the hero and the celebrity: "The hero was distinguished by his achievement; the celebrity by his image or trademark. The hero created himself; the celebrity is created by the media. The hero was a big man; the celebrity is a big name."[35]

In his style, Kennedy seemed most unlike other prominent political figures of his time—men like Truman, Eisenhower, Nixon, Johnson, or Humphrey. Eisenhower may have been a military hero, but Kennedy and his supporters judged him a tired old man. Norman Mailer, in an adulatory article about Kennedy the candidate, went so far as to call Eisenhower an "anti-Hero" because he failed to engage the imagination of the nation.[36] Kennedy, on the other hand, better fit the definition of a celebrity. He was young and articulate; he wore his hair long; he sailed and played touch football; he consorted with Hollywood stars and Harvard professors alike; he spoke beautifully and cited ancient writers; he was rich; he was an accomplished author. His wife, moreover, was beautiful and glamorous; and the two Kennedy children were as photogenic as their parents. The American people had never seen anything like the Kennedys, except perhaps in the movies. Kennedy saw that a president must not only lead but entertain too.

President Kennedy was America's first president—and the only one so far—successfully to marry the role of politician to that of cultural celebrity. Some of his successors—Bill Clinton and Barack Obama—have tried to bring off that combination but have not succeeded to the degree Kennedy did. It would not have occurred to Harry Truman or Franklin Roosevelt that they might burnish their political credentials by seeking a Pulitzer Prize. Nor would either man have had much interest in hanging about with Hollywood stars and starlets as Kennedy did. Kennedy was quite the opposite of Ronald Reagan, who moved into politics from the world of celebrity, while Kennedy bridged that divide from the other direction. Reagan may have represented Hollywood's past, but Kennedy represented its future. His success in linking liberalism with celebrity was greatly responsible for turning Hollywood into the liberal-left fortification that it later became.

Kennedy achieved this through what Schlesinger called his "cool" style, which gave the appearance of a man at the cutting edge of new cultural trends, in contrast to other politicians (like Nixon or Eisenhower) who generally represented the established patterns and morals of middle-class life. Sorensen acknowledged that Kennedy at his inauguration deliberately played up the stylistic contrast between himself and his tired predecessor.[37] Schlesinger saw in Kennedy's style a substantive statement in and of itself: "His coolness was itself a new frontier. It meant freedom from the stereotyped responses of the past. It offered hope for spontaneity in a country drowning in its own passivity."[38] Mailer saw Kennedy as an "existential hero," a man who would risk death in quest of authentic experience. With Kennedy in the lead, "America's politics would now be also America's favorite movie,

America's first soap opera, and America's best-seller." Kennedy's youth, good looks, and beautiful wife, according to Mailer, were not merely accessories to the man but necessary instruments for inspiring new acts of national creativity.[39] Mailer was writing from the stand-point of the "new" radicalism—the idea that politics must involve the redefinition of culture in the direction of liberation, experimentation, and the casting off of traditional assumptions about family, sex, and education. He saw Kennedy as a potentially important cultural model.

While Kennedy understood political leadership to involve facing down communism or putting a man on the moon, Mailer and others were thinking of "a revolution in the consciousness of our time." It is true that Kennedy cultivated a style, but it is also obvious that many read into it far more than was really there. In projecting their hopes onto Kennedy, liberals like Schlesinger and cultural radicals like Mailer were redefining liberalism more as a style or a posture toward the world than as a coherent body of ideas about government and politics. Indeed, by investing so much in Kennedy's style they came dangerously close to creating a cult of personality around him, thereby linking liberal ideals too closely to Kennedy the man. Because Kennedy embodied sophistication, he was seen after his death as a more authentic liberal than figures like Johnson or Humphrey who labored for legislative victories but appeared hopelessly old-fashioned in style and comportment.

Through this contrast with conventional figures, Kennedy added to his popularity by standing for a style of life to which many aspired, especially the college-educated young, who mistakenly thought his style was a rejection of the bland conformity of middle-class life, when in fact it reflected more the ways of the American aristocracy to which he and his wife belonged. In the new age of television, more-over, glamour and celebrity were suddenly assets to a political career as they had not been before. Television had created a vast audience of voters who judged political leaders by the way they appeared on the screen. Intellectuals, journalists, and commentators, along with their own audience on college campuses and elsewhere, had created a new constituency that was as attentive to matters of style as to policy. After his death, Kennedy was admired more for his attractive and sophisticated style than for any breakthroughs in policy. ~~the cult of~~

Victor Lasky, along with Kennedy's critics from the left such as ~~personality~~ Garry Wills and Christopher Lasch, noted that this was a manufactured and manipulated image at odds with a darker reality.[40] This is largely true though perhaps it misses the point, since all celebrity is based on the careful crafting and manipulation of images for wider consumption. To some extent this is true of political life itself, a fact which facilitates the merging of the world of politics with that of celebrity, particularly in the age of television and movies. Kennedy understood this far better than any other politician of his time. Still, there were facts about his "real" life (unknown to the public at the time) that would only have enhanced his reputation as a hip cultural figure—namely, his use of drugs and his reckless pursuit of sex, two activities that just a few years later would define the youth culture of the 1960s. Kennedy, however, was on to these amusements long before the youngsters discovered them. In essence, he anticipated these new directions in the culture. Here too, Kennedy behaved more like a Hollywood star than like a conventional politician.

* * *

It is Kennedy's status as a cultural figure that is responsible for the enduring interest in the man and his presidency and his transfiguration into a liberal hero. He was not in office long enough for the wear and tear of politics to have stripped away his cultural luster, and his untimely death only magnified his cultural appeal. Moreover, in seeming to stand above and apart from the conventions of middle-class life, he opened up new possibilities for cultural politics and cultural criticism that were eventually absorbed into the mainstream of liberal reform, so much so that within a few years liberals seemed more preoccupied with cultural issues—feminism, sexual freedom, and gay rights—than with the traditional issues of economic security that had animated Roosevelt, Truman, and even Kennedy himself. It was thus through the opening that Kennedy provided that the ideas associated with cultural radicalism began to blend with the broader movement of liberal reform. Yet it was perhaps this immersion in cultural politics following Kennedy's death that as much as anything brought about the end of the liberal era. Liberals after Kennedy identified their doctrine with his style and his sophistication while, in many areas, abandoning the substance of his ideas.

Kennedy's unique achievement was to have maintained this cultural stance in combination with his ardent patriotism and emphasis on national defense—a balancing act that proved impossible for his liberal successors to sustain. Kennedy was a decorated war veteran and an outspoken nationalist, but at the same time a symbol of cultural sophistication, a combination that appealed to both traditional Americans and the new cultural reformers. After Kennedy's death, these two groups divided into conflicting camps, thereby establishing the terms for the culture war that still continues today between cultural liberals and traditional middle-class Americans.

Kennedy was thus a bridge between the old liberalism and the new—between the programmatic liberals who followed FDR and the cultural liberals and radicals who gained influence following Kennedy's death. Daniel Bell and other liberal analysts of the postwar period turned out to have been correct when they suggested that "the end of ideology" in the 1950s might eventually lead to new forms of radicalism focused on issues of culture. Yet they could not have foreseen the surprising way by which this came about. Kennedy made politics seem interesting and exciting, albeit through the avenues of celebrity and glamour. His sudden death left a void that could not be filled by programmatic liberalism.

CHAPTER TWELVE

JFK & Camelot

Few events in the postwar era have cast such a long shadow over our national life as the assassination of President John F. Kennedy, now more than a half century ago. The murder of a handsome and vigorous president shocked the nation to its core and shook the faith of many Americans in their institutions and way of life.

Those who were living at the time would never forget the moving scenes associated with President Kennedy's death: the Zapruder film depicting the assassination in a frame-by-frame sequence; the courageous widow arriving with the coffin at Andrews Air Force Base still wearing her bloodstained dress; the throng of mourners lined up for blocks outside the Capitol to pay respects to the fallen president; the accused assassin gunned down two days later while in police custody and in full view of a national television audience; the little boy saluting the coffin of his slain father; the somber march to Arlington National Cemetery; the eternal flame affixed to the gravesite. These scenes were repeated endlessly on television at the time and then reproduced in popular magazines and, still later, in documentary films. They came to be viewed as defining events of the time.

In their grief, Americans were inclined to take to heart the various myths and legends that grew up around President Kennedy within days of the assassination. Though the assassin was a communist and an admirer of Fidel Castro, many insisted that President Kennedy was a martyr to the cause of civil rights who deserved a place of honor next to Abraham Lincoln as a champion of racial justice. Others held him up as a great statesman who labored for international peace.

But by far the most potent element of the Kennedy legacy was the one that associated JFK with the legend of King Arthur and Camelot. As with many of the myths and legends surrounding President Kennedy, this one was the creative contribution of Jacqueline Kennedy, who imagined and artfully circulated it in those grief-filled days following her husband's death.

* * *

On the weekend after the assassination and the state funeral, Mrs. Kennedy invited the journalist Theodore White to the Kennedy compound in Hyannis for an exclusive interview to serve as the basis for an essay in a forthcoming issue of *Life* magazine dedicated to President Kennedy. White was a respected journalist and the author of the best-selling chronicle of the 1960 campaign, *The Making of the President, 1960*, which portrayed candidate Kennedy in an especially favorable light and his opponent, Richard Nixon, in a decidedly negative way. White had also known Joseph Kennedy Jr. (John F. Kennedy's older brother) while a student at Harvard in the late 1930s. Mrs. Kennedy reached out to White in the reasonable belief that he was a journalist friendly to the Kennedy family.

In that interview, Mrs. Kennedy pressed upon White the Camelot image that would prove so influential in shaping the public memory of JFK and his administration. President Kennedy, she told the journalist, was especially fond of the music from the popular Broadway musical *Camelot*, the lyrics of which were the work of Alan Jay Lerner, JFK's classmate at Harvard. The musical, which featured Richard Burton as Arthur, Julie Andrews as Guinevere, and Robert Goulet as Lancelot, had a successful run on Broadway from 1960 to 1963. According to Mrs. Kennedy, the couple enjoyed listening to a recording of the title song before going to bed at night. JFK was especially fond of the concluding couplet: "Don't ever let it be forgot, that once there was a spot, for one brief shining moment that was Camelot." President Kennedy, she said, was strongly attracted to the Camelot legend because he was an idealist who saw history as something made by heroes like King Arthur (a claim that White knew to be untrue). "There will be great presidents again," she told White, "but there will never be another Camelot." In this way, and to her credit, Mrs. Kennedy sought to attach a morally uplifting message to one of the more ugly events in American history.

Following the interview, White retreated to a guest room in the Kennedy mansion to review his notes and compose a draft of the essay. His editors were at this hour, late on a Saturday evening, holding the presses open at great expense while waiting to receive his copy over the telephone. When White later phoned his editors to dictate his text, with Mrs. Kennedy standing nearby, he was surprised by their reaction: they instinctively rejected the Camelot references as sentimental and inappropriate to the occasion. Mrs. Kennedy, interpreting the gist of the exchange, signaled to White that Camelot must be kept in the text. The editors quickly relented. White later wrote that he regretted the role he played in transmitting the Camelot myth to the public.

The Arthurian images were contained in White's essay in the special issue of *Life* that hit the newsstands on December 3, 1963. *Life* at that time had a weekly circulation of seven million and a readership of more than 30 million. The extensive distribution of the issue guaranteed that the essay would receive the widest possible circulation here and abroad. Though the Camelot motif has been ridiculed over the years as a distortion of the actual record, it has nevertheless etched the Kennedy years in the public memory as a magical time that will never be repeated.

Mrs. Kennedy had very likely read *The Once and Future King*, the

Arthurian novel by T. H. White (no relation to the journalist) that formed the basis for *Camelot*, the Broadway musical and later a Hollywood movie. The book was published in 1958 but composed of four parts that the author had written separately beginning in 1938. Perhaps Mrs. Kennedy had shown her children the cartoon version of *The Sword in the Stone*, the first part of the novel, that Walt Disney produced in 1963. *The Once and Future King* became one of the most popular and widely read books of our time. Reviewers called it "a literary miracle" and "a queer kind of masterpiece." The reviewer for the *New York Times* described it as "a glorious dream of the Middle Ages as they never were but as they ought to have been, an inspired and exhilarating mixture of farce, fantasy, psychological insight, medieval lore and satire all involved in a marvelously peculiar retelling of the Arthurian legend." In contrast to traditional versions of the Arthurian story, which celebrated knighthood and chivalry and portrayed Arthur as a brave warrior, White's modern version poked fun at the pretensions of knights and princes and pointedly criticized war, militarism, and nationalism. White presented King Arthur less as a military leader than as a peacemaker who tried (but failed) to subdue the belligerent passions of mankind.

There were biting ironies in Mrs. Kennedy's attraction to a legendary kingship that unravels due to the consequences of betrayal and infidelity, and in her association of the central myth of English nationality with the United States' first Irish president. Nevertheless, she looked past these contradictions to focus on the central message of White's novel: its representation of war as pointless and absurd. President Kennedy, like King Arthur, was a peacemaker who died in a campaign to pacify the warring factions of mankind.

The final section of the novel (and the final act of the play), titled "The Candle in the Wind," concludes with a scene around a campfire on the eve of Arthur's final battle, in which he would lose both his kingdom and his life. There the king, ruminating on his failures and the dissolution of his kingdom, sees a boy preparing for the next day's battle. Now searching for a way to perpetuate his ideals, Arthur urges the boy to abandon the battle and go forth to spread the noble principles for which he and his knights have stood. "Thomas," he says to the boy, "my idea of those knights was a sort of candle. I have carried it for many years with a hand to shield it from the wind. It has flickered often. I am giving you the candle now—you won't let it out?" The boy pledges to carry the flame into the future as the enduring symbol of Arthur's ideals of peace and justice.

Is the eternal flame burning on President Kennedy's grave a replica of King Arthur's candle in the wind? Though Mrs. Kennedy never made any declaration on this point, the answer is probably yes, given her explicit campaign to associate her husband with the Camelot legend, and in particular with T. H. White's modern retelling of the Arthurian myth.

* * *

One cannot help but admire Mrs. Kennedy for the skill and composure with which she deployed these images in the sad aftermath of her husband's death. Our retrospective view of President Kennedy is now filtered through the legends and symbols she put forward at that time. The hardheaded politician devoted to step-by-step progress was transformed in death into the consummate liberal idealist. The Cold War leader who would "pay any price, bear any burden" to ensure "the survival of and the success of liberty" was subsequently viewed as an idealistic peacemaker in the image of *The Once and Future King*. Difficult as it may be to accept, the posthumous image of JFK reflected the idealistic beliefs of Mrs. Kennedy more than the practical political liberalism of the man himself.

But the Camelot image as applied to the Kennedy presidency had some unfortunate and unforeseen consequences. By turning President Kennedy into a liberal idealist (which he was not) and an almost legendary figure, Mrs. Kennedy inadvertently contributed to the unwinding of the tradition of American liberalism that her husband represented in life. The images she advanced had a double effect: first, to establish Kennedy as a transcendent political figure far superior to any contemporary rival; and, second, to highlight what the nation had lost when he was killed. The two elements were mirror images of one another. The Camelot myth magnified the sense of loss felt as a consequence of Kennedy's death and the dashing of liberal hopes and possibilities. If one accepted the image—and many did—then the best of times were now in the past and could not be recovered. Life would go on but the future could never match the magical chapter that had been brought to an unnatural end. As Mrs. Kennedy said, "there will never be another Camelot."

The Camelot myth posed a challenge to the liberal idea of history as a progressive enterprise, always moving forward in spite of setbacks here and there toward the elusive goal of perfecting the American experiment in self-government. Mrs. Kennedy's image fostered nostalgia for the past in the belief that the Kennedy administration represented a peak of achievement that could not be duplicated. The legend of the Kennedy years as unique or magical was, in addition, divorced from real accomplishments as measured by important programs passed or difficult problems solved. Instead, the magical aspect of the New Frontier was located in its style and sophisticated attitude. Mrs. Kennedy, without intending to do so and without understanding the consequences of her image making, put forward an interpretation of John F. Kennedy's life and death that magnified the consequences of the assassination while leaving his successors with little upon which to build.

⤝

A version of this chapter appeared on the website
The Daily Beast, November 2013.

CHAPTER THIRTEEN

Revisiting the Kennedy Assassination after Fifty Years

It has been over fifty years since President John F. Kennedy was cut down on the streets of Dallas with rifle shots fired by Lee Harvey Oswald, a self-described Marxist, recent defector to the Soviet Union, and ardent admirer of Fidel Castro. Since 1963, more than 1,400 books about JFK and his assassination have been published, with many more appearing in 2013 and 2014 to mark the anniversary of his death. The passage of time does not appear to have dimmed the public's fascination with President Kennedy and the Kennedy family, or to have allayed the confusion and controversy surrounding JFK's assassination.

There should have been little confusion because the evidence condemning Oswald was overwhelming: the bullets that killed President Kennedy were fired from his rifle; the rifle was found on the sixth floor of the warehouse where he worked and where he was seen moments before the shooting; witnesses on the street saw a man firing shots from a sixth-floor window in that building and immediately summoned police to provide a description of the assassin. Forty-five minutes later, a policeman stopped Oswald on foot in another section of the city to question him about the shooting. As the policeman stepped from his squad car, Oswald pulled out a pistol and pumped four shots into him before fleeing to a nearby movie theater, where he was captured, still carrying the pistol with which he had killed the policeman. Two days later, Oswald was himself assassinated while in police custody by a nightclub owner distraught over Kennedy's death.

Kennedy's very public murder, recorded in amateur films and news photos, was a shock that many Americans could never quite get over. Those who were taken with Kennedy's style and idealistic rhetoric could not help but feel that the ensuing disasters—the war in Vietnam, the urban riots, the assassinations of Robert Kennedy and Martin Luther King, Nixon's election—were in some way connected to the irrational act of violence that claimed President Kennedy's life. And so they returned to it again and again as the years passed. The act could not be undone, though if it could at least be explained or understood, or if blame could be fairly apportioned and punishment meted out, then the world might again be set right. But it proved to be singularly difficult to understand or explain in terms satisfactory to the prevailing assumptions of the age. Before long, the assassination came to be encrusted in layers of myth, illusion, and disinformation strong enough to deflect every attempt to understand it from a rational point of view.

Today, despite the evidence, relatively few Americans believe that Lee Harvey Oswald shot President Kennedy, or that he acted alone if he did. A recent poll found that a remarkable 75 percent of American adults believe that JFK was the victim of a conspiracy, usually of a right-wing variety. This is not surprising because most of the popular books published on the assassination since the mid-1960s have elaborated one or another conspiracy theory. Right-wing businessmen, disgruntled generals, CIA operatives, and Mafia bosses are the typical villains in these fanciful and fact-free scenarios.[1] The conspiracy mania surrounding the JFK assassination has at length transformed the event from tragedy into a macabre parlor game in which new entrants devise speculative theories to explain how the murder might have been carried out and who might have had motives to commit it. The hard facts of the case seem less interesting: that President Kennedy was assassinated by a communist seeking to protect the Castro regime from JFK's campaign to overthrow it.

The public confusion surrounding the Kennedy assassination makes it unique among politically consequential assassinations that have occurred throughout history. The assassination of Julius Caesar led to a long civil war and eventually to the defeat of the republican faction in Rome. The assassination of Lincoln complicated efforts to return the Southern states to the Union on the basis of civil rights for all. The assassination of Archduke Franz Ferdinand of Austria in 1914 ignited a series of events that led to a disastrous world war. No one doubts that these assassinations were consequential in the extreme: they provoked powerful reactions against the assassins and the parties with which they were associated. There was no doubt in any of these cases as to who the assassins were and why they committed their crimes. The Kennedy assassination was different: its consequences flowed from widespread confusion about the meaning of the event, the individuals or groups responsible for it, and even what John F. Kennedy really stood for.

* * *

In the days and weeks following the assassination, the idea took hold that a climate of hate in Dallas and across the nation established the conditions for President Kennedy's murder. Racial bigots, the Ku Klux Klan, followers of the John Birch Society, fundamentalist ministers, anticommunist zealots, and conservatives of all kinds—these were the battalions of the American right that sowed hatred and division in national life. They had been responsible for manifold acts of violence across the South against Negroes and civil rights workers in the months and years leading up to the assassination. It made perfect sense to suppose that these same forces must have been behind the attack on President Kennedy.

Given such assumptions, it followed that President Kennedy, like Abraham Lincoln, was a martyr to the great causes of civil rights and racial justice. Liberal writers had warned throughout the 1950s and into the 1960s about the undercurrent of bigotry and intolerance that ran through American culture and the political dangers arising from the "radical right." Now it appeared that their warnings had come to pass in the murder of a president.

This explanation for the assassination did not drop out of thin air but was circulated immediately after the event by influential leaders, journalists, and journalistic outlets, including Mrs. Kennedy, Lyndon Johnson, Chief Justice Earl Warren, Democratic leaders in Congress, Arthur Schlesinger Jr., James Reston, Drew Pearson, and any number of other liberal spokesmen. The *New York Times* through its editorial page and columnists insisted that a climate of hate brought down President Kennedy, even as the paper's news reporters documented the evidence against Oswald and his communist connections.

On the day after the assassination, the *New York Times* ran a banner headline across the front page: KENNEDY IS KILLED BY SNIPER AS HE RIDES IN CAR IN DALLAS; JOHNSON SWORN IN ON PLANE. In the middle column, the editors ran a signed article by a reporter on the scene about Lee Harvey Oswald, the suspect arrested for the crime. The headline read, LEFTIST ACCUSED; FIGURE IN PRO-CASTRO GROUP IS CHARGED. The article went on to summarize the accused assassin's left-wing and pro-communist associations, along with the array of physical evidence that linked him to the crime. The key facts contained in that article were compelling as to Oswald's role in the crime, and none of those points was ever impeached by later investigations.

Adjacent to that article on the front page, however, readers found an opinion article penned by James Reston, the Washington bureau chief of the *Times* and dean of national political journalists. The article was titled "Why America Weeps: Kennedy Victim of Violent Streak He Sought to Curb in Nation." Reston wrote: "America wept tonight not alone for its dead young president but for itself. The grief was general, for somehow the worst in the nation had prevailed over the best. The indictment extended beyond the assassin for something in the nation itself, some strain of madness and violence, had destroyed the highest symbol of law and order." Reston seemed to be searching for an explanation for the assassination that reached beyond the assassin himself and his possible motives. "The irony of the president's death," he continued, "is that his short administration was devoted almost entirely to various attempts to curb this very streak of violence in the national character." Reston went on to observe that "from the beginning to the end of his administration he was trying to tamp down the violence of extremists from the right." Reston returned to this theme in subsequent columns, pointing the finger at hatred and a spirit of lawlessness in the land as the ultimate causes of the presidential assassination. In the process, he (like others) ignored the mountain of evidence that pointed to a communist as the probable assassin.

Also expressing this line of thought was Chief Justice Warren, soon to head the official commission that investigated the assassination, who declared, "A great and good President has suffered martyrdom as a result of the hatred and bitterness that has been injected into the life of our nation by bigots." Late in the evening of November 22, Chet Huntley, chief newscaster for NBC, told millions of viewers that the assassination had been brought about by "the sickening and ominous popularity of hatred" across the United States and more particularly by influential "pockets of hatred" within the country. The president's death, he said, is "thundering testimonial of what hatred comes to and the revolting excesses it perpetrates." Both Huntley and Warren pointed to domestic factors as causes of the assassination, and specifically to "right-wing" hatred.

They were far from alone in doing so. Pat Brown, governor of California, and Charles Taft, mayor of Cincinnati, organized a series of candlelight vigils across the nation "to pledge the end of intolerance and to affirm that such a tragedy shall not happen in America again." The Reverend Adam Clayton Powell (also a congressman) issued a statement shortly after the assassination: "President Kennedy is a martyr of freedom and human rights and a victim of injustice as promulgated by Barnett and Wallace," here referring to the segregationist governors of Mississippi and Alabama. Less than a week after the assassination, Drew Pearson published one of his syndicated columns under the title "Kennedy Victim of Hate Drive." Many took this case a step further to declare that all Americans were complicit in President Kennedy's death because they had tolerated hatred and bigotry in their midst. This idea even appeared in a popular song by the Rolling Stones a few years later, with the line: "I shouted out: Who killed the Kennedys? When after all it was you and me." This was the nearly universal response to the assassination: a strain of bigotry and hatred in American culture was culpable for President Kennedy's murder.

For his part, President Johnson saw that his job as national leader in that time of crisis was to supply some meaning to Kennedy's sudden death. "John Kennedy had died," he said later, "but his cause was not really clear. I had to take the dead man's program and turn it into a martyr's cause." In his first speech before Congress on November 27, just two days after Kennedy's state funeral, Johnson proclaimed that "no memorial could more eloquently honor President Kennedy's memory than the earliest possible passage of the civil rights bill for which he fought so long." The civil rights bill, which Kennedy belatedly proposed in mid-1963, was approved in 1964 with bipartisan majorities in Congress.

On the international front, Johnson feared a dangerous escalation of tensions with the Soviet Union and another McCarthy-style "witch hunt" against radicals should the American public conclude that a communist was responsible for the assassination. He was well aware that Oswald's pro-communist background might provoke a backlash among the American people against the Soviet Union and Cuba. From Washington's point of view, it was better to evade that danger by deflecting blame for the assassination from communism to some other vague or unpopular target.

In doing so, the U.S. government adopted a line similar to that being pushed by the Soviet Union and communist governments around the world. Those governments were understandably concerned that they might be blamed for the assassination and thus sought to deflect blame in other directions. Within hours of the assassination, the Soviet press put out reports declaring that "rightists" were responsible for the assassination and that plots were being hatched to blame the crime on a communist. A Soviet spokesman said that "Senator Goldwater and other extremists on the right could not escape moral responsibility for the president's death." Leftists around the world were quick to disown Oswald out of fear that his deed might contaminate their cause.

Mrs. Kennedy took the lead in declaring her husband a martyr to the causes of civil rights, racial justice, and international peace, even though she was told hours after the assassination that Oswald had been arrested for the crime. She soon gave instructions to aides to make her husband's funeral rites "as Lincolnesque as possible" in order to cement the connection between the two fallen leaders. The implied connection between Lincoln and Kennedy was not lost on the millions who viewed the funeral in person or on television. Mrs. Kennedy also crafted the symbolism of Camelot and King Arthur's court to frame the Kennedy presidency as a near-magical enterprise guided by the highest ideals of international peace and domestic justice.

These were the myths, illusions, and inventions that attached themselves to the Kennedy assassination. All evidence to the contrary notwithstanding, they are still widely believed, and not only by members of a credulous public. The claim that JFK was a victim of hatred and bigotry or a martyr in the crusade for civil rights or that the New Frontier was a peak moment in American history—these are now basic elements in the liberal interpretation of the postwar era. Arrayed against Kennedy the liberal hero and martyr is a roster of villains: bigots, conservatives, anticommunists, militarists, and agents of the radical right. From a liberal point of view, the Kennedy assassination was the moment in which the battle between the "good" America and the "bad" America was expressed in its most dramatic and memorable fashion.

Taylor Branch, in his award-winning biography of Martin Luther King, summed up the liberal consensus that has grown up around the JFK assassination:

> In death, the late president gained credit for much of the purpose that [Martin Luther] King's movement had forced upon him in life. No death had ever been like his—Reinhold Niebuhr called him "an elected monarch." In a mass purgative of hatred, bigotry, and violence, the martyred president became a symbol of the healing opposites. . . . President Johnson told the nation that the most fitting eulogy would be the swift passage of his civil rights bill. By this and other effects of mourning, Kennedy acquired the Lincolnesque mantle of a unifying crusader who had bled against the thorn of race.[2]

The Kennedy legend, incorporating the myths about his assassination, is closely intertwined with the history of modern liberalism: JFK came to represent a liberal ideal and his assassination the threat posed to it by the dark forces of bigotry, intolerance, and the radical right.

* * *

To the extent he can be called a martyr at all, President Kennedy was a martyr in the Cold War struggle against communism. Lee Harvey Oswald was not in any way, shape, or form a product of a "climate of hate" as found in Dallas or anywhere else in the United States. He defected from the United States to the Soviet Union in 1959, vowing when he did so that he could no longer live under a capitalist system. He returned to the United States with his Russian wife in 1962 in disappointment with life under Soviet communism but without giving up his Marxist beliefs. By 1963, Oswald had transferred his political allegiance from the Soviet Union to Castro's communist regime in Cuba. Nor was Oswald a bigot; he supported the civil rights movement and the ideal of racial equality. In his eyes, racial bigotry was an evil inseparable from American capitalism. He hated the United States, the capitalist system, and everything associated with the "radical right." Oswald was a creature of the far left, not of the far right. In contrast to academic or armchair radicals, he was on the lookout for opportunities to act out his ideological convictions.

In April 1963, seven months before he killed President Kennedy, Oswald took a shot (and missed) at Edwin Walker, a retired general, as he sat at his dining table working on his income tax return. Walker was the head of the Dallas chapter of the John Birch Society and a figure then in the news because of his public opposition to school integration and his demand for the overthrow of the Castro regime. Only weeks earlier, Oswald had purchased a scoped rifle (later used to shoot President Kennedy) by mail order for the purpose of assassinating General Walker.

A month later, fearful that he might be identified as the assailant in the Walker shooting, Oswald left Dallas to take up residence in New Orleans, where he established a local chapter of Fair Play for Cuba, a national organization dedicated to gaining diplomatic recognition for Castro's regime. While in New Orleans, Oswald was arrested and detained for a brief period following an altercation on the street with several anti-Castro Cubans who were upset about the pro-Castro leaflets he was distributing. He even appeared on local television in a debate with a conservative and an anti-Castro Cuban, and his adversaries revealed to the audience that Oswald had once defected to the Soviet Union and lived there for three years. This information supported accusations that Fair Play for Cuba was a communist front and that Castro's regime was a "puppet" government of the Soviet Union.

His enterprise in New Orleans in ruins, Oswald traveled to Mexico City in late September to visit the Soviet and Cuban embassies in desperate pursuit of a visa that would allow him to travel to Cuba. Before taking this step, he discussed with his wife the possibility of hijacking an airliner to take them to Cuba (an idea she rejected). Oswald took along a dossier of news clippings on his pro-Castro activities in New Orleans for the purpose of establishing his revolutionary bona fides with embassy personnel. He returned to Dallas empty-handed after being told by embassy officials that his application would take weeks or even months to process. He was still waiting to hear on his application six weeks later when he read that President Kennedy's forthcoming visit to Texas would include a motorcade through the downtown streets of Dallas and past the building where he worked. FBI agents, having been informed by the CIA of Oswald's visits to the embassies in Mexico City, were still trying to track him down on the day President Kennedy arrived in Dallas.

Oswald's motives in shooting President Kennedy were undoubtedly linked to a wish to protect Castro against efforts by the Kennedy administration to overturn his government. From 1961 to 1963, the Kennedy administration was preoccupied with two large issues: the civil rights crusade at home and the Cold War abroad, with Cuba as its central flashpoint. Oswald was preoccupied with Cuba and the Cold War, while JFK's domestic supporters focused on civil rights and the injustice of the racial caste system in the South.

Kennedy failed to oust Castro in 1961 in a U.S.-sponsored invasion of the island carried out by Cuban exiles opposed to the regime. In response, and on Castro's invitation, the Soviet Union placed offensive missiles in Cuba, thereby provoking a crisis in 1962 that brought the United States and the Soviet Union to the brink of nuclear war. In settlement of that crisis, the Soviet Union withdrew its missiles and Kennedy pledged to abandon efforts to overthrow Castro's government by force. But the war of words between the two governments continued, and so did clandestine plots (unknown to the public at that time but revealed in the 1970s) by the Kennedy administration to assassinate Castro.

In late April 1963, Castro asserted that the United States may have given up plans to invade Cuba but was continuing to sponsor plots to assassinate Cuban leaders. His remarks were made in response to Kennedy's observation from the previous day that Castro would no longer be in power in five years. Returning to that theme in early September, Castro stated in an interview that "United States leaders should be mindful that if they are aiding terrorist plans to eliminate Cuban leaders, they themselves will not be safe." A transcript of the interview was circulated by the Associated Press and published in many American newspapers, including the local paper in New Orleans, where Oswald was then living. It was probably this statement that sent Oswald off on his urgent trip to Mexico City in search of a visa for travel to Cuba.

U.S. intelligence officials were alarmed at this escalation in Castro's rhetoric and the implied threat it conveyed. Was Castro aware of U.S. plots to assassinate him? If so, how did he know? Did he intend to retaliate by organizing reciprocal plots against American leaders? They concluded that among various things Castro might do, he was unlikely to risk an assassination attempt on a U.S. leader. In any case, Castro's threats had little effect on Kennedy's determination to get rid of him. On November 18, four days before he was killed, Kennedy delivered a speech in Miami in which he described the Castro government as "a small band of conspirators that has stripped the Cuban people of their freedom." He pledged to restore U.S. assistance and friendship "once Cuban sovereignty has been restored." Oswald, an admirer of Castro and other Third World revolutionaries, was acutely attentive to the smoldering war between the U.S. and Cuban governments and to the personal and ideological war of words between Castro and Kennedy.

The JFK assassination was thus an event in the Cold War, but it was interpreted by the liberal leadership of the nation as an event in the civil rights crusade. This interpretation sowed much confusion as to the motives of the assassin and the meaning of the event. It made little logical sense to claim that Kennedy was a martyr to the cause of civil rights while acknowledging that the assassin was a communist and a supporter of Fidel Castro. In deciding which of the two should go—the facts or the interpretation—many decided to jettison the facts, or at least to ignore them. Even the Warren Report, while setting forth conclusive evidence that Oswald acted on his own (without any Cuban or Soviet assistance) in killing President Kennedy, contributed to the confusion by suggesting that he did so for a mix of personal reasons unrelated to his communist ideology or his admiration for Castro. In this way, the report carried forward the "official" view that required the suppression of ideological motives in the assassination. Before long, the vacuum of meaning surrounding the assassination was filled by a host of conspiracy theories claiming that JFK was a victim of an elaborate plot orchestrated by right-wing elements in American life.

The fruitless fifty-year debate over who killed Kennedy was a direct consequence of the tendentious interpretation assigned to the assassination in 1963. Needless to say, there would never have been any such debate nor any speculation about conspiracies had President Kennedy been killed by a right-winger whose guilt was confirmed by the same evidence as condemned Lee Harvey Oswald.

* * *

According to Robert Caro, author of a multivolume biography of Lyndon Johnson, the liberal explanations for Kennedy's assassination may have served a good purpose in helping the nation weather a crisis. Although Caro has a decidedly negative view of Johnson's career as a whole, he gives him high marks for holding the country together in the wake of the assassination. Johnson tamped down Cold War tensions that might have gotten out of control in response to Kennedy's death; he skillfully used the symbolism of "Kennedy as martyr" to generate the political momentum needed to pass his civil rights bill; and he put the Democratic Party in a position to claim a sweeping victory in the 1964 elections.[3] From Caro's perspective, the civil rights interpretation of the assassination may have been a distortion or even a lie, but if so it was a noble lie because it brought about a great deal of good while causing little in the way of damage.

This argument makes sense if one confines the effects of the assassination to the twelve or eighteen months following the tragic events in Dallas when President Johnson and a Democratic Congress pushed through the Civil Rights Act, a Keynesian tax cut, the Voting Rights Act, the Medicare and Medicaid programs, and countless other pieces of reformist legislation. Kennedy's death and Johnson's skillful handling of the transition provided the necessary momentum for these liberal victories. Yet these legislative successes in 1964 and 1965 turned out to be the high-water mark for postwar liberalism. Before long, the deeper implications of Kennedy's death set in, with lasting consequences for the liberal movement and the nation at large.

The official interpretation of the assassination—that JFK was a martyr in the struggle for civil rights or a victim of the national culture—had some unforeseen repercussions. Because of this interpretation, Kennedy's reputation as a liberal was magnified but Oswald's motives as a communist were diminished in the aftermath of the event—an interpretive coupling that led to disorienting consequences. The first heightened the sense of loss felt as a result of Kennedy's sudden death; the second rendered that loss meaningless, absurd, and impossible to understand. The widespread feeling that the national culture contributed to Kennedy's death encouraged an attitude of anti-Americanism that became a pronounced aspect of the radical and countercultural movements of the 1960s. This was an outlook that never entirely disappeared from the worldview of the American left.

By any logic, the assassination of a popular president by a communist should have generated a revulsion against everything associated with left-wing doctrines. Yet something very close to the opposite happened in the wake of JFK's assassination, and for many of the reasons outlined above. Within a few years, radical ideas and revolutionary leaders—Marx, Lenin, Mao, and Castro among them—enjoyed a greater vogue in the United States than at any previous time in our history, converting college students by the thousands to an anti-American and anticapitalist creed. Soon those students were taking over campuses and joining protest movements in support of a host of radical and revolutionary causes. Socialism and revolution—causes that Kennedy resolutely fought against—were the watchwords of the New Left that emerged within a few years of his death.

By the time of Martin Luther King's assassination in early 1968, the country was far along in a process of unraveling that began shortly after President Kennedy's death. The violence and disorder that Americans witnessed on college campuses and in major urban centers made the earlier antics of the far right look like child's play. No one could any longer say that the main threat to public order and democratic civility came from the far right. Now, with little advance warning, it came from a different direction altogether—in particular from the protest movement against the war in Vietnam and from riots in the cities that developed after the legislative successes of the civil rights movement. These protest movements arose from different sociological sources but they shared some common ideological themes, especially the claims that America was a nation deeply corrupted by the evils of bigotry, violence, and militarism.

A few days after President Kennedy was killed, James Reston wrote in the *New York Times*, "The death of President Kennedy and the shock and brutality that caused his death have changed the direction of American politics from extreme conflict toward moderation." It would be hard to find a political prediction that turned out to be more profoundly mistaken. Kennedy's death set off a period of intensifying political conflict in the United States that originated in attacks from the far left against liberals and moderates. In the 1960s, following Kennedy's death and partly as a consequence of it, radicals began to compete with liberals as spokesmen for the American left.

The assumption of national guilt, which surfaced in innocent form in the wake of the assassination, spread quickly through the institutions of politics, academe, and journalism that shaped liberal culture. The United States—*Amerika* in the lexicon of the New Left—was now an out-of-control colossus, a world superpower that suppressed Third World peoples abroad and minorities at home. The attributes that Americans value most in their nation—its prosperity, market economy, and representative political institutions—were denounced by the radicals as wicked or hypocritical. The reformist spirit in American liberalism was pragmatic and forward-looking (and well represented by John F. Kennedy), but it now appeared tired and complacent when set alongside these radical critiques of American life. The friction between the older liberalism and the new radicalism created a rupture within the Democratic Party that was fully on display in the general mayhem that attended the party's national convention in Chicago in 1968.

In just a few years, from 1963 to 1968, the liberal movement, under pressure from the new radicalism, absorbed a skeptical disposition toward the American past and the major institutions of American society. It would not be an exaggeration to label this disposition "anti-American." Among those who maintained a foothold in the liberal camp, there was a tendency to accept the left-wing assessments of American society as vulgar, violent, and racist. The radicals and the liberals might differ on style and strategy, but they agreed that real change must come about not through programmatic reforms but through cultural criticism that leads to a revolution in thought and conduct.

There is little doubt that the animus that pushed liberals and radicals onto this path had its origins in the aftermath of the Kennedy assassination. Once having accepted the claim that JFK was a victim of the national culture, many found it easy to extend the metaphor into other areas of American life, from race and poverty to the treatment of women to the struggle against communism. These were no longer seen as challenges to be met and overcome, but as indictments of the nation. The new mood was at odds with the genuine convictions of John F. Kennedy, even though many who upheld this indictment of the United States continued to look back on JFK as the ideal liberal statesman. Nor did the new mood promise a more constructive approach to national problems than did the tradition of reform liberalism that Kennedy represented. In a bizarre paradox, Kennedy's archenemy, Fidel Castro, was elevated to a status of revolutionary hero by many of those young people who mourned JFK's death in 1963. In an even more bizarre paradox, Kennedy's assassination came to be cited by the radical left as a principal exhibit in their indictment of the national culture.

The radicalism of the 1960s, mixed as it was with anti-Americanism and romantic conceptions of socialism and Third World dictators like Castro, may not have developed as it did if blame for the Kennedy assassination had been properly assigned to a communist acting out of ideological motives. In that case, the admiration that many felt for President Kennedy would have been in obvious conflict with the radical doctrines responsible for his assassination. Such an account could have been advanced in a responsible way without inciting calls for war against the Soviet Union or Cuba. As things turned out, the tactic of interpreting Kennedy's death as a landmark in the history of civil rights introduced confusion on top of tragedy, eventually turning the assassination into a weapon aimed at the nation itself.

* * *

In his book on *Lincoln in American Memory,* the historian Merrill Peterson wrote that "the public remembrance of the past…is concerned less with establishing its truth than with appropriating it for the present." Remembered history, he suggests, "is always penetrated with myth," and there is always a gulf between the public memory of an event and the way it actually transpired. This was true to some degree with Abraham Lincoln as he passed into public memory as a martyr and savior of the Union following his assassination, as Peterson documents. Yet there is no precedent in American history for the vast gulf that immediately opened up between the public memory of President Kennedy's assassination and the actual facts of the case. Looking back through the decades, it is easy to see how different the two assassinations—Lincoln's and Kennedy's—were in their character and in their political effects.

The public memory of Lincoln, as Peterson writes, was fashioned out of the victory of the Union Army and his assassination just a few days later. These events turned the politician who eight months earlier was certain that he would lose his bid for re-election into a martyr for the Union cause. Like Lincoln, Kennedy too was viewed as a martyr, albeit in devotion to a most uncertain cause. Here was a source of much bewilderment about the man and the event. The great difference between Lincoln and Kennedy is that the former died at his moment of victory while the latter was killed before he was able to achieve any great success. Lincoln was assassinated at the end of a civil war, Kennedy at the beginning of a culture war. Lincoln was mourned but also celebrated for his magnificent achievement; Kennedy was mourned in a spirit of frustrated possibility and dashed hopes. Lincoln's assassin was a Southern partisan whose motives were easy to understand; Kennedy's was an enemy, too, but something of a cipher whose motives may have been obvious but also difficult to accept in the political atmosphere of the time.

In the end, John Wilkes Booth achieved far less than he intended. Few saw him as a hero; even in the South his deed was widely repudiated. Lincoln's death united the North; no one after the assassination voiced agreement with Booth's description of Lincoln as a tyrant like Caesar. Indeed, Lincoln was immediately held up as a symbol of republican liberty.

Oswald, on the other hand, achieved more by his violent act than he might have hoped or expected. Lyndon Johnson, once in power, soon phased out assassination plots against Castro and withdrew U.S. support from Cuban exiles bent on staging another invasion of the island. Plans for another invasion of Cuba were permanently shelved. Johnson soon reoriented Cold War policy away from its focus on Cuba toward the challenge of communist revolutions in Southeast Asia. Kennedy's death led to a "hands off" policy toward Cuba that provided Castro with the latitude he required to survive over these many decades. If such was Oswald's goal, then there is little doubt that he achieved it—and then some.

Walt Whitman suggested in 1879 that the ending of a "heroic-eminent life" such as Lincoln's could serve to "condense a nationality" and unite a people more effectively than armies or institutions could do:

> The final use of the greatest men of a nation is not in reference to their deeds in themselves, or their direct bearing on their times or lands. The final use of a heroic-eminent life—especially a heroic-eminent death—is its indirect filtering into the nation and the race, and to give, often at many removes, but unerringly age after age, color and fiber to the…youth and maturity of that age and of mankind. Then there is a cement to the whole people, subtler, more underlying than anything written in the constitution, or courts or armies—namely, the cement of a death identified thoroughly with that people, at its head, and for its sake. Strange is it not that battles, martyrs, agonies, blood, even assassination, should so condense a nationality?

Lincoln's death, shocking though it was, unified the nation, or at least the Northern section of it, around the ideals of union and liberty for which the Civil War was fought. For Whitman, as for many at the time, Lincoln's "heroic-eminent death" provided "cement" for the Union in ways that the Constitution and the laws had failed to do.

The effect of the Kennedy assassination has been quite different. More precisely, the stories told about it divided the nation and introduced an element of confusion, bitterness, and distrust into national life. The assignment of guilt for Kennedy's death to the nation at large; the belief that there had to be something deeply wrong with the country in order for such an event to have occurred;

the search for conspiracies to account for the assassination; the claims that a distinguished body of American leaders deliberately covered up the truth behind the event; the denial that communism or the Cold War could have played any role in the tragedy; the emphasis on civil rights as the political context in which the event should be understood—all of these contributed to the poisoning of the political atmosphere in the United States for decades afterward. For this reason, the Kennedy assassination is coming into view as one of the signal events of the postwar era.

It was wrong for national leaders in 1963 to invent a story of President Kennedy's assassination that deflected responsibility from the real assassin to the nation's culture or to a group of Americans who played no role in the president's death. In formulating a story that fit comfortably with the assumptions of the time, even though it was at variance with the facts, they sowed the seeds of distrust and division in the body politic that are still with us today.

A version of this chapter appeared in
The Claremont Review of Books, October 2013.

CHAPTER FOURTEEN

Was JFK a Conservative?

After President Kennedy's assassination in 1963, as we have seen, his family, friends, and members of the White House inner circle portrayed him as a liberal hero and a martyr to the causes of civil rights and international peace—overlooking the fact that he was shot by a communist. Kennedy loyalists Theodore Sorenson and Arthur Schlesinger Jr. soon published histories of the New Frontier in which they highlighted JFK's liberal accomplishments and lamented all that was left undone by his premature death. Some maintained that he should be honored next to Abraham Lincoln as one of the nation's great champions of racial equality. Mrs. Kennedy suggested that the Kennedy White House should be remembered, like King Arthur's Camelot, as a special place devoted to peace and justice.

These images of the late president as a hero and a martyr to his ideals have had remarkable staying power in American culture over the five decades since he was killed. In recent opinion polls, American adults have placed JFK at or near the top in rankings of the greatest American presidents. This explains why Democratic presidential candidates since the 1960s—especially George McGovern, Michael Dukakis, Bill Clinton, Al Gore, and John

Kerry—have tried to outdo one another in associating themselves with JFK's liberal legacy. Barack Obama's campaign for the presidency received an early boost when the Kennedy family endorsed him as the candidate most likely to carry forward that legacy. The salacious revelations over the years about scandals in the Kennedy White House have done little to dim the luster of the Kennedy name or to undermine JFK's reputation as a liberal statesman.

Those who knew or served in government with Kennedy and scholars who have studied his life and career have tried to deflate the overblown image of JFK as an idealistic liberal. Kennedy, they point out, was in reality a moderate or pragmatic liberal, a conventional representative of the postwar consensus that emphasized economic growth at home and fighting the Cold War abroad as the two great challenges of American public life. He was never on good terms with Hubert Humphrey, Adlai Stevenson, or other leaders of the liberal wing of the Democratic Party. Far from being a bold and innovative leader, JFK was a cautious politician who never wanted to get too far out in front of public opinion. He was slow to embrace the cause of civil rights and did so only in 1963 when events in the South forced his hand. He saw the Cold War abroad as a more important struggle than the campaign for civil rights at home.

* * *

Now Ira Stoll has come along to take the argument a step further. Stoll makes the startling case that JFK was not a liberal at all, but in reality a conservative who, had he lived, might have endorsed Ronald Reagan for president and might today be comfortably at home writing editorials for *National Review* or the *Wall Street Journal*. Most readers are likely to be skeptical of this thesis and to think the author has gone a bit too far with his revisionist history. Yet Stoll, who is also the author of a fine biography of Samuel Adams and former managing editor of the *New York Sun*, makes a strong case that conservatives should stake a claim to President Kennedy as one of their own. *JFK, Conservative** is a finely crafted brief for this interpretation, and it comes close to winning the case.

When Kennedy rose to power in the 1940s and 1950s, Stoll reminds us, both major parties had liberal and conservative wings, and it was far from clear which one was the liberal and which the conservative party. Rising politicians did not move into one party or the other for ideological reasons but rather for a mix of cultural, religious, and historical factors. Kennedy said that the main reason he was a Democrat was that he was "born one." JFK disdained the liberals of his day because, he said, they preferred to posture rather than get things done. Kennedy went out of his way to correct anyone who called him a liberal. He ran to the right of Henry Cabot Lodge in the senatorial election of 1952 by courting the supporters of the conservative senator Robert Taft. He positioned himself similarly against Richard Nixon in the 1960 campaign when he accused the Eisenhower administration of allowing the Soviet Union to gain an advantage in the arms race. According to Stoll, Nixon was the liberal in that race and JFK the conservative.

Stoll emphasizes one theme that has never been widely appreciated: Kennedy was a devout Catholic who prayed and attended mass regularly. He grew up in a Catholic family guided by a religiously devout mother. Stoll recounts many occasions on which JFK interrupted official trips or campaign tours to attend church. His mother was surprised (and pleased) to encounter him at church on the morning of his presidential inauguration. In the heat of the Cuban missile crisis, he pulled aides aside to accompany him to church for prayer. He spoke frequently about the religious foundations of America's political institutions. "The informing spirit of

---

* Houghton Mifflin Harcourt, 2013.

the American character has always been a deep religious sense," he said during his first campaign for office in 1946. The apparent conflict between the devout Catholic and the promiscuous husband is one that the author is unable to resolve.

Kennedy's religious faith was the foundation for his generally conservative outlook. It is well known that JFK was an ardent cold warrior and a dedicated foe of communism. Less well known is that he grounded his opposition to communism in religious principles and viewed the Cold War as a spiritual contest between two irreconcilable views of man and society. Sounding very much like a conservative, Kennedy declared in the 1960 campaign that the Cold War "is not a struggle for supremacy of arms alone—it is also a struggle for supremacy between two conflicting ideologies: freedom under God versus ruthless, Godless tyranny." He saw the spiritual and material dimensions of the struggle as connected, and he believed that the Cold War might be won through a confrontation of ideas and by sustained focus on the achievements of the free world in comparison with those of the Soviet bloc. That, as Stoll argues, was the point of his speech in 1963 in Berlin, where he challenged communists and fellow travelers to compare the quality of life in the two sectors of the city: "There are those who say that communism is the wave of the future. Let them come to Berlin."

Kennedy's policy as president was to confront and not merely to contain communism. Stoll rejects the claim, made first by Arthur Schlesinger Jr. and later by a battalion of liberal writers, that Kennedy softened his opposition to communism in the last year of his life following the dangerous showdown over nuclear missiles in Cuba. As he points out, such a shift was not evident in JFK's rhetoric in Berlin, in his efforts in 1963 to hold off the communist insurgency in Vietnam, or in his continuing campaign to get rid of Castro's regime in Cuba.

JFK's brief presidency is notable in retrospect as a time when Cold War tensions reached their most perilous point, involving clashes with the Soviet Union over Cuba, Berlin, and South Vietnam. Kennedy meant it when he vowed in his inaugural address to challenge Soviet ambitions in Europe, Latin America, and Southeast Asia. As Stoll puts it, "Kennedy felt encircled, embattled, under siege by a menacing, expansionist subversive Communist empire. Fighting back was a top priority." Having studied Hitler's near-conquest of Europe in 1939 and 1940, Kennedy accepted the lesson of Munich that when free nations fail to prepare, dictators will take advantage of their weakness. He thus supported a build-up of American arms in order to fight the Cold War on the basis of "peace through strength."

President Kennedy was not only a conservative cold warrior but also a fiscal conservative and a tax cutter. He favored efficiency in government and aimed to cut wasteful spending. He came to office pledging to balance the federal budget over the life of the business cycle. His top domestic priority in 1963 was a general reduction in personal and corporate income taxes to spur consumer spending and to promote faster economic growth. He proposed to cut the top marginal tax rate from 91 to 65 percent and the lowest rate from 20 to 14 percent, and also to reduce long-term capital gains taxes from 25 to 19.5 percent. He pushed this proposal against the opposition of liberals like John Kenneth Galbraith and Senator Albert Gore Sr. who called for more government spending to stimulate growth. A version of JFK's proposal was passed into law in 1964, and the payoff came in the mid-1960s, when the U.S. economy grew at average rates of more than 6 percent per year.

Many of Kennedy's central ideas, as Stoll points out, were later picked up by Ronald Reagan and other conservatives but generally abandoned by the liberal Democrats who came along in the 1970s and 1980s. This was true of Kennedy's principle of "peace through strength," his belief that the Cold War might eventually be won through a policy of confrontation, and his conviction that tax cuts rather than government spending are the best means to promote economic growth. Kennedy was also optimistic about America's future, an outlook he shared with President Reagan though not with some of his dour successors in the Democratic Party like Jimmy Carter.

* * *

Stoll makes a strong case that JFK was neither the idealistic liberal of legend nor even the pragmatic liberal that the historical consensus suggests he was. Does that make him a conservative? That is a much harder case to make.

Stoll does not explain why, if JFK was a conservative, he sought to extend the New Deal, courted labor unions, supported federal aid to local schools, promoted a system of health insurance for seniors (later passed as Medicare), proposed a cabinet department for housing and urban affairs, blasted business leaders who raised prices beyond his administration's wage and price guidelines, endorsed a federal agency to support the arts, advocated an expansion of welfare payments—in short, promoted many policies that conservatives opposed then and still do today. The surviving Kennedy brothers, Robert and Edward, had few doubts as to where President Kennedy belonged on the left-to-right spectrum. Both did their best to extend JFK's legacy by identifying it with the leftward drift of liberal culture in the late 1960s. If their brother was a conservative, it was not obvious to them.

No prominent conservative at the time saw JFK as a potential friend or ally. *National Review* refused to endorse either Nixon or Kennedy in the 1960 election. Barry Goldwater's *The Conscience of a Conservative*, published in 1960, took issue with virtually all of JFK's positions, and Goldwater looked forward to challenging

Kennedy in the 1964 election. One of the more popular conservative books of that time was Victor Lasky's *J.F.K.: The Man and the Myth* (1963), which portrayed the young president as an empty suit preoccupied with his image and ill prepared to tackle the great issues of the day. William F. Buckley Jr. concurred, writing in 1963 that "this efficient and likeable young man hasn't the least idea how to maneuver through the greatest crisis in world history." Conservatives viewed Kennedy as a hopeless representative of the postwar consensus that called for the preservation of the New Deal at home and the containment of communism abroad. Buckley launched the conservative movement in the 1950s in opposition to that consensus, calling instead for a "rollback" of both communism and the New Deal.

JFK appears more conservative to us today than he appeared to his contemporaries because liberalism moved so far to the left in the years after he was killed. As it did so, some liberals of the old school broke away from the Democratic Party and established a new tendency in national politics that endorsed the New Deal and a tough line against communism, but was skeptical of the Great Society and opposed to the new cultural politics of the 1960s. The neoconservatives held many principles in common with JFK, especially in the areas emphasized in Stoll's excellent study. *JFK, Conservative* adds still another dimension to JFK's tangled legacy, not by proving that Kennedy was a conservative, but by providing the basis for a quite different suggestion: that he may have been our "first neoconservative."

⌖

A version of this chapter appeared in *National Review*,
November 25, 2013.

PART FOUR

The Politics of Higher Education

CHAPTER FIFTEEN

The Left University

The college commencement ceremony, once an inspiring spring-time rite, has evolved over the past few decades into a battlefield of political correctness. According to the Foundation for Individual Rights in Education, there have been more than a hundred cases in the last five years of college commencement speakers who withdrew their names or had their invitations revoked because of protests by students and faculty. It should not surprise anyone to learn that most of these protests have been ginned up by leftists upset at the prospect of hearing—or allowing others on campus to hear—a conservative or a Republican, or anyone who has offended the reigning leftist pieties in some way.

In 2013, Dr. Ben Carson withdrew from a commencement address at Johns Hopkins University following protests against his political views. In 2014, the former secretary of state Condoleezza Rice was forced to withdraw from commencement exercises at Rutgers University due to protests against her association with the Bush administration and the war in Iraq. Christine Lagarde, managing director of the International Monetary Fund, was judged by student protesters to be unacceptable as a commencement speaker at Smith College on the grounds that she represents "privileged white women" and is "a symbol of imperialism and oppression." Michael Bloomberg was the target of protests at Harvard University because of his support for "stop and frisk" police procedures while he was mayor of New York City; but at least he was allowed to speak in the end. As a consequence of such protests, political liberals and leftists dominate the yearly roster of college commencement speakers.

The protests, moreover, go beyond the matter of commencement speeches, where students might argue that a unifying official event should not be marred by divisive politics. Many students believe that people whose views they find "offensive" should not be allowed to speak on their campus at all, even if those views fall within the mainstream of American society. Several years ago, for example, Justice Antonin Scalia was the target of faculty protests and petitions when he appeared at Amherst College to speak. In 2012, Fordham University rescinded a speaking invitation by the College Republicans to Ann Coulter because of student protests against her political views. Charles Murray, a distinguished fellow at the American Enterprise Institute, was disinvited from speaking at Azusa Pacific University in April 2014. George Will was disinvited from giving a speech to students at Scripps College in California later in the year. It would take up several pages to catalog all of the similar events that have occurred on college campuses over the past five or so years.

Most Americans do not understand why academics throw a temper tantrum whenever they are brought face to face with someone holding a different political view. After all, most people deal with conflicting opinions in the workplace, in social circles, even in family settings. Our treasured legal and political institutions— courts and elections, for example—are based upon adversarial procedures that require people to weigh conflicting arguments. Many people even appreciate hearing both sides of an argument before making up their minds. As John Stuart Mill wrote in *On Liberty*, "he who only knows his side of a case knows little of that." One

would think that academics, given their claims to be more toler-
ant and open-minded than everyone else, would welcome visits by
dissident speakers as opportunities to demolish their arguments.
Unfortunately, that is not how they think.

After many years of campus controversies over speakers deemed
unacceptable, there should not be any confusion as to the sources of
the academic distemper. By and large, liberals and radicals have tak-
en over the American university, and many of them, though certainly not all, view the campus as an arena for mobilizing like-minded
allies and waging political warfare against ideological enemies. This
can be a difficult kind of warfare to carry on when there are few
vocal conservatives on most campuses, which is probably why leftist
ideologues are so eager for battle when conservatives or Republicans
dare to invade their strongholds from without. Like leftists everywhere, they are all for free speech and open discussion when they
are out of power, but they turn into advocates of repression and the
enforcement of "community values" once they are in charge.

There is abundant empirical evidence for the claim that liberals and radicals control the American campus. In 2005, a national survey of college faculty by Stanley Rothman, Robert Lichter,
and Neil Nevitte showed that over 72 percent held liberal and
left-of-center views, while just 15 percent held conservative views.
The survey also found that academic opinion has moved steadily leftward over time, and especially since 1980, as the generation
shaped by the 1960s has taken control of academe. In the humanities and social sciences, where political views are most closely related to academic subject matter, the distribution of opinion is even
more skewed to the left. In a survey of faculty opinion conducted
in 2007 by Neil Gross of Harvard University, just 4 percent of
professors in the humanities and social sciences were identified as
conservatives, as against more than 60 percent who were on the
left. Unlike professors in the past, moreover, many teachers today

believe it is part of their mission to promote their political views in the classroom—and also to shield students from contrary views whenever conservative speakers show up on campus.

The survey by Rothman, Lichter, and Nevitte also found that more than 50 percent of college faculty voted for Democrats, compared with 11 percent for Republicans, while the remainder claimed to be "independents." Other scholars have reported even more lopsided distributions. Daniel Klein, an economist at Santa Clara University, found in a national survey of professors that Democrats outnumbered Republicans on college campuses by a ratio of at least 8 to 1, and in social science and humanities departments by even greater proportions. When professors were asked which party they typically voted for, 80 percent of respondents listed the Democrats and just 8 percent the Republicans. Klein estimates that in fields like anthropology, sociology, and history, the ratios are nearly 30 to 1 in favor of Democrats. Judging by such biased distributions, the American university has evolved into something very close to a one-party state. Spokesmen and defenders of the contemporary university are inclined to discount the significance of those statistics by claiming that professors do not bring their political views into the classroom or do not try to impose them on students. These arguments are not persuasive in view of the statements to the contrary made by many activist professors, the number of openly ideological programs and courses at colleges and universities today, and the persistent efforts of some faculty members to censor speech on campus.

Some observers have suggested that the American campus has evolved into a "base" for the Democratic Party and that the two institutions participate in a mutually beneficial political relationship. That is not a far-fetched proposition, given the partisan ratios cited above. There are obvious similarities in the guiding principles of the two institutions. In particular, there is a shared emphasis on the representation of women and minority groups, and a common embrace of the "diversity" ideology according to which the United States must compensate those groups for discriminatory practices in the past. Quota systems for minorities and women arrived on campus at exactly the moment in the early 1970s that the Democratic Party imposed similar requirements for the selection of delegates to its national convention. The two institutions have proceeded on parallel political paths ever since.

The leaders of most academic institutions are Democrats; or at least, it is rare to find a Republican at the head of a major university. It would be difficult in any case for a Republican in this day and age to lead a faculty made up almost entirely of Democrats. Both institutions—the Democrats and the universities—are heavily invested in public sector budgets, the Democrats to redistribute funds to voting blocs and the universities to gain funds to pay for faculty research and student tuition. Both, in addition, are closely intertwined with a broader network of liberal and left-wing institutions that includes the movie industry, public sector unions, large charitable foundations, and the national news media.

This portrait of the "left university" may upset those who understand the academic world in ideal terms as a "community of scholars" operating independently of society and outside of party politics. Such an ideal has never been operational, not in the past and certainly not today. The American university—speaking broadly of the top two hundred or so institutions—now operates comfortably within the parameters of the nation's postwar political regime, with its emphasis on federal leadership and government funding, social spending, identity politics, and the courting of constituent groups. As between the two parties, the Democrats are the more reliable advocates of this regime—and thus it is easy to understand why the universities should have found their way into the Democratic coalition.

While American universities have been "political" in the past, they have never been as uniformly partisan and ideological as they are today. Many look at this situation and wonder what is wrong with the universities and how they might be fixed. Others raise a more troubling question: What does it mean for the American polity that it has created a partisan and ideological university system? Politicized universities, after all, are more characteristic of "banana republics" than of a modern democratic superpower like the United States. In the less-developed world, universities fan the flames of ideological conflict and discourage compromise as "selling out" to enemies. If our universities are showing similar behavior and if they are on the cutting edge of society, as many say they are, that does not bode especially well for the future of the United States.

* * *

For the greater part of America's colonial and national history, from the founding of Harvard College in 1636 down to around 1900, colleges and universities played only a marginal role in the economic and political developments that shaped the nation. Through the colonial period and into the early nineteenth century, when states began to launch their own public universities, institutions of higher learning were built on a British model and were founded or controlled by Protestant denominations, usually Congregational, Episcopal, or Presbyterian. The purpose of these institutions was to shape character and to transmit knowledge and right principles to the young in order to prepare them for vocations in teaching, the ministry, and the law. Few thought of these institutions as places where new knowledge might be generated or where original research was conducted. In England, as in America, research and discovery were sponsored by nonacademic institutions like the Royal Society in London or the American Philosophical Society in Philadelphia, the latter founded by Benjamin Franklin.

Nevertheless, several of the prominent founders of the nation were interested in the role that academic institutions might play under the new government. Many of the leaders of the American Revolution and authors of the Constitution had attended one or another of the nine colleges that then existed in the fledgling nation. Alexander Hamilton, Gouverneur Morris, and John Jay, for example, had studied at King's College (later Columbia) in New York City, William Livingston at Yale, Thomas Jefferson at William and Mary, and James Madison at the College of New Jersey (later Princeton). Benjamin Franklin had been a founder of the University of Pennsylvania. Benjamin Rush, a signer of the Declaration of Independence, was a leading medical scientist in the early republic and a founder of Dickenson College in Pennsylvania. James Wilson, also a member of the Philadelphia convention, graduated from St. Andrews University in Scotland and studied in Edinburgh with David Hume and Adam Smith.

Madison and Jefferson in particular were first exposed to the ideals of liberty and limited government in college, where they studied the works of John Locke, Adam Smith, Hume, and other leading figures of the English and Scottish enlightenments. The colleges they attended were centers of republican thought owing to the presence of influential professors: John Witherspoon at Princeton, and William Small at William and Mary. At these colleges, Madison and Jefferson absorbed the philosophy that they later used to shape the institutions of the new nation. They did not think of themselves as academics or scholars, but rather as members of what Jefferson called a "republic of letters."* They were broadly learned in history and philosophy, and they studied ancient languages and politics in order to apply the lessons of the past to practical challenges of the present.

------

* The concept goes back to the fifteenth century in Europe, where it inspired a sense of international community among civic-minded men who were educated in Latin and ancient literature. It took on more of a political dimension in the Age of Enlightenment.

Jefferson was much taken with the idea of a university that would prepare the young to enter such a republic of letters and to take their place as wise leaders of the American republic. He understood, as did Madison, that the new republican order they had helped to establish required academic institutions that were more secular and philosophical, less religious and vocational than those existing at the time. During their presidencies, both Jefferson and Madison proposed the creation of a national university with precisely this aim, but the proposals went nowhere in Congress. Many early American leaders believed that the security of the republic rested more on the design of its institutions and the temper of its people than on the education of a leading class—a point that Madison himself had made in the debates over the Constitution.

In his later years, therefore, Jefferson turned his energies to the creation of the University of Virginia, which he conceived as the prototype for a new "republican" university. It was to enroll the best students in his state and provide them with a secular education in the languages and history of Greece and Rome, the practical sciences, and the correct understanding of the Constitution. Jefferson saw his dream realized when he attended the university's inaugural banquet (along with Madison and Lafayette) in 1824, two years before he died.

But Jefferson's vision of a new university for a republican polity did not develop according to his hopes and expectations. The sharpening sectionalism of the nation from the 1830s onward, and the growing preoccupation with slavery and expansion, undermined the Jeffersonian ideal of a republic of letters that transcended geography, personal backgrounds, and narrow interests. The emerging Jacksonian culture that celebrated equality and the common man, so well portrayed by Alexis de Tocqueville in *Democracy in America*, was likewise suspicious of an institution that appeared to be theoretical, impractical, and aristocratic. Andrew Jackson and his followers ridiculed the idea of a national university as undemocratic and an affront to the common man. Pioneer democracy was notoriously mistrustful of expert knowledge and the claims of educated elites. Thus, as new colleges were established, most were guided by religious or vocational objectives rather than by Jeffersonian ideals.

During most of the nineteenth century, academic institutions operated at some distance from the swirling economic and political events that were transforming the nation. They had little to do, for example, with the Protestant revivals of the 1820s and 1830s, with the Jacksonian or the abolitionist movements, with the emergence of the Republican Party, with secession in the South, with the rise of industry after the Civil War, or even with some of the intellectual movements of the time such as Transcendentalism, which developed in protest against college culture. The great entrepreneurs of the time, such as Andrew Carnegie, John D. Rockefeller, or George Pullman, were self-made men with little or no academic experience. Two of the most important presidents of the century, Jackson and Lincoln, had little formal schooling at all. Colleges sponsored no activities that would have brought them wide public attention, such as athletic contests or intellectual debates. Their exclusive focus on teaching meant that their influence could not reach beyond local circles, and also that the academic enterprise could not develop any center or hierarchy. College alumni at the time were not sufficiently numerous to exercise political or intellectual leadership as a distinctive group. At the close of the Civil War, therefore, academic institutions had important professional and educational purposes, but little in the way of political influence.

* * *

Laurence Veysey, in *The Emergence of the American University*, describes how the modern academic enterprise took shape between the years 1870 and 1910. During this period of reform and invention, colleges and universities began to break their ties to religious bodies, embraced the secular principles of science, progress, and democracy, and adopted the practices of research and academic freedom that define higher education to the present day.

The modern structure of the university, with its division into departments and colleges supervised by a class of administrators, was laid out in these years. It was also during this period that two great innovations, the graduate school and the elective system, were incorporated into the academic enterprise. This was the first of two academic revolutions that created the universities we know today and propelled them into the prominent place they hold in contemporary life.

A rapid expansion of higher education occurred in the last few decades of the nineteenth century, encouraged by the end of sectional hostilities, the closing of the frontier, the rise of science and industry, and the accumulation of great wealth in the hands of men prepared to direct some of it to new academic institutions. From the end of the Civil War to 1890, the number of colleges and universities in the United States doubled from about 500 to 1,000, and the number of students tripled to more than 150,000. By 1910, student enrollment had grown to 350,000. Many of our most influential universities were created during this time, including the University of Chicago, Johns Hopkins, Stanford, Vanderbilt, and Clark—all underwritten financially by wealthy entrepreneurs. The academic revolution of this era was directed and largely implemented by bold and visionary university presidents, including Charles Eliot of Harvard, Daniel Coit Gilman of Johns Hopkins, Andrew White of Cornell, William Rainey Harper of Chicago, David Starr Jordan of Stanford, and Woodrow Wilson of Princeton. It was a measure of the public esteem in which college presidents were held that Wilson, while president of Princeton, was recruited in 1910 to run for governor of New Jersey.

The intellectual inspiration and institutional model for this revolution came not from Jefferson and the University of Virginia, or from any American source at all, but from German idealists who brought about an academic revolution in that country in the early 1800s. The University of Berlin, established in 1810 by Wilhelm von Humboldt, was a fruitful model for academic innovation for much of the nineteenth century. Humboldt, the Prussian minister of education, operated under the influence of the idealist philosophers Fichte, Kant, and Hegel, who asserted that the task of the scholar was to search for the truth in science, philosophy, and morals, without interference from political or religious authorities. The University of Berlin, the original research university, was based on the idea that truth is not something known and passed on, but the product of persistent inquiry and continuous revision. It incorporated faculty autonomy in the selection of subjects for research and coursework, and conceived of students as junior partners in the research enterprise—that is, as researchers or professors in training.

This new institution thus moved the university's purpose away from theology, tradition, and the vocations, turning it in the direction of science and secular studies. It also discarded the practice of looking to ancient writers for moral lessons and political guidance. The new university thus placed the faculty rather than students, religious bodies, or public officials at the center of the enterprise, for it was the faculty that in the end would decide what was studied and taught.

The model of the German research university spread rapidly in the United States in the decades after the Civil War, starting with the founding of Johns Hopkins University in 1876 as the original American institution organized around graduate research. The sociologist Edward Shils referred to this as "perhaps the most decisive single event in the history of learning in the Western hemisphere." This innovation, as Shils believed, put pressure on other institutions to establish their own programs of research and graduate study. Harvard soon created its own Graduate School of Arts and

Sciences in order to keep pace with Johns Hopkins. Stanford University was established in 1891 along similar lines, which induced the University of California to follow suit. The University of Chicago, underwritten by John D. Rockefeller, was established in 1892 with research as the basis for faculty appointment and promotion. Other institutions in the Midwest, especially the flagship universities in Michigan, Wisconsin, and Illinois, were then in the process of embracing the research model. Through this multidecade competition for influence, the modern American university was born.

Shils was right to emphasize the far-reaching consequences that followed in the United States from the adoption of the German university model. In the United States, as in Germany, the research model transformed the status of the professor from a teacher to an independent scholar and researcher. Professors would no longer pass along established truths and traditional moral ideals, but would subject these truths and ideals to scrutiny in the search for new knowledge. The faculty, as the new priesthood of the research enterprise, would shortly claim authority to decide all matters dealing with curriculum, new faculty appointments, and promotions. The modern doctrine of academic freedom, which gives professors wide latitude to teach and conduct research as they wish, also followed from these premises in due course. Much as Oliver Wendell Holmes said that the law is what the judges say it is, the reformed university would henceforth be whatever the faculty decided it would be.

As the modern university took shape, faculties began to organize themselves into specialized departments, or disciplines, with their own formal rules for study, research, and publication. This was an important step in the professionalization of the research and teaching enterprise. It was in this period that the various academic associations were formed, including the American Historical Association (1884), the American Economic Association (1885), the American Physical Society (1899), the American Political Science Association

(1903), and the American Sociological Association (1905). These were national membership associations that held annual conventions and published their own journals containing research studies representing authoritative work in the respective disciplines. These associations were national communities that reoriented the attention of professors away from students at their own colleges and toward colleagues working in the same discipline at other institutions across the country. The status of professors in their various disciplines was based on their published research, which established in turn a new basis upon which to rank departments and entire institutions.

The emergence of the modern university thus created a new class of professional intellectuals—that is, men (and a few women) who worked with ideas for a living. Until this time, intellectual life in America, such as it was, had been dominated by ministers and patricians (the Founding Fathers), and then in the nineteenth century by independent writers who generated income by publishing books and articles. Few professors in the antebellum era were known as writers or intellectuals. Now for the first time, university professors, such as Charles Beard, Frederick Jackson Turner, William James, and John Dewey, became famous for their lectures, books, and articles.

Humboldt and the prominent philosophers who held positions at the University of Berlin were continental liberals in the old sense of that term, sympathetic to liberty and reason and to the Enlightenment critique of religion, theology, and tradition. It is in this sense that we can refer to their academic innovation as a "liberal" university, as it was based on reason, science, free inquiry, and the pursuit of new knowledge.

The new university, devoted to creating new knowledge and questioning old truths, was bound to form a frictional relationship with an American polity that was also liberal but shaped by a different and somewhat conflicting intellectual tradition. The American Revolution and Constitution were grounded in the writings of Scottish and English thinkers of the eighteenth century, but the modern university was shaped more by continental ideas arising out of Germany and France. Professor Morton White, a Harvard historian, wrote in *Social Thought in America: The Revolt against Formalism* that the intellectual leaders of the university revolution were sharp critics of the Scottish Enlightenment and the tradition of British empiricism. These figures—Dewey in philosophy, Thorstein Veblen in economics, Charles Beard and James Harvey Robinson in history, Holmes in law—asserted that the philosophical ideas of the English and Scottish enlightenments were too abstract, were not grounded in experience, and could not address the concrete problems of modern life. Many, especially Dewey and Robinson, arrived at these judgments through exposure to the German school of historical thought originating with Hegel, which emphasized culture and historical evolution as the keys to understanding society and politics.

It was from this standpoint that Veblen and other economists rejected Adam Smith and classical political economy, that Dewey attacked Hume for his skepticism and reliance upon tradition as the main source for ethical principles, that Beard and Robinson criticized traditional narrative historians who failed to connect the past to the problems of the present, and that Holmes attacked legal theorists who thought that the words of statutes and the Constitution answered the basic questions about the law. These thinkers were not only academics but more importantly graduates of the new university: Dewey and Veblen had studied together as graduate students (along with Woodrow Wilson) at Johns Hopkins, and Robinson earned a doctorate in history at the University of Freiburg in Germany. All save for Holmes, who was not an academic, concluded that the Constitution and the philosophy behind it were inadequate to the challenges of modern life. This led them to search for new intellectual foundations for politics, history, economics, law, and (in Dewey's case) education.

It was through these theories that the modern university laid the intellectual groundwork for political progressivism and the reorientation of liberal doctrine in the direction of state regulation and reliance on nonpartisan experts. In many circumstances, universities provided more than just philosophical and theoretical ammunition. The first large-scale experiment with Progressive policies occurred in the early 1890s, when the University of Wisconsin offered its research services to the governor and legislature of the state. The "Wisconsin idea," as it came to be called, and which served as a model for other institutions to emulate, envisioned a partnership under which the university would provide information, statistics, and technical expertise to the state so that effective and intelligent legislation might be enacted. More than this, as Frederick Jackson Turner argued, the university would train experts who might serve as judges and commissioners to mediate between contending economic interests—for example, between business and labor. Though the university was meant to serve a nonpartisan role, the underlying objective of the enterprise was to bring big business to heel through legislation and regulation, which was understood soon enough by business leaders in the state. This nonpartisan aspiration was genuine, however, since the Progressive agenda had not yet found a home in either of the major political parties and would not do so until the 1930s, when Progressives settled for good into Franklin D. Roosevelt's Democratic Party.

The Wisconsin idea brought out into the open a new role for the university, which was to bring experts and expert knowledge into the political process. This was one of the clearest links between the emerging university and the Progressive movement, since the university was the logical source for the experts needed to design and implement Progressive policies. As time passed, more and more universities established research centers on the Wisconsin model, which eventually led to the creation of public policy schools and an entire profession of academic public policy experts.

This development in turn led to a new disjunction in American political life, with trained academics replacing public figures as sources of the ideas that shaped the country. For the eighty or so years from the formation of the Union to the close of the Civil War, the theorists who designed institutions and policies were one and the same with the political leaders who put them into place. This was true of Madison, Jefferson, and Hamilton, and also of subsequent figures such as Daniel Webster, John C. Calhoun, and Abraham Lincoln. With the rise of the university, political theories and programs were increasingly devised by academics, like Dewey, Beard, or the Wisconsin professors, all of whom operated outside of electoral politics and whose experience was of a far different kind. The reliance on experts introduced into liberal ranks a permanent ambivalence toward representative government and the common man—for while the experts purported to act in the name of the people, they did so on the basis of expert knowledge that was not democratically available to all.

The modern university in America thus developed in tandem with the new ideology of progressivism—later in the 1930s to be called "liberalism." They were purveyors of common themes: the discovery of new knowledge through research, the important role of experts in government as representatives of the public interest, and the obsolescence of the ideas that shaped the founding of the nation. From that time forward to the present, the fortunes of liberalism in America have been entwined with those of the university such that the two have evolved in parallel and mutually enforcing ways. It is not an exaggeration to say that modern liberalism originated with the emergence of the modern university.

* * *

The American academic system continued to evolve into the 1960s according to patterns that were established during that formative generation. The research university, now supported heavily by public funds, expanded exponentially. A gulf developed between populous and well-funded research universities and the smaller liberal arts colleges. Faculty governance was institutionalized. The elective system was applied more or less universally, leading to debates about the "core" curriculum and concerns that specialization and the emphasis on expert knowledge had gone too far. Students and parents viewed a college degree as a key requirement for professional employment and upward mobility. By the 1960s, public officials and academic leaders were nearly unanimous in the view that a college education should be made available to all, and that the expansion of higher education was an important component of national strength and economic growth.

From the 1920s through the 1950s, many leading institutions, Columbia and Harvard prominent among them, made sustained efforts to leaven the new emphasis on specialization and expertise with broader curricula in the arts, humanities, and social sciences—as these fields came to be called when the universities turned in a secular direction. Jefferson's ideals regarding humanistic learning were not completely abandoned in the modern university. Columbia inaugurated its widely emulated course in "Contemporary Civilization" in 1919 to give students (in the wake of the world war) a general understanding of how modern institutions came into being and to expose them to the great literature of Western civilization dating back to the ancient Greeks; additional courses later joined the core requirements. Following World War II, the Harvard faculty sought to combat specialization with its General Education curriculum, which included broad courses in science, history, literature, and American democracy. These thoughtful innovations provided a counterweight of sorts to the Progressive emphases on expertise and political reform; moreover, they provided intellectual weight to the academic enterprise itself by linking it to the American past and to the civilization out of which the nation and the university evolved.

Despite these campaigns, the liberal university grew larger and more complex and multifaceted in its operations in the postwar era. In 1963, Clark Kerr, president of the University of California, coined the term "multiversity" to describe this evolution. "Today," he noted in his book *The Uses of the University*, "the large American university is a whole series of communities and activities held together by a common name, a common governing board, and related purposes." The "multiversity" serves society, he wrote, but it does so in many ways through specialized research, service, consulting to industry and government, and graduate and undergraduate education. It also evolved in the postwar era as a "federal grant university," expanding through federal support for research and specialized studies in new fields, student scholarships and graduate fellowships, and the construction of new facilities. This process was bringing about a "second transformation" in the American university through which (he predicted) it would educate unprecedented numbers of students, respond to expanding claims and demands from government and industry, and adapt to new intellectual currents in society. Kerr, along with other academic leaders, looked ahead to the full development of the "multiversity" that had the potential to knit together the important educational, commercial, and political currents in American society.

By 1965, the American university was at a high point in public esteem. Academic scientists had played a leading role in the discoveries that had led to victory in World War II. Veterans returning from the war enrolled in colleges and universities in large numbers, contributing a sense of maturity and seriousness to the academic enterprise that it had lacked before (and lacks today). Though academics leaned in a liberal direction, there were many prominent conservatives on major campuses in the 1940s and 1950s. Several distinguished Republicans—Milton Eisenhower, Harold Stassen, and John Hannah, to name three of them—headed up major institutions in that period and were also leading spokesmen for higher education. Professors in all fields, including the arts and humanities, enjoyed wide prestige, and several professors at leading schools were featured on the cover of *Time* magazine in 1966. College sports reached large audiences through national television broadcasts. As the baby-boom generation—the largest in the history of the nation—began to enter university life, enrollments more than doubled (from 3.5 million to 8 million) between 1960 and 1970.

* * *

In the decade or so after 1965, the American university would change as fundamentally as it had in the formative years between 1870 and 1910—and not always in the directions that Clark Kerr anticipated. The political and cultural upheavals spurred by the civil rights movement and opposition to the war in Vietnam, combined with the demographic explosion, brought about a second revolution in higher education and created an institution (speaking generally) that was more egalitarian, more ideological, and more politicized in its preoccupations, while being less academically rigorous than was previously the case. It was in this period, from the mid-1960s to the mid-1970s, that the left university emerged in place of the liberal university.

The changes that took place in that short period of time were unprecedented in the history of American higher education: single-sex colleges all but disappeared; college regulation of student morals disappeared as well; government regulation of employment expanded, putting pressure on institutions to hire women and minorities for faculty positions; the line between teaching a subject matter and advocating political positions was blurred or even eliminated altogether as the new campus radicalism asserted that all teaching is political in nature; core curricula were eliminated at most institutions in favor of "open curricula"; the liberal underpinnings of academic culture—the freedom to teach and conduct research—were attacked and eroded in the name of political correctness; the unifying character of the humanities was subverted and discredited when they were said to represent an oppressive tradition formed by white European males; new fields, usually with ideological preconceptions, were created outside the traditional departments and areas of study, thus expanding the positions available for radical faculty; serious academic requirements, including foreign language proficiency, were softened or eliminated. Faculty opinion, already skewed in a liberal direction in the 1950s and 1960s, moved decisively to the left. All of these changes were blasted into place in the tumultuous decade from the mid-1960s to the mid-1970s, and were institutionalized in the decades that followed.

In many important ways, the left university reversed or modified the assumptions and practices of the liberal university. The architects of the liberal university were optimistic about the prospects for the nation and looked ahead to the advancement of democracy and liberty, but the leaders of the left university tend to be pessimistic about the American future and decidedly negative about its history. The liberal academics believed in progress through the application of reason and knowledge, but the academic left asserts that reason and knowledge are masks for corporate or conservative interests. While the old liberals carved out a role in politics for experts and expert knowledge, the left disdains expertise and embraces the doctrine of diversity, which is based on the assertion of group interests. The liberals believed in academic freedom for all, but the academic leftists support academic freedom only for themselves, not for conservative or moderate faculty, not for speakers who disagree with them, and not for students who wish to learn from a nonideological standpoint. The liberals of a century ago took over the university with an intellectual vision grounded in nineteenth-century philosophy, while the radicals of our time seized control through politics and political pressure by organizing demonstrations and protests and by shrewdly leveraging assistance from governmental regulatory bodies. The liberals were theoretical; the leftists are nakedly political.

There was, in addition, a powerful countercultural element in the left university that was never a significant dimension of the liberal university. While liberals had pressed for practical reforms in American capitalism and the Constitution, the radicals of the 1960s went further to launch a wholesale attack on American culture and the middle-class way of life, which they condemned as repressive and uninteresting. The cultural radicalism of the 1960s promised something beyond political reform—namely, a different way of life with a revised set of morals, new styles of dress, and an alternative to conventional careers. The campus became a place where faculty and students could experiment with different lifestyles. In the past, Americans in search of bohemia or a refuge from middle-class life would flee to communes in the countryside, or to European outposts as Hemingway and other writers did in the 1920s, or to Greenwich Village or San Francisco, but now they found homes on the modern campus.

There were some obvious weaknesses in the liberal university that the radicals were able to exploit in executing their takeover. The leaders who built the liberal university a century ago erected a set of effective defenses against attacks coming from the outside world— from conservative businessmen, trustees, and donors who disagreed with the political views of professors, or from legislators or politicians who sought to punish universities for the unconventional views of some faculty. As things turned out, the protections of academic freedom were much less effective in dealing with internal attacks from organized students and left-wing faculty who disrupted classes, picketed faculty homes and offices, took over administration buildings, issued threats to faculty and administrators, and generally used the tactics of street politics to bring about changes to their liking.

Liberal academics like Clark Kerr did not anticipate a revolt from within their own family, and did not know how to respond to it without betraying cherished beliefs about rational discourse and authority legitimized by achievement—ideals that in any case the radicals denounced as fraudulent. The liberals, moreover, had invited the contempt of the radicals by erecting a comprehensive critique of American capitalism and the Constitution, based on theories developed from the Progressive Era forward through the 1950s, but then failing to accomplish anything significant in the way of real change—a failure that made them appear ineffective and weak. The generation in charge was used to debating against socialists and reactionaries, but had difficulty dealing with the new claims of identity politics, group rights, and diversity, which had direct implications for the organization of the university. The advocates of these new academic doctrines demanded new courses of study for women and minorities, the hiring of new and different kinds of professors to teach them, and changes in the campus culture designed to neutralize opposition to these initiatives. Within a short time, this new doctrine of group representation took hold in the universities.

* * *

The American university has passed through two important revolutions in the past century, the first driven by ideas of progressive reform, and the second by left-wing doctrines of diversity, group rights and representation, and cultural change. The first revolution created the liberal university and the second the left university. Both were far-reaching in the sense that they contributed to a reformulation of liberal or leftist doctrine and were linked to broader movements for political reform that found a home in one or both of the major political parties. Throughout this period, the university has been "political" in the broad sense of that term, but in markedly different ways.

The left university has now been in place for more than a generation. Many of its post-1960s innovations have been institutionalized by this time and are no longer considered quite so radical as before. Nevertheless, they are still behind the embarrassing flare-ups that periodically occur on campus, as when speakers are heckled or "disinvited," or when radical professors level unfounded accusations at colleagues or student organizations, often for the purpose of scoring political points and gaining additional funding for their programs. Such events have taken a toll on the popularity of the academic world with the general public, and on the willingness of taxpayers to fund public universities as generously as in the 1950s and 1960s.

There are many problems with a politicized university, and one of them has to do with the limits and failures of ideological scholarship. Those who view the world through ideological lenses are bound to misunderstand it in profound ways. One could draw up a long list of events and developments in the world that academic experts did not foresee and still do not understand because of the ideological blinders they have put on.

For example, academic experts pronounced the Soviet Union and communism to be in good shape up until the day they collapsed. First socialism and then the welfare state were discredited at the same time that the market revolution gained force in Central Europe and Asia. The emergence of the United States as the world's sole superpower confounded international relations experts who were convinced that a multipolar world was in the making or, alternatively, that the communist and capitalist systems would eventually converge at some point close to the Swedish welfare state. In the domestic policy arena, academic experts claimed for thirty years that welfare programs were in no way implicated in urban poverty, crime, family breakup, or teen pregnancy—an ideological view that was refuted by the success of welfare reforms in the 1990s. Nor could academics, committed as they are to secular doctrines, foresee or comprehend the recent rise of fundamentalist religion around the world, even with all their professed commitment to appreciating cultural "diversity."

For a generation now, universities have promoted research and coursework in "multiculturalism," a doctrine that purports to foster an understanding of foreign societies and cultures. Looked at from an abstract point of view, this is the kind of study that academic institutions should encourage—and, indeed, have frequently encouraged in the past. Yet it turns out that "multiculturalism" does not mean in reality what it appears to mean in the abstract. After the terrorist attacks in 2001, we quickly learned that the nation had trained few specialists in the Arabic language or Islamic cultures who might have helped us understand and counter this new threat. The stress on multiculturalism should have given us some experts with a grasp of the language, culture, and politics of the Islamic world; but multiculturalism is not at all about studying foreign cultures and languages, since that requires real effort. Instead, it is about mobilizing various ethnic groups to exert political influence within the United States. In terms of content, multiculturalism is a hollow shell of political slogans.

Step by step, the outside world is debunking the ideological prejudices of the left academy and exposing the emptiness of its pretensions. Academics have been wrong about many of the important developments of our time, and mainly because of the insular ideology that they have adopted. University faculties outside the sciences are losing the capacity either to understand or to influence the external world. Private research centers and independent scholars and journalists are taking their places as sources of knowledge and understanding about the wider world. Centers like the Manhattan Institute, the Brookings Institution, the American Enterprise Institute, and the Hoover Institution have had far more influence in the public policy arena in recent decades than all the schools of public policy combined. Various independent magazines and journals have seized intellectual leadership from the academy in the arts, humanities, and public affairs. Many of the most prominent and influential historians writing today are nonacademics, like David McCullough, Rick Atkinson, and Ron Chernow, who, along with documentary film makers like Ken Burns, have done far more than "race and gender" academics to revive the study of American history. In the 1950s and 1960s, academics and academic programs fulfilled these purposes; today the marketplace is finding ways to fill the intellectual vacuum left behind by the retreat of the academics into ideological studies.

The failures of the left university, along with the excesses of some of its more vocal representatives, are gradually leading trustees and donors, and even some presidents and deans, to ask some long-overdue questions about the path their institutions have followed. How, for example, can a college or university carry out its responsibilities if all faculty members think the same way, if genuine debate over vital questions is discouraged, if ideological rhetoric crowds out thoughtful discussion, if students know more about the civil rights movement than the Constitution and more about Ward Churchill than Winston Churchill? They are right to raise these questions.

American colleges and universities are under pressure today from several sources—from online competitors offering degrees at far lower prices, from the rising costs of their programs and the unwillingness and inability of students to pay escalating tuition, from Congress and other legislative bodies demanding greater accountability in the use of public funds, and from a public concerned that political correctness on the campus has gone too far. While such pressures may bring about some changes on the margin, they will do little to alter the fundamental character of the higher education industry. These institutions are deeply implicated in the postwar political regime, and are unlikely to change in any fundamental way as long as that regime remains standing.

Several decades ago, the historian Corelli Barnett wrote in *The Collapse of British Power* that the insularity of British universities in the late nineteenth century was one of the factors that left the nation unprepared for the rising German threat. The academics of that time, he wrote, were far too complacent about British power and the durability of empire and too absorbed in academic matters to notice troubling developments arising on the continent. As a result, British leaders and civil servants were ill equipped to meet the economic, political, and strategic challenges they faced in 1914, and also after the war when the loss of British power was too obvious for anyone to deny. For Barnett, the condition of the universities was both a symptom and a cause of the collapse of British power.

A parallel development is unfolding in the United States, though today the main threat facing American power is not from external aggression but rather from internal fragmentation, polarization, and dissolution. For several decades, the United States has been dividing into hostile political and cultural camps, with the political parties controlling different states and regions, conservatives and liberals getting their news from different sources, and Americans dealing on a daily basis only with like-minded people. In the best of worlds, the university might have evolved as an institution where these different factions could come together to exchange views and work out their differences in a spirit of toleration. That has not happened—and is not likely ever to happen. The American university has joined the "left nation," and has successfully walled itself off from the views of the "right nation" in an effort to render them illegitimate. By promoting polarization and fragmentation, the left university is both a symptom and a cause of the fraying of America's postwar order.

※

A version of this chapter appeared in *The Weekly Standard*, October 3, 2005.

CHAPTER SIXTEEN

Reflections on 'The Closing of the American Mind'

It has now been more than a quarter century since Allan Bloom published *The Closing of the American Mind* (1987), his best-selling broadside against the ideas and conceptions that animate the contemporary university. The general theme of Bloom's book is encapsulated in the subtitle: *How Higher Education Has Failed Democracy and Impoverished the Souls of Today's Students.* Bloom's thesis was striking precisely because it ran against the grain of conventional commentary on the academy.

Following the upheavals of the 1960s, educators took pride in the degree to which they had reformed the American university in the direction of democracy, equality, and openness. They sought, as they said, to create an academic environment in which students might explore various ways of thinking and living in order to find their authentic selves. Those academic leaders were convinced that they had served democracy and enriched the educational experience of students by all the reforms, curricular and noncurricular, that they had engineered in response to the student revolts. Now here was Bloom bluntly saying that they had actually done something quite different: in the quest for openness and democracy, the academics had closed off genuine thought and intellectual exploration, and in so doing they had undermined the case for democratic institutions.

Bloom's book appeared at a propitious time in the late 1980s when the turmoil of the 1960s had fully run its course, but the academic and political causes of that period—the open curriculum, diversity and affirmative action, feminism and racial studies, co-education, and the deregulation of student life—had been fully institutionalized in the major colleges and universities of the nation. The radical leaders of the 1960s were now coming into their own as tenured professors, deans, and, in some cases, college presidents. *The Closing of the American Mind* represented the first serious attack, from a philosophical point of view, on everything brought into the university by the student upheavals.

Many readers bought the book with the sense that some of the reforms of that period had gone too far, thus compromising the educational and research purposes of the university. Others may have picked it up under the misconception that "the closing of the American mind" referred to the baleful effects of the Reagan administration on American life. Naturally, those who had been active in the student movements of the 1960s and remained in the academy did not take kindly to Bloom's assault on what they regarded as justified and much-needed reforms on the campus. Opening up opportunities for women and minorities, eliminating old-fashioned course requirements, and replacing traditional works by white men with those representing oppressed groups were steps toward a more democratic and intellectually stimulating university, they believed. Their fury was amplified by Bloom's suggestion that the radicals of the 1960s resembled nothing so much as the Nazis and their sympathizers who used threats of violence to seize control of German universities in the 1930s.

* * *

The Closing of the American Mind has been interpreted as one of those influential salvos in the culture wars of recent decades between reformers and traditionalists on the campus and between conservatives and liberals in the society at large. It has also been heard as a call for curricular change in the direction of a core curriculum focused on the study of the great books—a cause that Bloom certainly favored. An article by Rachel Donadio in the *New York Times Book Review* commemorating the twentieth anniversary of the publication of the book was titled "Revisiting the Canon Wars," suggesting that the main target of Bloom's attack was the college curriculum and the books that students are assigned to read.

If this were all that Bloom had to say, his book would have added little to what had already been said more than a generation before by Robert Maynard Hutchins and Mortimer Adler, two of Bloom's predecessors at the University of Chicago who were advocates of an education in the great books. Indeed, many aspects of the debate over *The Closing of the American Mind* were prefigured by a debate in the 1930s over Hutchins's book *The Higher Learning in America*, in which he attacked the academy for its emphasis on vocational training and disciplinary research, and for its generally anti-intellectual culture. "The people think that democracy means that every child should be permitted to acquire the educational insignia that will be helpful in making money," Hutchins wrote. "They do not believe in the cultivation of the intellect for its own sake."

According to John Dewey, Hutchins's mistake was to suggest that there are fixed truths applicable at all times and in all places. An education in the great books, Dewey said, is one that relies on an "authoritarian" approach in which students are told that a few writers possess the answers to the great questions of life and society. Such an education is divorced from actual experience and the movement of history. In his view, new "truths" are being discovered continuously with the movement of history; new generations must discover their own truths. Dewey said that a real education is not one that relies on Plato and Aristotle or on other authorities, but on

the knowledge and society of our own time. Dewey and his supporters won this argument in the 1930s, and Hutchins and Adler lost it,
much as their successors would lose it in the 1960s and thereafter.

Bloom, however, understood that trying to change the curriculum without addressing the more fundamental ideas that have
shaped it would be like treating the symptoms of a disease without understanding their underlying cause. Bloom claimed that
the West faces an intellectual crisis because no one any longer can
make a principled defense of its institutions or way of life. This was
most evident in the university, which over the decades had reorganized itself around the doctrines of openness, tolerance, relativism,
and diversity—all of which claim that no political principles, institutions, or way of life can be affirmed as being superior to any
others. This is the near-universal view among students and faculty
at leading colleges and universities today. The tragedy, according to
Bloom, is that relativism has extinguished the real motive behind
all education, which is "the search for the good life." If all ideas and
ideals are equal, there is little point in searching for the best ones.

This open-mindedness, as Bloom said, is thought to be a moral virtue that counters a dangerous vice called "absolutism," which
involves the affirmation of any set of principles or morals as objectively true. It is assumed that anyone who asserts that an idea
is objectively true will soon begin to suppress others who disagree
or who hold some other view. Any assertion of absolute truth leads
inevitably down the path to tyranny and oppression. Hitler, it is believed, was an absolutist; his crimes followed from his absolute conviction that he was right and that Germans were a superior people.
By contrast, democracy and freedom seem to rely on tolerance and
openness, and on the belief that no one has access to absolute truth.

The curriculum and the organization of the academy are operational reflections of these ideas. This is why there is no required
core curriculum at most leading institutions, why contemporary

authors have replaced the great thinkers of the past on academic reading lists, why there is no structure to the curriculum, why there is no clear body of ideas that students are expected to master before graduation, and why language requirements have disappeared. If no structure or hierarchy of knowledge exists, then it makes little sense to maintain a structured curriculum or to insist that some things are more important to learn than others. Openness requires an open curriculum. In the absence of any foundation for knowledge, however, it was inevitable that academics would turn tolerance into an absolute. That is why students and faculty often voice outrage when a speaker appears on campus to express a view that contradicts their doctrine of tolerance.

To Bloom, it was hardly surprising that the academic commitment to tolerance should have led to political correctness on campus. He tried to challenge the philosophy—such as it is—that has shaped the academy, and only incidentally to reform the curriculum. This was the conversation that he wanted to ignite with his controversial book: What are the foundations of tolerance, openness, and relativism? Are they true? Does it matter?

The great question in Bloom's eyes was whether a political order founded on principles believed to be true here and everywhere (as expounded in the Declaration of Independence) can survive when they are no longer believed to be true or when they have been reinterpreted in the form of vague notions like openness and tolerance. This is one of the ways by which the academy has failed democracy, according to Bloom. Students and teachers believe fervently in democracy but cannot tell us why.

A related failing of the academy is that, instead of acting as a check on the extreme impulses of a democratic order, it encourages them by a thoughtless embrace of relativism, equality, and diversity. Bloom argued that the university in a democratic society should be a refuge from democratic impulses, a place where excellence is encouraged and pursued, where students consider ideas that run against the grain of democracy and equality, where for a short period of time they step outside our democratic regime to consider the best that has been thought and written through the ages. This was his ideal of a liberal education. By encouraging this kind of inquiry, the academy might contribute to the elevation of democratic life instead of pandering to its natural impulses. By seeking to shape society in ever more democratic and egalitarian ways, the academy has betrayed its true function in a free and democratic society.

Underlying this outlook, as Bloom argued, is a coherent philosophical doctrine that arose in Germany in the nineteenth century and asserts that the culture and institutions of any society are entirely manmade, lacking any objective anchors in nature, truth, or God. Nietzsche, known for his doctrine of nihilism and the "will to power" and for his attack on Christianity, was the most influential philosophical figure behind this movement and the thinker to whom Bloom devoted the most attention. He regarded Nietzsche as the deepest and most penetrating of all modern thinkers but also one whose thought tended to dissolve established institutions because he understood truth and morality as representations of power. Though Nietzsche's thought is sometimes associated with Hitler and the political right, Bloom claimed that the contemporary left has seized selectively on his writings and has used them as bludgeons against the institutions of liberal societies. "Liberty," "rights," or "the rule of law" lack any real foundations, are therefore arbitrary, and are instruments by which the strong oppress the weak—or so it is claimed. In this way, the self-evident truths of the Declaration of Independence are discredited and replaced with—what? That is a good question, because the same claims that dissolve liberal institutions will similarly dissolve any alternative put in their place. Because today's academics do not really take ideas seriously, they are untroubled by the moral implications of nihilism—that there can be no moral compass by which to guide the life of society. They are, as Bloom called them, "easy-going nihilists."

This link to German thought was one of the original and creative aspects of Bloom's book, and a thesis that few critics attempted seriously to confront. Bloom worried that the academy, having placed itself on this new philosophical foundation, represented the leading edge of change in the character of the American regime as a whole. Once they had taken over the academy, it was only a matter of time until those ideas would bleed out into the wider society and undermine the institutions by which the public orders its life and governs itself. That is why he believed that the battle over the academy was so important—and why it is so troubling today that his case was so clearly lost.

* * *

Before the publication of his book, Bloom was all but unknown outside a small circle of devoted students who knew him as an inspiring teacher, as the author of works on Shakespeare and Rousseau, and as the translator of modern editions of Plato's *Republic* and Rousseau's *Emile*. Bloom studied both as an undergraduate and as a graduate student at the University of Chicago, where he received his doctorate in 1955 in the Committee on Social Thought. There he came into close contact with a curriculum focused on the great books and with the teachings of Leo Strauss, who had recently joined the Chicago faculty and had generated a following in Hyde Park with his attacks on historicism and relativism from the standpoint of ancient philosophy. Bloom then began his teaching career at Yale before moving in the early 1960s to Cornell, where he watched the life of the campus being turned upside down in 1969 by radical students who seized the student union, brandishing weapons in the process and threatening violence unless their demands were met. The capitulation of the faculty to those threats had a shattering effect on

Bloom, compromising his faith in the university and suggesting that some intellectual disorder had overtaken Cornell and the American academy at large. After the disorders in Ithaca, Bloom soon resigned his position at Cornell, moving first to the University of Toronto before returning to the University of Chicago in 1977.

Among his students, Bloom was seen as something of a Johnsonian figure, an unusual mixture of brilliance and eccentricity in the manner by which he taught the classics of political philosophy. His classroom lectures were presented in a rapid-fire manner, his thoughts punctuated by tics, stutters, and unpredictable gestures and expressions. He was known to lecture with unusual intensity, so much so that he sometimes lost track of time and the planned subjects of his lectures. There were moments of tension in the classroom, as one student recalled, when Bloom would light the filtered end of a cigarette. Bloom was not to every student's taste, but for those with a philosophic bent he was a luminous figure on campus. He encouraged his students to follow a philosophic life, to address the great questions of life and politics through the study of the great works of Western civilization. Before 1987, he had a well-earned reputation as a teacher, not as an author or writer, least of all a popular writer.

All of that changed when *The Closing of the American Mind* turned Bloom into an international celebrity. Between March 1987, when it was published, and December of that year, the book sold more than half a million copies. It maintained a place on the bestseller list for nearly a year after it first appeared there on April 26, 1987. During the summer of 1987, *The Closing of the American Mind* was number one on the *New York Times* list for ten weeks. A paperback edition, published in 1988, also spent several months on that list. Bloom was now in demand on the college lecture circuit; journalists followed him around the Chicago campus, crashing his lectures, trying to figure out what in fact he was trying to say and asking themselves and anyone who would listen why such an obscure and idiosyncratic book should have become a national and international sensation. Bloom, who had been chronically in debt because he could not underwrite his expensive tastes with a professor's salary, became a millionaire many times over.

The Closing of the American Mind had its origins in a short essay titled "Our Listless Universities," published in *National Review* in 1982. Here Bloom developed the key themes that would form the basis for his book, explaining,

> I begin with my conclusion: students in our best universities do not believe in anything, and those universities are doing nothing about it, nor can they. An easy-going American kind of nihilism has descended upon us, a nihilism without terror of the abyss. The great questions—God, freedom, and immortality—hardly touch the young. And the universities, which should encourage the quest for the clarification of such questions, are the very source of the doctrine which makes that quest appear futile.

Under pressure from this doctrine, colleges and universities have gradually gotten rid of their traditional liberal arts curricula and have largely abandoned the study of great books in favor of books that represent the thought of different cultures or groups.

With the encouragement of Saul Bellow, his friend and colleague at the University of Chicago, and Erwin Glikes, then an editor at Simon & Schuster, Bloom was persuaded to turn the essay into a full-length book on the contemporary university. The publisher paid a modest advance of $10,000 on the outside chance that the book might sell enough copies to recoup the investment. By the time Bloom finished the manuscript, however, Glikes had departed for another publishing house (The Free Press), thus placing final editorial revisions in the hands of another editor, Robert Asahina.

By all accounts, Asahina performed indispensable editorial services in turning Bloom's manuscript into the compelling document that was released for public sale. It was Asahina who suggested to Bloom that he should abandon his original title, "Souls Without Longing," in favor of a more captivating one—and thus was born *The Closing of the American Mind*. He also encouraged Bloom to begin the book with his discussion of contemporary students, with his unsparing comments on their relationships, the books they read, and the music they liked— rather than with his more difficult and obscure discussion of German philosophy. Perhaps as the editor anticipated, Bloom's attack on rock music as a narcotic that diverts the energy of young people away from learning and toward tactile pleasures was an aspect of the book that attracted much attention. Several reviewers depicted Bloom as an old fogy who did not understand rock music and did not appreciate its creativity. "The Pop Culture that Bloom despises," one reviewer wrote, "is one of America's great original contributions."

*   *   *

The early reviews of the book were surprisingly favorable and encouraging, which certainly played a role in launching it on a track to the bestseller lists. Roger Kimball, writing in the *New York Times Book Review*, described the book as "essential reading for anyone concerned with the state of liberal education in this society." In the same review he wrote that it is "that rarest of documents, a genuinely profound book." The editors, unwittingly helping Bloom's cause, assigned as the title to Kimball's review "The Groves of Ignorance." Christopher Lehmann-Haupt, reviewing the book in the daily *Times*, wrote that "it commands one's attention and concentrates one's mind more effectively than any book I can think of in the last five years." William Kristol wrote in the *Wall Street Journal* that "No other recent book so brilliantly knits together such astute perceptions of the contemporary scene with such depth of scholarship and philosophical learning." The *Washington Post* also weighed in early with a favorable review by S. Frederick Starr, president of Oberlin University.

The critics soon entered the fray—too late, however, to blunt the momentum given to the book by those early reviews. Many of the critics were harsh, though none rose to the high level of Bloom's argument. David Rieff, writing in *The Times Literary Supplement*, compared Bloom to Colonel Oliver North, who had recently testified to Congress on the Iran-Contra scandal, called him a reactionary, and said that his book was one that "decent people would be ashamed of having written." He also asserted, more than a little foolishly (at least to anyone who had ever known Allan Bloom), that the author was a front for corporate interests because his research center at the University of Chicago was underwritten by grants from the John M. Olin Foundation. Benjamin Barber, a political science professor from Rutgers, said that Bloom was a "philosopher despot" whose ideas were elitist and antidemocratic. Martha Nussbaum, in an essay in the *New York Review of Books*, challenged Bloom's interpretation of ancient thought and suggested, contrary to Bloom, that ancient thinkers were in fact far more sympathetic to the ideals of democracy and equality than Bloom suggested. "The Right Absolute Allan Bloom" was the title given to an article in the *Washington Post* on the best-selling author, which served to confirm Bloom's thesis about relativism and absolutism. Even the feminist Betty Friedan got into the act, challenging Bloom's portrayal of feminism as "anti-family and anti-man." Bloom's book ignited a fierce debate over the intellectual foundations of democracy and equality that continued for months and even years before it died out in the happy-go-lucky conformity that now envelops the contemporary academy.

With few exceptions, the assessments of Bloom's book predictably broke down into liberal and conservative camps—the former attacking him for his elitism and negative view of the 1960s, the latter endorsing his criticisms of equality and relativism and his calls for a return to a traditional liberal arts curriculum. Strangely enough, liberals like Nussbaum, Barber, and Rieff, who frequently criticize American culture on egalitarian grounds, attacked Bloom for his supposed anti-Americanism, which they said was evident in his comments on the young and on American popular culture. They did not credit Bloom with the attempt to look at America "from the outside." While it is true that Bloom was sufficiently *sui generis* as a thinker to defy attempts to pigeonhole him into any political camp, reviewers were in little doubt as to the generally conservative drift of his book—and rightly so. There can be little doubt, after all, as to the political allegiances of an author who attacks relativism, diversity, egalitarianism, multiculturalism, affirmative action, feminism, the open curriculum, free sex, rock-and-roll music, the 1960s, and our general cultural obsession with the here and now. If Bloom was not a conservative, in the sense that he did not endorse market capitalism or evangelical religion, he spoke like one in many areas.

This latter point represents a sign of the great change that has overtaken intellectual life in the United States over the last half century. When Hutchins and Dewey debated the great books, they did so from within the perspective of liberal thought—Dewey appealing to democracy and experience in his rejection of the great books, and Hutchins appealing to the ideals of liberal culture with its emphasis on rational principles as alternatives to revealed religion. In 1964, Richard Hofstadter won a Pulitzer Prize in history for his book *Anti-Intellectualism in American Life*, which criticized American culture in general and the university in particular for their practical emphasis and disdain for intellect. Hofstadter singled out conservatives—especially fundamentalist ministers, businessmen, and anticommunists—for the role they played in lowering the sights of cultural life in the United States. In those years, liberal culture was a form of "high culture" and something distinct from popular culture as expressed in television, the movies, and popular music. This ceased to be the case after the upheavals of the 1960s. Popular culture invaded the universities and obliterated all distinctions between the high and low in the intellectual and cultural spheres. Thus, by the time Bloom published his book, it was possible to launch a broad attack on America's intellectual culture that dismissed it as crude, unreflective—and popular.

The editors of the *Wall Street Journal*, in an editorial on the meaning of the Bloom phenomenon, wondered whether his bestseller might make a permanent difference in American life or if "the United States will display its remarkable ability to absorb both serious ideas and silly fads without being changed by them." The editors at that time were rather optimistic that Bloom had inspired fresh thinking in the university. Now, from the perspective of over twenty-five years, we can see that trends have moved even further in the directions that Bloom criticized—which makes all the more urgent the efforts taking place on campuses across the country to restore programs in Western civilization or in the great books, so that students may at least be given a choice whether to embrace the current trends or to pursue the kind of education in the classics that Bloom prescribed in *The Closing of the American Mind.*

* * *

In an essay on Samuel Johnson written fifty years after the poet's death, Thomas Macaulay commented on the ironic change that had overcome Johnson's literary reputation over the previous decades. This was due primarily, as Macaulay wrote, to the wide circulation of Boswell's popular biography of the literary giant. Johnson assumed that he would be remembered for his poems, stories, and literary criticism, but the influence of Boswell's biography caused successive generations to remember him more for his manners and conversation. As Macaulay wrote, "The reputation of [Johnson's] writings, which he expected to be immortal, is every day fading; while those peculiarities of manner and that careless table talk, the memory of which he probably thought would die with him, are likely to be remembered as long as the English language is spoken in any quarter of the globe." That is, unfortunately, still an accurate judgment.

In his novel *Ravelstein*, written in 2000 and based loosely on Bloom's character, Saul Bellow wrote about his protagonist:

> Well, his friends, colleagues, pupils, and admirers no longer had to ante up in support of his luxurious habits. All of that was a thing of the past. He was now very rich. He had gone public with his ideas. He had written a book—difficult but popular—a spirited, intelligent, warlike book, and it had sold and was still selling in both hemispheres and on both sides of the equator. The thing had been done quickly but in real earnest: no cheap concessions, no popularizing, no mental monkey business, no apologetics, no patrician airs. His intellect had made a millionaire of him. It's no small matter to become rich and famous by saying exactly what you think—to say it in your own words, without compromise.

This was indeed what Bloom had done—but in doing so he brought about a reversal in his reputation that was every bit as striking as that which had overcome Johnson's. Following the publication of his book, his premature death, and the influence of Bellow's biographical novel, the inspiring teacher with the unusual style and manner, known through most of his career to but a small circle of dedicated students, will henceforth be remembered by a vast reading public as the author not simply of a popular book, but of a book that has taken its place as an American classic.

A version of this chapter appeared in *The New Criterion*,
November 2007.

CHAPTER SEVENTEEN

What's Wrong with Our Universities?

The Closing of the American Mind did not spark the kind of fruitful conversation that Allan Bloom hoped for concerning the way that academic relativism has failed our democracy; much less did it inspire a systematic effort to rectify the errors of modern academia. Today's college students say they believe in democracy but cannot explain why, and neither can they explain what they are actually getting with their college education. In the past half century, higher education has gone through a democratizing revolution, with the result that more and more students are being sold an increasingly expensive product that neither their professors nor the deans and presidents of their colleges can even begin to define.

A college education is now deemed one of those prizes that, if good for a few, must therefore be good for everyone, even if no one in a position of academic authority can specify what such an education is or should be. College enrollments have grown steadily year by year, more than doubling since 1970 and rising by nearly one-third since the year 2000. This year, more than twenty million students will enroll in the four thousand or so degree-granting colleges and universities now operating in the United States. More than 70 percent of high school graduates enroll in a community college, a four-year residential college, or one of the new online universities, though only about half of these students earn their degrees within five years. The steady growth in enrollments is fed by the widespread belief that a college degree is a requirement for entry into the world of middle-class employment.

Higher education is a growth industry in America—one of the few that foreigners (now mostly Asians) are willing to support in large numbers. College tuition and expenses have grown by five times the rate of inflation over the past three decades, forcing parents and students far into debt to meet the escalating costs. Fed by a long bull market in stocks, college and university endowments have exploded since the mid-1980s, providing even more resources for salaries, new personnel, financial aid, and new buildings and programs.

A handful of prestigious colleges and universities, mainly private, are overwhelmed each year by applications from high school seniors seeking to have their tickets punched for entry into the upper strata of American society. But these institutions are far from representative of higher education as a whole. The vast majority of colleges and universities—90 percent of them at least—admit any applicant with a high school diploma and the means to pay. Given the availability of financial aid, any high school graduate who wishes to attend college can do so.

Many universities, and not a few colleges, have come to resemble Fortune 500 companies with their layers of highly paid executives presiding over complex empires that encompass semiprofessional athletic programs, medical and business schools, and expensive research programs along with the traditional academic departments charged with providing instruction to undergraduate students. Like other industries, higher education has its own trade magazines and newspapers, influential lobbying groups in Washington, and paid advertising agents reminding the public of how important their enterprise is to the national welfare.

In contrast to business corporations, whose members generally agree on their overall purpose, colleges and universities have great difficulty defining what their enterprise is for. What is a college education? What are students supposed to learn during their four years on campus? On just about any campus at any given time, one can find faculty members in intense debate over what a college education entails and what the mission of their institution should be, and one will find little consensus on the answers. Few businesses would dare to offer an expensive product that they are incapable of defining for the inquiring consumer. Yet this is what colleges and universities have done at least since the 1960s, with surprising success.

The most trenchant criticisms of these developments in higher education have come primarily from the conservative end of the political spectrum. From the time William F. Buckley Jr. published *God and Man at Yale* in 1951, conservatives have been the main critics of the evolution of colleges and universities away from their traditional role as guardians of civilization and into the political-corporate institutions that they have gradually come to resemble. Over the decades, conservatives like Russell Kirk, Allan Bloom, and Roger Kimball have criticized academic institutions for dismembering core curricula, offering trendy but intellectually worthless courses, surrendering to political correctness, and providing comfortable sinecures for faculty paid for by hardworking students and their parents. Conservatives were always skeptical of the campaign to democratize higher education, arguing that it was bound to lead to lowered standards and loss of purpose. Events have confirmed their predictions, even if their diagnosis has done little to alter the path of the American university.

Liberals have been more reserved in their criticisms of higher education, no doubt because they (in contrast to the conservatives) have been in charge of the enterprise over these many decades. To the extent that they have called for reform in higher education, it has usually been to urge colleges and universities to move more rapidly down the path on which they were already traveling—that is, in the direction of more diversity, easier access, more student choice in courses and curricula, more programs for special groups, and so on. Because they have operated inside the walls of academe, liberals (and leftists) have never had much difficulty in translating their proposals into academic policy.

Yet a curious thing is now happening in the ever-expanding commentary on higher education: many of the criticisms formerly made by conservatives are now being reprised by liberals, or at least by authors who are in no way associated with conservative ideas or organizations. At least two distinguished academic leaders, Anthony Kronman, former dean of the Yale Law School, and Harry Lewis, former dean of students at Harvard, have published stern critiques of colleges and universities for failing to challenge students with the great moral and political questions that were once at the center of the liberal arts curriculum.* (Kronman's book is discussed in Chapter 19 below.) More recently, several books written from a liberal point of view have taken colleges and universities to task on various counts: they are too expensive; the education they offer is subpar, especially in relation to costs; they are administratively top-heavy; their faculties are too specialized; they do not emphasize teaching; their catalogs are filled with bizarre courses; and, importantly, they are not providing the liberal arts education that students need and deserve.

---

* Anthony T. Kronman, *Education's End: Why Our Colleges and Universities Have Given Up on the Meaning of Life* (New Haven: Yale University Press, 2007); Harry Lewis, *Excellence without a Soul: Does Liberal Education Have a Future?* (New York: PublicAffairs, 2006).

These are serious charges, especially when one considers who is making them. What lies behind them? And what do the authors propose to do about them?

* * *

The most comprehensive of these indictments is set out by Andrew Hacker and Claudia Dreifus in a book titled *Higher Education? How Colleges Are Wasting Money and Failing Our Kids—and What We Can Do about It.** The authors cannot be accused of being outsiders to the industry or lacking in understanding of their subject. Hacker is a distinguished political scientist, author of many academic books, formerly a professor at Cornell, and now an emeritus professor at Queens College in New York City. Dreifus writes for the Science section of the *New York Times* and is a faculty member at Columbia University's School of International and Public Affairs. It is surprising, even refreshing, to encounter a wide-ranging critique of higher education by authors with such impeccable credentials. Yet one would never call this a dispassionate analysis. It is meant to arouse indignation and to bring forth remedies for the ills it diagnoses.

Hacker and Dreifus begin from the premise that higher education has lost its way and no longer fulfills its basic obligations to the rising generation of Americans. As they write, "A huge—and vital—sector of our society has become a colossus, taking on many roles, and doing none of them well." The central purpose of higher education, and of the liberal arts in particular, is to turn students into "thoughtful and interesting human beings"; but colleges and universities have weighed themselves down with so many ancillary activities, from technical research to varsity athletics, that they have lost sight of their basic mission.

---

* Henry Holt & Co., 2010.

The authors write from the standpoint of a pre-1960s liberalism, which assumed that democratic education and the liberal arts should operate in harmony. Thus they assert that every student can learn, that a college education should be available to all, and that such an education should revolve around the liberal arts, loosely defined. They are unable to come to terms with how the campus upheavals of the 1960s succeeded in overthrowing the traditional liberal arts curriculum in the name of democracy, diversity, and inclusion. The authors think that the older synthesis can be resurrected on campus if only some institutional encrustations like disciplinary research, administrative bloat, and varsity athletics can be peeled away. Though they are undoubtedly wrong about this (since the problems go much deeper), their book contains much valuable evidence that something has gone wrong in the world of higher education.

Hacker and Dreifus point to a basic contradiction in the higher education industry: students enroll to receive an education, and many pay dearly for this service, but faculty members are paid and promoted on the basis of disciplinary research that is unrelated to teaching. In the authors' view, in fact, "there is an inverse correlation between good teaching and academic research." A heavy emphasis on research causes professors to short-change teaching responsibilities and to view colleagues at other institutions as a more important audience for their work than their own students. It also encourages faculties to load up college catalogs with narrow and arcane courses as young professors "teach their dissertations" and veteran professors teach their latest research projects. In this way, the research agenda in the various disciplines invades the undergraduate curriculum. The tenure system, originally created to protect the freedom of faculty to conduct research, now insulates professors from incentives to perform in the classroom. Given the evolution of First Amendment protections on campus, tenure is no longer needed to guarantee academic freedom for dissident professors.

Moreover, since research professors must have graduate students, major departments at large research universities must have their own Ph.D. programs whether or not their graduates have any hope of finding positions in the academy. The authors cite a telling statistic: from 2005 to 2007, American universities awarded 101,009 doctoral degrees but created just 15,820 assistant professorships. Given such a ratio, few young men and women who have spent between four and eight years earning their doctoral degrees can entertain hopes of pursuing careers in academic teaching and research. Many of these redundant Ph.D.'s wind up in fields unrelated to their studies and for which an advanced degree is probably more of a handicap than a qualification. Some are recruited back to campus as adjunct professors to teach courses for nominal sums that are a fraction of what tenured professors are paid. The authors estimate that 70 percent of all college teaching is performed by adjuncts, graduate assistants, and other nonfaculty personnel.

The expansion of administration—or administrative "bloat"—is a major factor in the escalating costs of higher education. The ratio of administrators per student has doubled over the past three decades, from about 30 to more than 60 administrators per 1,000 students. At many of the prestigious colleges and universities, the ratios are far higher. At Williams College, roughly 70 percent of the employees are occupied in pursuits other than teaching. Administrative expansion at Williams has not taken place through the hiring of groundskeepers, janitors, health and safety personnel, or cafeteria workers, but by the creation of positions like Babysitting Coordinator, Spouse-Partner Employment Counselor, and Queer-Life Coordinator (really).

This is a common pattern at top-ranked institutions that probably have more money than they need to operate high-quality educational programs. Their superfluous funds therefore underwrite superfluous activities. The *Chronicle of Higher Education* routinely runs advertisements for positions like Sustainability Director, Credential Specialist, and Vice-President for Student Success. Wouldn't students be better served if, instead of filling positions like these, colleges and universities hired more philosophers, classicists, and physicists? From the authors' point of view, the question answers itself.

All of these administrators not only cost money (with their generous salaries) but invent work that requires still more of their kind, thus diverting institutional attention from learning and instruction to second- and third-order activities. A portion of administrative bloat is a function of the growing complexity of academic institutions, some of it self-imposed and some of it flowing from governmental requirements related to financial aid, research contracts, and civil rights laws. In many cases the new administrators serve as advocates for special causes, demanding the hiring of more faculty and administrators in fields like feminism, environmentalism, and "queer studies." Thus, administrative expansion also grows from the politicization of the modern campus.

The most obvious expression of the administrative takeover of higher education is the emergence of "hired gun" presidents who move from institution to institution gaining bigger salaries for themselves and their peers as they do. The president of Ohio State University—who previously held top positions at Brown University, the University of Colorado, and West Virginia University—had a pay package exceeding $2 million before he resigned last year. The president of the University of Chicago has a compensation package that exceeds $3 million. It is not uncommon today for college presidents to receive salary packages exceeding $1 million, courtesy of student tuition payments and taxpayer subsidies, while the average faculty member receives a salary one-tenth of that sum. Do these presidents fill the role of academic and intellectual leader on their campuses, as college and university presidents (like Robert Maynard Hutchins and Charles William Eliot) did at one time? The answer in almost all cases is no. They are hired mainly to raise money, manage complex bureaucracies, and keep their faculties happy. The emergence of this new kind of academic administrator is one of the more obvious signs of the overall loss of intellectual purpose in higher education.

Hacker and Dreifus reserve their strongest criticisms for a handful of elite institutions—the "Golden Dozen," as they call them—that set the tone for higher education as a whole. The list is familiar: the eight Ivy League institutions, plus Duke, Stanford, Williams, and Amherst. These are the prestigious schools that attract applications from ambitious students across the country and around the world. The existence of this elite stratum of institutions seems to violate the authors' sense of democratic fairness; in their view, these schools are overrated and do not merit their hallowed reputations. They name several institutions of lesser rank (including the University of Mississippi and Arizona State University) that they believe do a better job of educating their students.

While all this may be true, the authors offer scant evidence for their conclusions. They do not try to assess the quality of education offered at these institutions, but try instead to assess how *successful* their alumni have been compared with the graduates of other institutions—an exercise that cuts against the overall purpose of their book. They conclude on the basis of an examination of entries in *Who's Who* that the alumni of the "Golden Dozen" do not fare any better in life than any other group of college graduates. Unfortunately, in using worldly success as a measure, the authors endorse the dubious proposition that what matters most in an academic institution is the financial and vocational status its students attain, rather than the substantive education they gain in the liberal arts.

In view of the intellectual vacuum that has developed on campus, it is entirely understandable that students should more and more express vocational aspirations in their selection of courses and majors. Hacker and Dreifus are disappointed that so many students choose majors like business, engineering, and communications over fields in the liberal arts like history, philosophy, and literature. Business is by far the leading major among undergraduates today, far surpassing in student popularity any of the traditional fields in the humanities or social sciences. Traditional liberal arts departments in classics, foreign languages, literature, and philosophy are contracting and some of them disappearing altogether for want of student interest. This is a lamentable outcome, as the authors say, but at the same time one that is easy to understand. If students are required to pay vast sums for their degrees, then they want value for the money spent—and this is found in vocational preparation of some kind. It is also hard to blame students for these choices when they never hear anyone on campus making a good case for the liberal arts as "an education for life." The long-running agitation for diversity, democracy, and inclusion on campus has at length displaced the traditional case for the liberal arts.

The authors propose several controversial but nevertheless justifiable remedies to lower the costs of higher education and return it to its central purposes. They would end tenure and sabbaticals for professors, emphasize teaching over research in all aspects of undergraduate education, curb the exploitation of adjunct professors, spin off university medical schools and research programs, eliminate varsity athletics, spread resources around to more institutions beyond the "Golden Dozen," reduce the costs of administration (especially presidential salaries), and take advantage of new technologies to improve classroom instruction.

These are generally good ideas, though perhaps also utopian in

current circumstances. Getting rid of varsity athletics, especially football, has long been a goal of academic reformers, and they
are no nearer their goal today than they were fifty or one hundred
years ago. Even so, some of these reforms, such as the elimination
of tenure and the scaling back of varsity athletics, may come about
in the coming years due to mounting financial pressures on colleges
and universities. The fact that universities exploit adjunct teachers
is a clear sign that they cannot afford to spread the costs associated with the tenure system across all instructional programs. As
costs escalate and available resources dwindle, all institutions will
be forced to confront basic questions as to which programs they can
afford to maintain. What advocacy and criticism cannot accomplish, the laws of economics may eventually bring about.

The central weakness of this otherwise useful critique is that
the authors never tell us what kind of education is most likely
to form "thoughtful and interesting human beings." What is an
education in the liberal arts? What should students learn during
their undergraduate years? Should every college have a core curriculum in the liberal arts, as most did a generation or two ago?
The authors make a case for the liberal arts but fail to tell us what
they entail or how they might be revived from their near-coma-
tose condition on campus.

The liberal arts are dying on college campuses today from the
combined effects of specialization, the diversity agenda, and an emphasis on vocational goals. (Actually, they have essentially expired
already, except at a handful of holdout institutions where undergraduate education is taken seriously.) The century-long campaign
to apply the scientific model to the humanities has at length yielded the consequences that Hacker and Dreifus document so well.
The various academic travesties that they cite are symptoms of this
deeper problem. Many of these—such as the proliferation of pointless courses—take place in humanities departments and not in the

sciences, where there still exists a ladder of learning and where research is linked to an ongoing search for knowledge.

The fundamental problems of higher education, especially as they relate to its overall loss of purpose, can be traced back to the collapse of the liberal arts. As a consequence, a large gulf has opened up between the sciences, where undergraduate teaching programs are generally very good (as long as resources are available), and the humanities, where teaching and research have lost their purpose and with it their value. Conservatives have known this for a long time. Now, some liberal critics are beginning to feel their way toward the same conclusion.

* * *

In elementary and secondary education, costs have risen exponentially over recent decades while student learning as measured by achievement tests has steadily declined. Likewise, college costs have risen severalfold since the 1970s (as Hacker and Dreifus amply document), even as academic rigor has declined, according to recent research by Richard Arum of New York University and Josipa Roksa from the University of Virginia.

Arum and Roksa, both sociologists, make their case in *Academically Adrift: Limited Learning on College Campuses.** Though burdened by some of the turgid language and ponderous methodology that are endemic to the social sciences, this book is a serious effort to find out if colleges and universities are delivering on their promise to educate all students. The authors have assembled empirical data showing that college students today are studying and writing less and learning far less than their peers of a generation ago, while our competitors abroad are passing us in measures of academic achievement and rates of college graduation. America's competitiveness in

---

* University of Chicago Press, 2011.

the global economy is thus at risk on account of declining standards in our colleges and universities.

Academically Adrift is one product of a movement to measure student learning that was set in motion in 2006 by a report from the Spellings Commission (named for Margaret Spellings, then the U.S. secretary of education). The report called for greater "transparency and accountability" in colleges and universities that receive federal aid, and for "better data about real performance" to allow students, parents, and policymakers to compare institutions on the basis of measurable outcomes. According to the commission, such measures are needed in order to determine if "the national investment in higher education is paying off." The report was a signal that "outcomes testing," long used in elementary and secondary education, was about to be introduced into higher education as well.

Arum and Roksa took up the challenge. To measure student learning, they drew upon results from the Collegiate Learning Assessment (CLA), a standardized test given to more than three thousand students at different institutions upon entry into college and then again at the end of their second and fourth years of undergraduate work. The CLA asks students to examine a complex problem, such as an argument in a political campaign about how best to reduce crime, and then to write up their assessments of different approaches along with their own recommendations. The test purports to measure critical thinking and complex reasoning as well as writing ability.

On the basis of the CLA, the authors report that large numbers of students show little improvement in these skills during their college years. According to this study, 45 percent of the students showed little evidence of improvement after two years of college, and 36 percent showed little improvement after four years. The performance gap between blacks and whites, already significant upon entry into college, widened further during the undergraduate years.

"An astounding proportion of students are progressing through higher education today without measurable gains in general skills," Arum and Roksa conclude. Even so, nine in ten students say upon graduation that they are satisfied with their college experience.

The authors locate the sources of these disappointing outcomes both in the culture of student life and in the lack of rigor in college curricula. Students spend the bulk of their time socializing with peers rather than studying, reading, or discussing academic subjects. According to the study, students spend on average only about thirteen hours per week studying, far less time than in the 1960s. The reason that students can get away with it today is that they encounter few courses that require much writing or significant amounts of reading. It is little wonder, then, that the culture of student life does not assign great value to learning and achievement.

Arum and Roksa agree with other authors about the basic problems of higher education. Colleges are bloated with administrators who have impressive-sounding titles, but none carries a mandate to improve student learning. Adjunct and part-time faculty teach too many courses. Professors do not spend enough time in the classroom or meeting individually with students. College trustees and presidents are preoccupied with fundraising, budgets, national rankings, and reputations. Students are viewed as "consumers," and thus are given too much choice in the selection of courses. Colleges devote too many resources to luxurious dormitories, student centers, and expensive athletic facilities, in a misguided effort to entertain students and keep them happy.

One conclusion they do not reach is that too many students are attending college who are not motivated or who lack the skills to do college-level work. The Council for Aid to Higher Education reports that "forty percent of students entering college do not read, write or perform math at a college-ready level," a figure that closely approximates the proportion of students reported by

Arum and Roksa that do not learn very much during their undergraduate years. Is it possible that 40 percent of the students we send to college are not prepared for the experience and are unable to benefit from it? Are faculty and administrators "dumbing down" their curricula to make it possible for these students to pass the requirements? Reasonable observers have answered both questions in the affirmative, even if such answers seem to violate a national commitment to guarantee a college education to every student who wants one.

Academically Adrift has been widely criticized in academic circles because (it is said) the Collegiate Learning Assessment does not really measure learning, but rather aptitude or something else unrelated to classroom instruction. While this is possibly so (although the makers of the test dispute it), results from the CLA are undoubtedly closely correlated with those of the SAT and ACT examinations that administrators use for admissions and which they claim are measures of learning rather than innate aptitude. If the CLA does not do the job, then critics have an obligation to come up with a better test.

It is probably the case, however, that no conceivable test can accurately measure what students should really learn during their college years. After all, the purpose of higher education is not to train students in the basic skills of reasoning and writing, but to take students who already have these skills and supplement them with something more important—namely, knowledge and understanding. The campaign to turn colleges into glorified high schools has been as misguided as the effort to turn the humanities into a science. It is not possible to educate students in something called "critical thinking" in the absence of a foundation of knowledge; and students who have taken the trouble to fortify themselves with knowledge will naturally develop the capacities both to criticize and to affirm, and to understand the difference between the two.

An education in the liberal arts, rightly understood, is one means by which educators in the past sought to engage students in the search for knowledge and understanding. Whatever the weaknesses of that approach, academic leaders have yet to find an effective substitute for it. Appropriately, Arum and Roksa call upon academic leaders to strengthen the general education requirements (that is, the core curricula) at their institutions in order to ensure that all students receive an education in the fundamentals of the liberal arts and the sciences.

* * *

While curricular debates have been going on for some time, the recent financial collapse has exposed and exacerbated structural weaknesses in our system of higher education. Mark C. Taylor argues that a situation of dwindling resources has led to a crisis on campus that will force academic leaders to reorganize their institutions if they are to survive. In a controversial op-ed article he published in the *New York Times* in 2009, Taylor called for the abolition of the tenure system and the elimination of permanent academic departments that he regards as the obsolete equivalents of assembly lines and small family farms. The title of that article, "End the University As We Know It," provides a sense of the ambitious— and inflated—aims of his proposals.

Professor Taylor, now chair of the Department of Religion at Columbia University and previously a longtime professor in the humanities at Williams College, decided to enlarge the essay into a book because of the popular response it provoked. "My analysis of the current state of higher education and proposals for change set off a firestorm of discussion and controversy," he explains. Well, perhaps—but he would have served the debate better by letting matters stand with the short statement of his position.

His book, *Crisis on Campus: A Bold Plan for Reforming Our Colleges and*

Universities,* unfortunately reads like an extended opinion piece, long on assertions and proposals but short on analysis and supporting information. Few of Taylor's proposals are new or bold. Like Hacker and Dreifus and many before them, he wants to end tenure, but in his case mainly to open up opportunities for young scholars who have worked for years to earn Ph.D.'s only to find no jobs when they are finished (which was not exactly a secret when they began). Like other critics, he thinks that colleges and universities encourage disciplinary research at the expense of teaching. He urges a national collaboration between elite and nonelite institutions to train and reward good teachers, certainly a worthwhile proposal. He thinks that computers and video games should be used widely to improve the quality of teaching and break down barriers between disciplines, and goes so far as to suggest that colleges and universities should be restructured to reflect the open and adaptable characteristics of computer networks.

He is especially keen to promote more cross-disciplinary activities that bring scholars from different fields—like art and physics or religion and international affairs—together to address new problems. There are many professors who resist such collaborations, preferring to focus on the subject matter in their disciplines. At the same time, and as Taylor notes, this kind of cross-disciplinary work has been going on for a long time on major campuses where new combinations of fields are continually evolving into new disciplines like regional science, biochemistry, the history of science, social psychology, and neuroscience. But these fields evolve out of existing disciplines and do not emerge *de novo*, as Taylor imagines that they can.

Crisis on Campus does have some ideas that are new and bold, but they are not necessarily constructive or practical. Taylor advances

---

* Alfred A. Knopf, 2010; quotation above on p. 7.

a bizarre proposal to eliminate permanent departments and re-constitute fields on the run to study particular subjects, such as water, time, money, law, and networks. After a few years, these fields would be dissolved, and professors and students would be dispersed to study new ones as they are formed. Graduate students could earn advanced degrees in any of these temporary fields, per-haps by producing films, video games, or websites in place of the traditional written dissertation.

In making such proposals, Taylor has let his imagination run far afield from the institutional realities of academic life. A college or university could never organize its affairs according to such a plan without turning its professors into dilettantes and its students into experts on the passing fashions of the hour. He expresses little ap-preciation for the way that scientists conduct their enterprise or how they establish new knowledge by painstaking, time-consum-ing research. It is good that some professors are given to flights of imagination, but also good that some have their feet planted firmly on the ground.

Nor is Taylor particularly sympathetic to the liberal arts as a dis-cipline through which the lessons and achievements of the past are transmitted from generation to generation. He is an enthusiast for the new: new technologies, new ways of learning, new and untested patterns of academic organization. It is unusual to encounter a hu-manist and philosopher so completely enchanted with the possibil-ities of computers and online networks—undoubtedly a sign that he knows little about them. Taylor's proposals would indeed "end the university as we know it." Would that be a good thing? The university is in real need of reform and perhaps even an upheaval, but not of the kind that Taylor envisions.

Taylor is undoubtedly correct on one point: the financial crash and the long recession have put new pressures on colleges and uni-versities to cut costs and eliminate superfluous programs and personnel. The "higher education bubble," as he calls it, is bound to burst sooner or later, like the other "bubbles" we have seen. The contemporary university is to a great extent the product of a postwar American affluence that is gradually waning. Rising tuition, escalating salaries, administrative overload, and doubling and redoubling endowments are all reflections in one way or another of a steadily growing economy and a historic bull market in stocks (and the nation's ability to borrow unlimited sums). As resources become harder to find, as families can no longer afford tuition prices, and as federal resources are withdrawn, college and university leaders will be hard pressed to maintain the gains of the past few decades. Many of the current excesses of higher education that grew out of affluence will be scaled back in an age of austerity.

* * *

A few preferred reforms in higher education based on the information contained in these three books would include these high on the list: (1) Shelve the utopian idea that every young person attend college, and along with it the dubious claim that the nation's prosperity depends on universal college attendance. (2) Terminate nearly all Ph.D. programs in the humanities and most of them in the social sciences. (3) Replace them with postgraduate programs in the liberal arts that allow students to earn graduate degrees based upon teaching rather than research and permit them to master broad fields that cross existing disciplinary boundaries. (4) Reverse the expansion of administrative layers, especially offices and programs created to satisfy campus pressure groups. (5) Bring back general education requirements and core curricula to ensure that every undergraduate student is exposed to the important ideas in the humanities and sciences that have shaped our civilization.

No one should expect that any of these changes is likely to occur easily or soon. Despite the liberal outlook of most professors, higher education is one of the most conservative of enterprises and one of the most resistant to reform. In recent decades it has been marked more by dissolution and disintegration than by constructive reform. Most of the traditional organizational patterns inherited from the last century—specialized departments organized into colleges, tenure, graduate programs, and externally funded research—remain intact today. Colleges and universities of the future are likely to look much as they do today, except that they will operate with fewer resources and much narrower margins for excess.

＊

A version of this chapter appeared in *The New Criterion*,
September 2011.

CHAPTER EIGHTEEN

Columbia Beats Harvard

In their historic football rivalry dating back to 1877, Harvard holds a commanding advantage over Columbia, the Crimson having won fifty-seven of their joint contests as against fourteen for the Lions. Harvard's most recent winning scores were 69-0 (in 2012), 34-0 (in 2013), and 45-0 (in 2014). Among Ivy League institutions, Harvard has long had one of the strongest football programs and Columbia one of the weakest. In a head-to-head contest between the undergraduate curricula at these two institutions, on the other hand, Columbia has more than held its own against its Ivy League rival.

For nearly a century, the two universities have stood as national models for diametrically opposed approaches to undergraduate education. Harvard, under the leadership of Charles William Eliot from 1869 to 1909, pioneered the elective system under which students were given broad choices in course selection and areas of study. Columbia, guided by luminaries like John Erskine, Mark Van Doren, and Jacques Barzun, began building a core curriculum in 1919 based upon the classic writings of Western civilization. Harvard, as Daniel Bell has written, became known for its lectures, Columbia for its small seminars. Over the subsequent decades, other colleges and universities across the country adopted one or the other of these two approaches to undergraduate education.

The established curricula at Harvard and Columbia survived the multicultural battles of the 1980s and 1990s with only minor and marginal concessions to their critics. In recent years, both institutions have undertaken reviews of their educational regimens in response to claims that they are out-of-date in a world of increasing diversity and globalization. In a joint nod to tradition, both schools reiterated the basic curricular commitments they originally made decades ago.

* * *

In 1945, partly in response to Columbia's curricular initiatives in the 1920s and 1930s and also to the experience of World War II, Harvard's faculty—under the guidance of the president, James Bryant Conant—approved a far-reaching reform in the school's undergraduate curriculum. Summarized in book form under the title *General Education in a Free Society*, often called the "Red Book" because it was published with crimson covers, it proposed a curriculum requiring students to pass general survey courses in three areas: the humanities, social sciences, and natural sciences. This General Education curriculum differed from Columbia's Core in important ways: first, it was not organized around the great books; second, it focused heavily on modern (twentieth-century) intellectual developments; and, third, students were given a fair amount of leeway in deciding how they would meet the requirements. Because of this last feature, Harvard's curriculum came to be known as a "distributional" approach to the undergraduate core.

This curriculum lost its focus in the 1960s and 1970s as professors began to shape the General Education courses in accordance with their own intellectual interests, and as the urgent political questions that prompted its creation gave way to new issues relating to civil rights, feminism, and the war in Vietnam. In 1978, the Faculty of Arts and Sciences—led by Henry Rosovsky as dean—implemented a new curriculum organized around a concept called "approaches to knowledge." It required students to take a class or two in a broad range of fields, from the sciences to the arts and humanities, in order to expose them to different methods of research and study. This system preserved the original distributional model but expanded the number of basic fields from three to eleven.

Harvard's new core curriculum was controversial when it was adopted because, as critics said, it elevated method over substance, or "approaches" over knowledge. It was based on the assumption that understanding or knowing about *Hamlet* or the U.S. Constitution is less important than knowing how these works are understood according to different methods of analysis or disciplinary points of view. Critics claimed that the curriculum more often reflected the disciplinary preoccupations of the faculty than the educational needs of students. Nevertheless, it was quite influential, as things first done at Harvard often turn out to be. Many colleges and universities soon abandoned their traditional knowledge-based curricula in favor of Harvard's "distributional" approach to undergraduate studies.

In 2009, after several years of study and debate, Harvard's faculty implemented another new Program in General Education to replace the so-called Rosovsky curriculum. This latest revision of the curriculum has been hailed as an improvement over the previous one because it discards the focus on methods, aiming instead (according to the course catalog) "to connect a student's liberal education—that is, an education conducted in a spirit of free inquiry, rewarding in its own right—to life beyond the college." The new curriculum implicitly acknowledges the principal weakness of the old one—that it was organized around disciplinary controversies that are important to faculty but to no one else. The new curriculum also announces a practical purpose: to prepare students for future lives as citizens and professionals. But by conceiving liberal education in terms of free inquiry rather than knowledge or understanding, this revision advances further down the path charted in 1978.

According to the report of the faculty committee that approved the Program in General Education of 2009, a new curriculum was needed to address the significant changes that have taken place in the world over the past generation. The report alludes not only to changes in science and technology but also to the onward march of globalization. A major purpose of the curriculum, according to the faculty report, is to help students understand the sources of change in modern life and how they can keep their bearings in the midst of it. Putting aside the boilerplate language about "change," the most challenging questions about a curriculum deal with what subjects it will include or exclude. Given the above rationale, one might have expected the new curriculum to contain required courses that would help students understand the rise of science in connection with the history of the West, why the scientific enterprise flourished in some places and not in others, and how "globalization" developed out of Western thought and institutions. Yet in fact the rhetoric about "change" is dimly reflected in the actual courses that students are required to take, which was perhaps to be expected given the hazy nature of the rhetoric and—more importantly—the way faculties are organized.

Thus, the rationale may be new but the curriculum looks like a warmed-over version of the old one. Instead of eleven different fields of study, the faculty has carved up the course catalogue into eight areas with new names: Aesthetic and Interpretive Understanding; Culture and Belief; Empirical and Mathematical Reasoning; Ethical Reasoning; Science of Living Systems; Science of the Physical Universe; Societies of the World; and United States in the World. As with the old curriculum, the new one requires students to take at least one course in each subject area but does not require a basic level of mastery in any of them. Consequently, the new curriculum closely resembles the distributional system it replaced.

Harvey Mansfield, the William R. Kenan, Jr., Professor of Government at Harvard, has called the new curriculum "insipid" and "vacuous" because it lacks substance and evades difficult decisions about what students should learn during their college years, instead deferring the question to student choice. According to the faculty report endorsing the curriculum, an important objective of a college education is to put students "in a position from which they can choose for themselves what principles will guide them." But as Mansfield points out, this formulation puts the cart before the proverbial horse, since we usually understand principles or philosophy to guide important choices rather than the other way around. What principles will guide the choice of principles? Are some ways of life superior to others? On these fundamental questions, the faculty report is silent, and so, essentially, is the curriculum.

Thus it is that the curriculum enshrines choice in courses but supplies no structure that might guide it. In most of the fields of study, students can meet their requirements by choosing one from as many as forty different courses from disparate departments. The requirement in Aesthetic and Interpretive Understanding, for example, can be satisfied by choosing one course from a list that includes "Gender and Performance," "The 19th Century Novel," "Virgil," and "Buddhism and Japanese Culture." The requirement in Culture and Belief can be met by choosing one course from among some thirty or forty courses in fields ranging from classics to economics to Slavic studies.

So it goes with the other fields as well. For United States in the World, students choose from an extensive list of courses that includes "Sex and the Citizen," "American Food: A Global History," and "American Health Care Policy." Students can meet this requirement without once coming into contact with the writings of Thomas Jefferson, James Madison, or Abraham Lincoln, or learning anything about the Revolution, the Constitution, the Civil War, or the Great Depression. In regard to America, such writings and events were the mainsprings of "change," but students are not required to learn anything about them.

Many of these courses, judged individually, are doubtless valuable and full of substance. At the same time, a course catalogue should not be confused with a curriculum. The committee that designed Harvard's curriculum made no effort to stipulate what kinds of knowledge students should acquire in different areas of study, but instead passed the buck to students to decide for themselves what courses they will take from the vast array of choices presented to them. There is not even a guarantee that Harvard's students will learn anything substantive about "change," vacuous as that concept may be as a guide to a curriculum in the first place. Though the new program is sometimes described as a core curriculum, it does not present students with a common intellectual experience, nor is it based on any assumptions about what an educated person should know after four years of college. Given this curriculum, one can make few assumptions about what a Harvard graduate will know after four expensive years of study.

* * *

Such is not the case at Columbia, where students are required to pass through a structured curriculum in which they encounter the great books and artistic creations of Western civilization. Much in contrast to Harvard's new curriculum, Columbia's has substance and structure and is guided by a coherent rationale. While Harvard's periodic curricular revisions are highly publicized, Columbia's stable and long-lived Core Curriculum receives far less publicity and recognition.

The first plank of Columbia's Core has been in place continuously since 1919, when a handful of faculty members envisioned an education in the classics to replace the disintegrating curriculum in Greek, Latin, and religion. The Core arose even more directly out of the urgent questions raised about democracy and civilization by the world war that had just concluded. "Contemporary Civilization," one of the courses that would become a mainstay of the Core, developed out of a "War Issues" seminar that Columbia's faculty offered to army officers in training for the purpose of codifying the great issues at stake in the war. When the war was over, the professors who were engaged in that enterprise crafted a new course for undergraduates on the foundations of Western civilization. At roughly the same time, Columbia's English Department, led by John Erskine, devised an honors course arranged around the reading and discussion of various classic works of literature (in translation) in small seminar settings; one of its purposes was to counteract the increasing specialization of departmental studies. This course gradually evolved into what is now called "Literature Humanities," the second major plank of Columbia's Core.

From Erskine's point of view, a course in the classics was path-breaking and liberating because it focused on the important ideas contained in those books and their influence on later authors, rather than emphasizing mental discipline and memorization. In mounting his course, Erskine had to overcome the resistance of colleagues who felt that the reading of these works in translation was dilettantish and unserious. That objection, however, missed the main point, which was not to have students master some aspect of Homer, Plato, or Aristotle in the manner of a doctoral candidate, but rather to expose them to the works of those seminal thinkers as a means of introducing them to the fundamental ideas that shaped our world. Students who wanted to go further in such inquiries could do so through graduate studies.

Columbia's curriculum grew out of concerns about the changing world that were not so different from those that more recently guided Harvard's revisions. The major difference is that Columbia's faculty addressed this challenge far more seriously. When Columbia's president Nicholas Murray Butler announced the new "Contemporary Civilization" course, he noted that its purpose would be "to give first-year students an outlook on the modern world as well as a point of view to help them understand their subsequent studies." In reference to the more directly political aims of the curriculum, Butler went on to say that, "for students enamored of the cruder forms of radicalism, early instruction on the origin and development of modern civilization and the part that time plays in building and perfecting human institutions is of the greatest value. For those afflicted with the more stubborn forms of conservatism, early appreciation of the fact that movement is characteristic of life and that change may be constructive as well as destructive is most desirable."

Since Butler's statement contained no snide references to political liberals, one may infer that he thought the new course to be more sympathetic to that point of view than to conservatism or radicalism—a judgment that, in relation to the great books, held up for many decades thereafter. It was only very recently that some critics began to claim, bizarrely, that a curriculum in the classics was part of a conservative plot to impose upon students a "white" or a Western point of view.

Columbia's Core Curriculum today is a set of courses required of all undergraduates and taught in small seminars of twenty or so students. Students must pass yearlong seminars in "Contemporary Civilization" and "Literature Humanities," in which they read and discuss one important book per week. The reading list for "Contemporary Civilization" includes selections from the Old and

New Testaments and the Koran, along with works by Aristotle, Plato, Machiavelli, John Locke, Adam Smith, Marx, Darwin, and from *The Federalist* (among others). In "Literature Humanities," students take up Homer's *Iliad* and *Odyssey,* Virgil's *Aeneid,* the plays of Sophocles, Euripides, and Shakespeare, Dante's *Inferno,* and the novels of Dostoevsky and Jane Austen (among other readings). Students are also required to take single-semester courses in art, music, and science, all of which are similarly organized around the great works in these respective subjects. Core requirements add up to seven semester courses, or about 20 percent of the typical student's four-year workload.

Columbia's Core is frequently described as a "great books" program, despite the best efforts of the faculty to resist this label. Faculty leaders object to the commercial and middle-brow association the term acquired during the mass-market campaign launched by the *Encyclopedia Britannica* in the 1950s, in which the illusion was circulated that all the knowledge an educated person needs to acquire is contained in a set of books that can be purchased and displayed on an average bookshelf. This was the kind of superficiality against which some early critics of the Core had warned. Faculty supporters of the program thus have always emphasized the difficulty of these works and the importance of reading and discussing them under the guidance of trained teachers.

Though the curriculum has undergone revisions over the decades, its original focus on the classics has survived intact, and so also has the dual emphasis on civilization and literature. When women were first admitted to Columbia College in the 1970s, Mary Wollstonecraft's *A Vindication of the Rights of Women* was added to the required readings in Contemporary Civilization and one of Virginia Woolf's novels was added to the Literature Humanities syllabus. Later, in response to criticisms that the reading list contained no works by black or Third World authors, *The Souls of*

Black Folk by W. E. B. Du Bois was added to the syllabus in Contemporary Civilization. While some observers viewed these steps as concessions made under pressure, others saw them as a way of making a great books curriculum more compelling to critics and to new groups arriving on campus.

The director of Columbia's Core, Roosevelt Montás (who also teaches in the American Studies program), argues that a structured curriculum is preferable to loosely tailored alternatives because few students at the beginning of their college careers are well equipped to choose the best educational program from the array of options available at most universities. Thus, a well-designed system of courses embodying the great works of the past and expressing the traditions of the institution can be of great value to students as they proceed through their college years. In addition, a structured curriculum, particularly one organized around the classics, provides a common vocabulary for all members of an institution and a baseline of knowledge on which academic specialization and discussions outside the classroom can build. In advanced courses, professors can make realistic assumptions about what students have read and what they can be expected to know.

Montás is an unusual figure to be heading up a traditional program. After immigrating from the Dominican Republic as a teenager, Montás entered Columbia as an undergraduate in 1991 ill prepared for the intellectual challenges of the Core Curriculum. By conventional campus logic, he was precisely the kind of student who should have rebelled against a course of study filled with the works of dead white Europeans. Yet he soon found that Columbia's academic requirements, instead of stifling his curiosity, gave him a sense of intellectual order that laid a foundation for further study and discovery. With that foundation, Montás proceeded to earn his B.A. from Columbia and later a Ph.D. in

English and comparative literature. Now, as the director of the Core, he serves as a thoughtful ambassador for a structured curriculum in the classics.

He is thus in a strong position to reply to critics on the campus and elsewhere who assert that the Core reflects the thought of a single culture and is too narrow for students preparing to enter a global economy. The Western tradition at the heart of the curriculum, Montás points out, is neither monolithic nor homogenous but rather one of debate, dissent, and surprisingly frequent upheavals in inherited doctrines and assumptions. The great books that students encounter in the Core encapsulate fundamental arguments over religion, morality, war, economics, and political organization that have shaped the history of the West and, indeed, of the entire world. Even the multicultural critique of the great books is built—albeit unreflectively—upon the theories of Nietzsche, Marx, and Freud, whose writings appear on the syllabus. There is no single line of thought inherent to the Core that bolsters the interests or outlook of any particular group. Far from being conservative, the works taken as a whole challenge and undermine contemporary habits of thought. The critic David Denby, in his chronicle of a year spent at Columbia studying in the Core, went so far as to conclude that the "core-curriculum courses jar so many student habits, violate so many contemporary pieties, and challenge so many forms of laziness that so far from serving a reactionary function, they are actually the most radical courses in the undergraduate curriculum."

The challenges to such a curriculum are not only ideological but also financial and pedagogical. It is expensive and administratively difficult to staff the large number of sections required by the small-class format. In any given semester, Montás must identify enough able teachers to schedule as many as sixty-five sections each of Contemporary Civilization and Literature Humanities.

Many senior professors at Columbia are not interested in teaching in the Core because it does not contribute to their research interests, leaving many sections to be taught by junior faculty, graduate students, postdoctoral fellows, and adjunct teachers. The growing specialization of academia makes it ever more difficult to nourish and recruit the kinds of generalists who can effectively teach sections of the Core. By contrast, Harvard's curriculum, which involves no special courses, is far less expensive and cumbersome to maintain.

Even so, Columbia, one of the most liberal universities in the nation, has managed to keep in place a most traditional curriculum—one that originated close to a century ago—through decades of change and upheaval on campus. This is largely because the Core Curriculum has always received strong support from a few members of the senior faculty, many of them with prominent public profiles. These include distinguished professors such as Jacques Barzun, Lionel Trilling, Moses Hadas, and Richard Hofstadter in decades gone by, and Gareth Williams, Andrew Delbanco, and even the former SDS leader Todd Gitlin today. Influential alumni have also turned out to be fervent supporters of the Core, an experience that they appreciate more and more as the years go by. Many undergraduates matriculate to Columbia precisely because they wish to study under the Core Curriculum.

After nearly a century with a common Core, Columbia's identity is now firmly associated with it. Nevertheless, even at Columbia such a curriculum would be difficult to introduce today in view of the ongoing departmentalization of the university. Professor Delbanco, a member of the English Department and head of the American Studies program, likes to quote a colleague who said, "The Core Curriculum is like the Interstate Highway System. It would be impossible to build today, but we are very glad to have it."

* * *

Today, among the four thousand or so colleges and universities across the country, Columbia is among the very few (less than 10 percent) that offer a core curriculum in which students are required to pass through a structured course of study in the liberal arts. Most institutions, perhaps as many as 90 percent of them, have adopted the distributional system pioneered at Harvard. In the competition between the two approaches to undergraduate study, Harvard's model appears to be winning out.

Yet that would be a shortsighted conclusion. An easygoing curriculum that asks little of students will often be more popular than a demanding one in which serious books must be read and discussed. Even so, the Core is surprisingly popular among students and junior faculty on Columbia's campus, probably more so today than it was a decade ago. In fending off a series of attacks, the curriculum seems to have revealed its deeper strengths and the advantages it holds over alternatives. As a Columbia College report concluded some years ago, "In contrast to the largely distributional curricula of other institutions, the Core is an oasis of order and purpose." And it is for these reasons that Columbia now finds itself in the company of an expanding list of colleges and universities offering courses of study in the great books, whether as core curricula or as elective options for students interested in such an education. Columbia's program may be unique for its longevity, but it is ever less so for its substance.

In contrast to Harvard's curriculum, which will require constant revision and new justifications because it must keep pace with changing conditions, Columbia's curriculum (and others like it) has a stable foundation because it is organized around timeless themes expressed in works that are unlikely to go out of style. If the objective of a liberal education is to identify the permanent and perennial issues in the midst of flux and change, then Columbia's

Core serves that purpose more directly than most alternatives. In judging the two curricula, one does not face a close call. Columbia and Harvard are playing in different leagues. If it were a football game, Columbia would beat Harvard by several touchdowns.

⌁

A version of this chapter appeared in *The New Criterion*,
September 2010.

CHAPTER NINETEEN

Liberalism versus Humanism

Writing nearly fifty years ago in *The New Industrial State*, John Kenneth Galbraith called on academics and intellectuals to seize the reins of national leadership that (he charged) were held by a bipartisan coalition of corporate managers, union officials, and machine politicians. Galbraith feared that these conventional leaders had defined the goals of the industrial system too narrowly in terms of production, consumption, and employment, when a much broader vision was needed to direct the goals of the new economy toward aesthetic, artistic, and intellectual interests, so that the lives of the American people might be elevated above mere work and consumption. Noting the growing influence of students and faculty within the Democratic Party, Galbraith judged that they were well positioned to compete for political leadership in the name of humane ideals.

While Galbraith sought to harness academic humanism to the purposes of liberal politics, campus radicals tried to take parallel action to bring national attention to the New Left. In the Port Huron Statement, written in 1962, the founders of a new campus organization, Students for a Democratic Society, decried the loss of meaning and humane ideals in a consumer-driven economy. "The goal of man and society," the students wrote, "should be human independence:

a concern not with image but with finding a meaning in life that is personally authentic." They claimed to raise profound questions that their elders had brushed aside in their headlong pursuit of money and comfort: What is really important? Can we live in a different and better way? If we wanted to change society, how would we do it?

The young radicals asserted that "meaning" had to be found not through study and reflection but through political action, and they astutely zeroed in on the university as "a potential base and agency in a movement for social change." They viewed the university in nakedly political terms as a far better institutional base for their activities than a new political party could be. For one thing, the campus archipelago that stretched across the nation was home to both liberals and socialists as well as to millions of young people yearning for "change." These would be the key constituent groups for a new left. For another, the university ethos gave wide scope for political activity. "The University," the radicals said, "permits the political life to be an adjunct to the academic one . . . ." There was nothing to stop professors or students from becoming spokesmen and activists for the new politics.

That the American university might be seized as a base for a political movement or that the humanistic ideals of the academy might be projected outward into the political process—these were novel and compelling conceptions, which together suggested that the academy had come of age as a partner in the institutional coalition that governed postwar America. Such propositions also pointed toward a reformulation of liberal doctrine away from the older emphasis on economic growth that held together the New Deal coalition. Liberals like Galbraith seemed to agree with the student radicals that the time had come for a new emphasis in liberal thought on cultural, humanistic, and "quality of life" issues that had not previously been viewed in political or partisan terms. For both liberals and radicals, the university would play a key role in guiding this reformulation and in giving it political expression.

Much of what the liberals and radicals called for in the 1960s eventually came to pass, albeit in the rough-edged way by which history is made. Galbraith's idea of using the university to elevate national politics backfired in spectacular fashion, but the vision of turning it into a base for liberal and radical politics was eventually achieved against only weak resistance from more traditionally minded academics. When the student movement ran out of steam at the end of the 1960s, many of its leaders settled back into the academy as graduate students and junior professors. They soon saw that they would have to reformulate their ideological notions into academically acceptable modes of study. As they did so, and as they pushed questions of race, gender, and multiculturalism to the front of the academic agenda, they unwittingly sacrificed the ideals of humanism and humanistic study that, according to liberals like Galbraith and the student radicals, had conferred on the university a degree of moral legitimacy that other institutions lacked. As political liberalism and radicalism advanced on the campus, humanism receded at a nearly identical pace.

* * *

Humanism is the name given to the various intellectual movements that have developed since the Renaissance that emphasize the secular achievements of man in the fields of art, literature, philosophy, and politics, using as starting points and models for study the civilizations of ancient Greece and Rome. Though humanism originally developed out of medieval Christianity, its main purpose then and afterward was to demonstrate the dignity and creative power of man. The major intellectual movements that shaped the modern world, including most especially the Renaissance and the Enlightenment, arose out of humanist ideals. Reason, science, free inquiry, the power of the human intellect—these have been the watchwords of humanist movements through the centuries.

Humanists have always pointed to the highest human achievements in order to promote understanding of what is great and noble in human affairs and to encourage efforts at emulation. Humanism—or the humanities—has long found a home in the great universities of Europe and North America. Indeed, those institutions have developed over several centuries as instruments for spreading the ideals of humanistic study. Until quite recently, the ideals of the university have been indistinguishable from those of humanism.

Liberal conceptions have now replaced traditional humanistic ideals in defining both the form and substance of the American university. Liberal ideals like freedom of choice, equality among all groups of people and fields of study, tolerance of disparate viewpoints and lifestyles, diversity, and compassion have pushed aside the tradition of humanistic study formerly pursued through a structured curriculum, mastery of ancient languages and literature, and immersion in the great books and intellectual controversies of Western civilization. Important historical figures or impressive works of art and literature that were once held up by humanists as models for emulation are now viewed through a "hermeneutics of suspicion" that unmasks the hidden political interests they actually represented. Since these interests are always framed in terms of money or power or some dishonorable calculation, such an approach has the pedagogical effect of reducing every subject of study to a common moral level. The point of these exercises is to establish equality as the conceptual prism through which all subjects must be viewed. This is a vision of equality—equality with a vengeance—that grows out of contemporary liberalism but which cannot be reconciled with the humanities as traditionally studied or with the ideals of classical humanism.

It is hard to know if the eclipse of humanism on campus is but a temporary setback for a venerable philosophy or if it marks the end of an intellectual tradition that for centuries provided the rationale and purpose for advanced academic study. The rise of liberalism as a counter-ideal has brought the university more into line with the norms of democracy and equality that are widely influential within American society at large—a development which (surprisingly enough) may have made it more legitimate in the eyes of parents, public officials, and philanthropists. From this point of view, humanism appears as an obstacle to the fulfillment of liberal goals both on campus and in the wider polity. Traditional humanists, as advocates for excellence, continuity, and disciplined learning, are easily portrayed as reactionaries or, worse, as enemies of equality and democracy. Because of the profound incompatibility between liberalism and humanism, the academic revolutions of the past half century may prove difficult to reverse or to modify.

At the same time, humanism has long been thought to be a necessary educational adjunct to liberal political doctrine. Beginning in the late 1600s, liberalism advanced as a political theory because it defined "liberty" as the individual's right to choose his own way of life, primarily in the area of religion but also, as time passed, in an expanding field of activities. Liberalism set individuals free but did not provide instruction as to how they should live or what they should value. As they promoted a revolutionary doctrine that placed limits on government, early liberal thinkers looked to classical traditions for instruction in important civic matters such as war, statecraft, and citizenship. For most people, religion filled the void opened up by liberalism in the area of private life and morals. Humanism did so as well for those who pursued advanced academic studies or who may have harbored political or literary ambitions. Liberalism, it was understood, was not the same as the liberal arts. However powerful it may have been as a political doctrine, liberalism (like science) was thought to be insufficient as a general guide to life and thus in need of support from other sources and traditions of thought. Liberalism, in other words, required support from humanism.

This awareness of the limits of liberalism is one source of calls for a revival of the humanities in higher education and also a reason for the wide readership gained by books critical of the academy like Allan Bloom's *The Closing of the American Mind*, Roger Kimball's *Tenured Radicals*, and Harold Bloom's *The Western Canon*. Such works, while routinely dismissed by college presidents and deans as reactionary tracts, point to a permanent problem in liberal thought that cannot be overcome by further reforms in the direction of more democracy, equality, and freedom on the campus. Such books, and the responses to them, have raised the main question: whether humanism is in fact an obstacle to the fulfillment of liberal ideals or a complementary philosophy that can supply them with a measure of content and purpose.

* * *

Anthony T. Kronman, a distinguished professor of law at Yale University, joins an expanding list of educators lamenting the loss of purpose in undergraduate education. The title of his useful and provocative volume, *Education's End: Why Our Colleges and Universities Have Given Up on the Meaning of Life*,* contains a deliberate irony that points at once to the enduring "ends" of higher education and to the terminal destination that our academic institutions now appear to have reached. The point of a college education, in his view, is to encourage reflection on the purposes of life; but it is obvious that academics no longer regard this as central to their mission. In keeping with his title, Professor Kronman seems alternately hopeful that such ends might be restored to undergraduate education and pessimistic that the strong countercurrents at work in the academy can ever be overcome.

One has to admire Kronman for subordinating his interests in professional education in order to make a case for the vital role played by the traditional humanities in the undergraduate curriculum. That such a case would be made by a law professor is per-

---

* Yale University Press, 2007.

haps a sign that it can no longer be made by professors of history, literature, classics, or philosophy. One has to admire the author also for the strong words he attaches to the various academic fads and practices that have led to the eclipse of the humanities, calling them "ruinous," "deadening," "destructive," "disastrous," "impoverished," "deformed," and "mistaken." At the same time, perhaps to counterbalance these strong words, he takes pains to present the case in a manner least likely to offend the academic gatekeepers who control the flow of ideas into the campus, refraining especially from chalking up the crisis in the humanities to the political upheavals of the 1960s (as other critics have done).

Professor Kronman reflects back nostalgically on his undergraduate years in the mid-1960s at Williams College, where he was exposed to something resembling a humanistic education that explored permanent questions about life's meaning and how the good life should be lived. Such a "quest for meaning" led the young Kronman, like other students of the time, to take a leave of absence from college to work as a community organizer in Chicago under the auspices of Students for a Democratic Society. Disappointed in what he was able to accomplish in that role, he returned to Williamstown to engage the questions of meaning through an academic route. In a seminar on existentialism, where he encountered authors like Kierkegaard and Sartre, he discovered something important that subverted his radical presumptions, namely, that "the meaning of life is a subject that can be studied in school." Thus as a young man he concluded that ultimate meaning in life is unlikely to be found in politics but rather through individual study and reflection.

In his view, colleges and universities took the wrong path when they jettisoned humanism in the 1960s in favor of the politicized doctrines that eventually won control over humanities departments. These doctrines are weak and mistaken in the academic setting precisely because they do not allow students to engage those ultimate questions that captivated him as an undergraduate. Kronman advocates a return to the secular humanism of that earlier period, which he defines as "the exploration of life's mysteries and meaning through the careful but critical reading of the great works of the literary and philosophical imagination." This was a twentieth-century version of humanism, which replaced the older humanistic focus on Greece and Rome with an emphasis on the continuity of Western civilization from those early sources to the influential works of the modern age. Kronman's view of humanistic education embodies an outlook advanced decades ago by Robert Maynard Hutchins, one of his predecessors as dean of Yale Law School, who wrote that "The tradition of the West is embodied in the Great Conversation that began in the dawn of history and continues to the present day." Like Hutchins and his colleague Mortimer Adler, Kronman advocates an education in the great books.

Professor Kronman suggests that the modern research university played a complex role first in the development of secular humanism and later in its destruction. In the decades following the Civil War (as related in Chapter 15), academic leaders reorganized their institutions along the lines of the German model, which asserted the autonomy of the professor to teach and conduct research free from control by religious or secular authorities. The research model also introduced the concept of the graduate school into higher education. The research university dedicated to the discovery of new knowledge thus replaced the traditional antebellum college, which emphasized humanistic studies but also placed these studies in the service of religious faith. What followed, from the 1870s into the 1960s, was something of a golden age for the American university—a time when the humanities were liberated from religion but not yet subordinated to science and specialization. The humanities were thus able to carve out an independent role at the center of the undergraduate curriculum.

Kronman parts company with critics like Bloom and Kimball

who attribute the collapse of secular humanism to the political movements that invaded the campus in the 1960s. Instead, he finds the cause in the relentless advance of the research ideal, which led academics to abandon the large issues of humanistic learning in favor of narrower (yet meaningless) subjects that are more amenable to scientific study. While the scientific approach may have been crucial to the advance of knowledge about nature and the physical world, it proved a disaster when applied to the humanistic fields, which could not be cut up into researchable parts without compromising their central purposes. The point of the humanities, after all, was to understand life from the broadest possible vantage point. Specialization, which is an integral part of the scientific enterprise, worked against the ideal of a "great conversation" extending from ancient Greece to modern times.

Thus by the end of the 1960s the humanities were compromised beyond redemption by the emphasis on research and publication. Intellectually curious students could no longer find answers to the nagging questions of life and politics in their courses in philosophy, literature, and history, since their professors were now more interested in narrower questions raised by their research agendas. Into this void flowed the "ruinous" and "destructive" concepts and modes of study that we associate with the contemporary university. All these doctrines, from multiculturalism to ethnic and gender studies, pointedly dispute the continuity of Western civilization or even the existence of such a civilization outside the minds of a handful of influential authors. While systematically attacking the assumptions of humanism, the new doctrines managed at the same time to accommodate the requirements of research and publication—a tactic that was instrumental to their success on campus. In Professor Kronman's view, these radical and antihumanistic approaches to learning were able to invade and subvert the humanities primarily because the research ideal had already emptied them of content.

* * *

The research ideal, while certainly detrimental to humanism, cannot finally be blamed for bringing onto campus the radical ideologies that have done so much damage to the humanities. Some of the most destructive rebellions of the 1960s took place at small colleges like Kenyon, Oberlin, Smith, and Wellesley, where the liberal arts were given the most serious attention and where the research ideal had yet to make any great headway. Cornell, Columbia, and the University of Chicago had built stellar reputations as centers of liberal learning in the postwar era, but these traditions did not inoculate them against student and faculty radicalism in the late 1960s. At Columbia in 1968 and Cornell in 1969, student radicals took over the campus demanding an end to racism and the war in Vietnam, along with a more "relevant" education than that being offered. The radical movement of that era was preoccupied with political issues whose sources were off campus, and it took aim at both the research ideal and the traditional humanities in equal measure. It is important to bear in mind that though the radicals did not destroy the modern research ideal, they did succeed in dismantling the traditional humanities curriculum. Research is alive and well on the American campus, while the humanities are all but dead.

The collapse of academic humanism has left a generation or more of undergraduates intellectually adrift in a sea of nihilism, relativism, and political correctness. Kronman believes that the rise of religious fundamentalism here and abroad is one consequence of the failure of the academy to address the ultimate questions from a secular point of view. Fundamentalist religion, leaving aside its blind spots, at least provides answers to the questions of life's meaning that every thinking person must consider. These answers are flawed, in Kronman's view, because they approach the crisis of meaning from the standpoint of dogma rather than reason, and because they represent a flight from reality rather than an engagement with it. Humanism (in his view) is superior to fundamentalism, and to religion in general, because it alone equips us with the resources of intellect and reason needed to face up to the crisis of meaning with honesty and composure.

Professor Kronman ends his book on a hopeful note, declaring that the age of political correctness will soon end and that the humanities will begin to recover from the abject state to which they have fallen. There is little evidence to justify that faith, as he acknowledges, other than the idea that since things cannot get much worse, they are bound to get better. One hopes this will be the case. If humanism is to advance, however, it must do so in the face of two well-entrenched adversaries: political correctness on the one side and research specialization on the other. As of now, humanism's troops on campus are still too few to engage this fight, let alone to win it.

Yet Kronman is able to point to some favorable straws in the wind. There is, for example, the Directed Studies Program at Yale, where he now regularly teaches and which offers a rigorous series of courses for freshmen in the great books of philosophy, literature, and politics. This is an elective rather than a required course of study, but it attracts far more applicants than can be accommodated with the faculty now on hand and within the current roster of courses. St John's College continues to offer a complete four-year curriculum in the great books and has little difficulty filling its classrooms with able and highly motivated students. Other institutions have begun to offer courses of study in Western civilization, the ideals of the American founding, the history of liberty and free societies, or various combinations of the above. So far, such concentrations have been offered on an elective basis for students who wish to pursue a traditional curriculum. Fledgling programs in Western civilization are now on offer to students at Emory University and the University of Texas, to name just a few institutions that are beginning to move in this direction. Faculty members at many other institutions are now thinking of mounting similar programs. These programs will give students an opportunity to "vote with their feet," as it were, and to send signals to administrators about the kinds of courses they wish to take and the kinds of faculty who should be hired. There is a growing awareness among many college teachers that the specialization found in graduate studies should be kept from spreading to the undergraduate curriculum.

If humanism and liberal learning are to be brought back into the academy, it will have to be accomplished through accommodations with the reigning dogmas of student choice, an open curriculum, and the freedom of professors to teach the courses they choose. Humanistic courses and programs are increasingly being offered at a modest number of colleges and universities as options for students and faculty on par with every other program of study. This is progress of an important kind, and it no doubt represents the only effective strategy available for those wishing to restore content to the humanities. On the other hand, the necessity of employing an elective strategy highlights the fact that humanism and liberalism are at odds in the contemporary university. For the time being at least, liberalism holds a decided advantage.

* * *

It is encouraging to read such an urgent call for a revival of the humanities as the one put forth by Professor Kronman—and even more so because of the case he makes for humanism as an instrument for discovering the meaning of life, or at least for pursuing that quest. Humanism has been advanced and defended in various ways in the past, but not often in modern times on these particular grounds. Sartre said that "existentialism is a humanism" because it demanded courage from the individual to face a world without meaning. There were others, like Erich Fromm, who said that "Marxism is a humanism" because it promised to end the alienation of man from himself, though the life of the individual had no meaning outside the process of history. According to both accounts, man does not discover but rather makes his own meaning through action and choice—and shapes his own character through the struggle with existence. It may be true, as some have suggested, that academics gave up on teaching about the meaning of life because they were finally convinced by these doctrines that there was no such meaning to be found.

There have been revivals and reformulations in the humanities in the past, though usually they have been provoked by impulses more powerful than the quest for meaning. Christian humanism was inspired in the fifteenth century by the rediscovery of the ancient world, with its works of art, literature, and philosophy that illuminated new paths of knowledge and understanding. The humanists of that time, such as Erasmus and Johann Reuchlin, did not aim to overthrow Christianity or the Church, nor did they see any deep conflict between humanistic studies and orthodox religion. They gained a foothold in the academies by setting forth an agenda of research and teaching based on this new knowledge, with the ultimate goal of discerning compatibilities between pagan learning and Christian doctrine. Ancient learning eventually took the humanists well beyond this limited agenda, in time creating an outlook that sought to free itself altogether from Christian influences.

In contrast to the religious focus of Christian humanism, the new German humanism of the nineteenth century developed out of the writings of Goethe and Schiller, who dreamed of building a new culture on the foundation of the ancient Greeks in order to fill a void left by the withering away of Christianity. The Greeks, it was said, represented an ideal form of life because they created a culture out of nature itself and without any human models to guide them. The new German research universities of that time were conceived as instruments to build such a culture through the scientific study of the culture of ancient Greece. This conception also suggested limits to the power of the state in relation to the university because only independent scholars possessed the requisite knowledge to build culture. Wilhelm von Humboldt, the founder of the University of Berlin and an associate of Goethe and Schiller, wrote that "The state must not demand anything from the university which would serve its purposes directly, but it should cherish the conviction that if the universities accomplish their ultimate aims, they will also serve its purposes from a loftier point of view." On this understanding, liberalism, humanism, and science were compatible and mutually reinforcing enterprises. Yet academic research grounded in science began, in time, to yield conclusions about classical culture that undermined the humanistic conceptions upon which the new universities were based. As a result, humanism gradually gave way to science in the German universities.

The decay and revival of the humanities have precedents in our cultural history. How and under what circumstances might they be revived today? In a scientific and politicized age, we are unlikely to follow the kind of humanistic path charted by Erasmus or Goethe. The restoration of a traditional "great books" curriculum now under way at several institutions is a welcome step, though it falls far short of igniting a genuine revival of the humanities. What is needed is not just a curriculum or even a new case for the humanities, but a renewed understanding of the liberal order, in which equality, freedom, and democracy are recognized as concepts that provide citizens with little guidance in ordering their lives. For generations, humanism has counterbalanced the inherent weaknesses of the liberal order by pointing to the human ends that the ideals of liberty and equality cannot prescribe. The collapse of the humanities is thus an aspect of the unfolding crisis in the liberal order, and it is unlikely to be reversed without a fundamental reassessment of what is required to sustain liberal institutions.

A version of this chapter appeared in *The New Criterion*, May 2008.

Beyond the Postwar Consensus

In early 2015, the Gallup organization published the results of a poll showing that the American public is now more divided politically than at any other time in the postwar era. A major source of the division, the poll suggested, revolves around Barack Obama and evaluations of his presidential performance, about which there is little in the way of a middle ground among American voters: Democrats overwhelmingly approve of his presidency while Republicans just as overwhelmingly reject it. According to Gallup, "Each of Obama's six years in office ranks among the most polarized in the last 60 years." Obama has certainly done much to polarize public opinion, pushing his health-care bill through on a narrow partisan vote, disdaining any compromise with Republicans over budget issues, and generally dismissing the results of the 2014 midterm elections that turned over control of both houses of Congress to Republicans. On the other hand, as the Gallup pollsters observed, the next most polarized period in the postwar era occurred between 2001 and 2009, during the presidency of George W. Bush, when Republicans had their turn to set the national agenda and Democrats pursued every opportunity to block and undermine it. Over the past fifteen years, neither party has been able to find much common ground with the opposition, which suggests that political polarization may be more deeply rooted in the structure of contemporary politics than most have been willing to acknowledge.

Politicians and pundits have pointed to various superficial factors as causes of this phenomenon—for example, the flood of money into politics, the increasing tendency of the two parties to appeal to their bases, the gerrymandering of congressional districts, and the fragmentation of political information due to the rise of cable news networks such as Fox News and MSNBC. For the most part, however, these are symptoms rather than causes of political polarization. Parties now raise vast sums by exploiting fears that the other side will gain power; they appeal to their ideological bases because these constituencies are far larger and more influential than they were a few decades ago; and the cable news networks respond to opportunities in the marketplace but do not create their audiences in the first place. As for gerrymandering, that has been going on since the early years of the republic, and because of Supreme Court decisions and judicial supervision of the districting process it is far less egregious today than it was fifty or a hundred years ago.

Then, much more seriously, there are those who blame the Republican Party for the dysfunction in Washington and the growing polarization between the parties. This is a popular view among liberal historians and pundits who think the political process worked better decades ago when Democrats were in charge and Republicans accepted their minority status as part of the natural order of things. From this point of view, it was mainly the rise of the conservative movement and its takeover of the Republican Party that disrupted the postwar consensus.

Geoffrey Kabaservice, a historian who studied and taught at Yale University, looks back nostalgically to the early years of the postwar era when the Republican Party was a force for moderation in national politics and worked with progressive Democrats to implement a bipartisan foreign policy and enact civil rights legislation. During that era, moderates and progressives like Dwight Eisenhower, Nelson Rockefeller, Thomas Kuchel, Earl Warren, and Everett Dirksen led the Republicans, while conservative southerners maintained outsized influence in the Democratic Party. Given the ideological splits within both parties, reformers needed to piece together bipartisan coalitions in order to pass legislation. In Kabaservice's view, the Goldwater insurgency in the early 1960s disrupted this arrangement by transforming the Republican Party from a mix of progressives, moderates, and conservatives into a rigidly conservative institution that attacks government, polarizes the national debate, and rejects compromises with Democrats. The rise of conservatism within the Republican Party thus ended the era of bipartisan compromise in Washington. "While there are many reasons to explain the present American political dysfunction," Kabaservice writes, "the leading suspect is the transformation of the Republican Party over the past half-century into a monolithically conservative organization."[1] Kabaservice thinks that the takeover of the party by conservatives made it weaker as an electoral force over the long run and less effective as a governing institution.

Thomas E. Mann and Norman J. Ornstein, both scholars at Washington think tanks, take this argument a step further and bring it up to date to take into account the battles in Congress over health care, entitlement spending, and the debt ceiling during the Obama years. These episodes, they argue, are manifestations of the current political "dysfunction" in Washington and of the failure of the political system to wrestle constructively with national challenges. In their view, the Republicans are largely to blame because they have allowed their party to evolve as an ideological force in a constitutional system ill equipped to deal with it. "The Republican Party," they write, "has become an insurgent outlier—ideologically extreme;

contemptuous of the inherited social and economic policy regime; scornful of compromise; unpersuaded by conventional understanding of facts, evidence, and science; and dismissive of the legitimacy of its political opposition."[2] Republicans, they claim, are a collection of radicals determined to overthrow the postwar consensus about the role of the federal government in American society. They view Democrats, on the other hand, as a collection of moderates and liberals willing to negotiate and make compromises to solve problems, if only they had a responsible opposition with which to work. The problem is that a willful and well-organized minority can exploit the levers of power to frustrate the majority and bring the affairs of government to a halt, which Mann and Ornstein say is what the Republican Party has now accomplished. Like Kabaservice, they identify the rise of conservatism within the Republican Party as the main cause of the polarization that now threatens to bring down the postwar order.

* * *

The main flaw in this argument is that it was the conservative insurgency, led first by Barry Goldwater and later by Ronald Reagan, that was largely responsible for the Republican Party's electoral and policy successes during the 1980s and 1990s. It is hard to argue, as Kabaservice does, that the Republican Party thrived during the 1960s and 1970s under the leadership of moderates like Richard Nixon and Gerald Ford, or that Democrats bent over backward to cooperate with them. Democrats, in fact, did everything they could to destroy Nixon and Ford, and they generally succeeded in doing so—and in this they played a central role in bringing down the moderate alternative in the Republican Party and opening up new opportunities for conservatives. At the same time, Democrats, led by Jimmy Carter and Walter Mondale, found themselves unable in the 1970s to come to grips with rising crime, inflation and unemployment, and a deteriorating international situation.

These two factors—the simultaneous failures of Republican moderates and Democratic liberals—paved the way for Reagan's capture of the Republican Party and his subsequent victory in the 1980 presidential election. (Reagan had failed to secure the presidential nomination on two previous occasions, against Nixon and Ford.) Reagan's successes in reviving the American economy, building up the U.S. military, and ending the Cold War made him the most successful president of the postwar period. At the same time, those successes strengthened the Republican Party as an electoral force and cemented the conservatives' control over the party. Conservatives prospered politically during that decade not because of recklessness or zeal, as these historians suggest, but because of the failures of existing alternatives and their own successes in addressing those failures. Had Reagan not succeeded, the postwar system might easily have collapsed in the 1980s.

The narrative of conservatives shattering the postwar consensus also ignores the important role played by liberal reformers in sharpening the divisions between the two political parties. It may be true that the Republicans have developed into the more coherent and cohesive ideological force of the two parties. Academic research suggests that this is the case. Yet many forget that in the late 1960s and early 1970s the Democrats reorganized themselves as well, adopting delegate quotas in national conventions for women and minority groups, and effectively expelling conservatives from the party. Beginning in 1972, the Democratic Party broke decisively with the policies of postwar Democratic presidents, moving quickly to the left on issues of economic growth and the Cold War. Republicans and many conservative Democrats responded by pointing out that the Democrats had abandoned the moderate and bipartisan politics of Presidents Truman, Eisenhower, Kennedy, and Johnson. Prior to 1980, most observers agreed that Democrats moved first in breaking up the postwar consensus, especially on foreign policy. In those years, public employee unions joined feminist and minority groups as new power brokers in the party, replacing urban mayors and private sector union leaders. In the process, the Democrats gradually turned themselves into a government party that relies on public employee unions for votes, money, and organization, and on government spending (along with high taxes) to maintain cohesion among the party's various constituent groups.

The Democratic Party today may appear less ideological than the Republican Party, but this is because it maintains internal coherence through government spending and regulation rather than through principled political appeals. Nevertheless, Democrats can be quite as single-minded in pursuit of their goals as Republicans are in theirs, as Obama has shown in his determined efforts to raise taxes and expand federal power over health care, banks and financial institutions, and the energy industry. While critics like Mann and Ornstein complain that Republicans have evolved into an "anti-government" party, they fail to note that Democrats have evolved into a "pro-government" party at the same time. This is one reason why compromises are now so difficult to come by in Washington: every expansion of government favors one party while every diminution favors the other.

The division between the two parties has now widened to the point that it cuts deeply through American society, which is one more reason why it makes little sense to blame conservatives for the breakup of the postwar order. There are, of course, the "red" and "blue" states that pursue widely divergent social and economic policies in keeping with deeply held views of voters and interest groups. In addition, Republicans and Democrats get their news from different sources, understand events and controversies from different perspectives, and generally congregate in different neighborhoods and jurisdictions with like-minded friends and associates. Conservatives dominate talk radio and cable television; liberals control broadcast news, establishment journalism, and the faculties of colleges and universities. Minority groups and secular liberals have gravitated to the Democratic Party; whites and religious Americans have moved in the opposite direction, toward the Republican Party. A large proportion of American adults can carry on their daily lives without ever coming into contact with supporters of the other party. Perhaps that is a good thing, considering the antagonistic views that Republicans and Democrats now hold about one another. A recent poll suggested that while parents were once concerned about a son or daughter marrying someone of a different religion, they no longer care so much about that but are now more concerned that he or she might marry someone of a different political party or ideology. Partisanship seems to have replaced religion as a source of cultural conflict in American society.

After seventy years of evolution, the postwar order has at length produced a sorting-out of Americans into conflicting and sometimes hostile political, social, and geographical groups. The most obvious historical precedent we have for such a configuration is the one that developed in the 1850s when slavery emerged as a national issue. That controversy divided the nation into geographical, social, and ideological coalitions, shattering the national consensus that took shape between the 1820s and 1840s about national power in the federal system, and causing the collapse of one established political party along with the creation of a new one. It also created a stalemate between the political forces in Washington, preventing national authorities from addressing other issues, such as organizing the western territories or settling on a route for a transcontinental railroad. We know how that split was eventually settled. The United States is not going to have another civil war in the twenty-first century, but it could easily pass through an extended period of stalemate as each party blocks the agenda of the other and a majority fails to form over any single approach to national challenges of growth, spending, debt, and the role of the United States abroad. It would probably take a crisis of some kind to break the stalemate, most likely a stock market crash or another deep and prolonged recession that would force a reckoning with the slow economic growth of recent decades.

* * *

In looking to the future and thinking about how such an impasse might eventually be resolved, one may be tempted to agree with Walter Russell Mead in concluding that the Democratic "blue model" is unlikely to succeed at restoring growth and dynamism to the American economy.[3] There are limits to the number of people who can be placed on the public dole without undermining incentives to work, and limits also in the amounts that can be paid to public sector workers in wages and benefits without causing a revolt among taxpayers who must pay for them. Public sector unions also contribute to inflexibility in public budgets, forcing jurisdictions to raise taxes before considering other alternatives to budget crises. The taxes required to underwrite this model must sooner or later impede economic growth and investment, cause workers and businesses to flee to other jurisdictions, and generally sap the resources necessary to sustain it. That model is already dead in cities like Detroit, Stockton, San Bernardino, and Harrisburg (Pennsylvania), and is on the ropes in states like Illinois, Connecticut, and California. The next recession will undoubtedly push more cities into insolvency, and force these states into some kind of reckoning with their financial affairs. This is a model that can survive in an era of rapid economic growth, but will inevitably be exposed in an era of stagnation and economic crisis.

Mead also doubts that we can restore a free-market regime of the kind in place in the United States between the Civil War and the Great Depression, and he is probably right about that. It will not be easy to dismantle Social Security, Medicare, and other pop-ular programs that constitute the entitlement state, even if such programs were acknowledged to be central to current troubles. In addition, the important role that the United States plays inter-nationally will require a substantial defense establishment in the years ahead. There are elements of the postwar system that should and undoubtedly will persist into any successor system.

Nevertheless, the outlines of that new system will necessarily look more like the "red model" than the "blue model"—that is, one that is more sympathetic to business and private sector growth than to public employee groups and beneficiaries of public spend-ing. There are likely to be at least three central elements to the new synthesis that must eventually replace the postwar order: (1) a focus on growth, and the fiscal and regulatory policies required to promote it, as an alternative to the emphasis on redistribution, public spending, and regulation that has characterized the Obama years and the "blue model" generally; (2) an emphasis on federalism both to encourage experimentation and innovation in the Amer-ican system and to remove issues from the national agenda where they contribute to division, stalemate, and endless controversy; and (3) a campaign to depoliticize the public sector by eliminating or strictly regulating public employee unions, so that governments themselves are no longer active in the political process and public workers can once again be viewed as "civil servants" rather than as active agents of one of the political parties.

Such a synthesis will require reorganization in both political parties, but especially in the Democratic Party because it has or-ganized itself around public spending and the "nationalization" of most political issues. In this sense, Democrats will have to ac-commodate themselves to a new system just as Republicans were forced to do once the New Deal and its various programs were in place. We do not know precisely what this new synthesis will look

like, though some of its features are already visible in some jurisdictions—for example, in Wisconsin, a traditionally liberal and
Democratic state where voters have sustained policies to decertify
and strictly regulate public sector unions in order to save taxpayers' money, introduce more flexibility into the public sector, and
promote economic growth. A century ago, the highly influential
"Wisconsin idea" was called upon as a national model for progressive government working in cooperation with the state university
to bring the latest research to bear upon public policy. This new
version of the "Wisconsin idea" may prove to be equally influential
in the decades ahead.

In any event, the postwar era is expiring, if it has not expired already. The consensus that sustained it is a thing of the past. It cannot be resurrected. Americans are an optimistic and forward-looking people: nostalgia for past successes must eventually give way
to efforts to build a new order on the foundations of the old, and
to open the way for a new chapter in the unfolding history of the
"American idea."

Acknowledgments

I am grateful to Roger Kimball, editor and publisher of Encounter Books, for his encouragement in undertaking this project and for his insightful editorial comments on earlier versions of the manuscript. Thanks are owed also to Thomas W. Smith, Kimberly Dennis, and William E. Simon, Jr., for their support and encouragement during the course of the project. Carol Staswick edited the manuscript with admirable professional care and attention, and suggested many revisions that greatly improved the final product. Heather Ohle, Katherine Wong, and Katherine Messenger ably guided the production and design of the book. The Thomas W. Smith Foundation and the Searle Freedom Trust provided financial support without which the project could not have been completed. The Earhart Foundation generously provided support for the chapters on higher education included in this volume. I am grateful to my wife Patricia and son Will for patiently listening to my theories and, on occasion, offering constructive suggestions. This book evolved out of a lecture delivered at Pepperdine University in early 2012 and a subsequent essay, "The Fourth Revolution," that appeared in the June 2012 issue of *The New Criterion*. I am indebted to the many friends, associates, and critics who commented on that lecture and article, and who encouraged me to elaborate on their general thesis.

Notes

CHAPTER ONE

1. Robert Skidelsky, *Keynes: The Return of the Master* (New York: Public-Affairs, 2009), chap. 6.

2. John Maynard Keynes, "Alfred Marshall," in *Essays in Biography* (1933; New York: W. W. Norton & Co., 1963), 141.

3. John Maynard Keynes, *The Economic Consequences of the Peace* (1919; New York: Skyhorse Publishers, 2007).

4. Ibid., 6.

5. Ibid., 7.

6. Ibid., 11. This was a theme to which Keynes would later return—that is, to the idea that the balance between saving and investment in an economy is based as much on moral and psychological dispositions as on purely economic calculations.

7. Keynes pointed more than once in the book to destabilizing effects of population pressure on resources. He speculated that the Russian Revolution was caused more by rapid increases in population than by Lenin's tactics or the czar's mistakes. Ibid., 8. Later, when addressing the challenges of feeding the peoples of Central Europe, he touched again on this Malthusian theme: "Some of the catastrophes of past history, which have thrown back progress for centuries, have been due to the reactions following on the sudden termination of temporarily favorable conditions which have permitted the growth of population beyond what could be provided for when the favorable conditions were at an end." Ibid., 131.

8. Ibid., 20.

9. Ibid., 23.

10. Keynes developed this remedy in detail in the last chapter of *The Economic Consequences of the Peace*, 154–61. This was essentially the proposal that was rejected at the Paris Peace Conference.

11. Ibid., 146.

12. Ibid., 81.

13. John Maynard Keynes, "The Reconstruction of Europe: An Introduction," *Manchester Guardian Commercial*, May 18, 1922.

14. This case was made most famously in Etienne Mantoux's *The Carthaginian Peace, or the Economic Consequences of Mr. Keynes* (Oxford, U.K.: Oxford University Press, 1946). Mantoux, a French economist, argued that Keynes exaggerated the flaws in the treaty and that his attacks on it later paralyzed Western leaders when Hitler repeated them. Mantoux's book was published posthumously (after he was killed in action in 1945 while fighting for the Free French Forces). For a more recent critique, see Stephen A. Schuker, "J. M. Keynes and the Personal Politics of Reparations: Part 1," *Diplomacy and Statecraft* 25:3 (2014), 453–71.

15. A good defense of Keynes against these charges can be found in Robert Skidelsky, *John Maynard Keynes*, vol. 1, *Hopes Betrayed, 1883–1920* (New York: Viking Books, 1986), 397–400.

16. On this subject see among several sources, Margaret MacMillan, *Paris 1919: The Peace That Changed the World* (New York: Random House, 2001), chap. 13–16.

17. Sally Marks, "The Myths of Reparations," *Central European History* 11:3 (September 1978), 231–55.

18. Sally Marks, "Mistakes and Myths: The Allies, Germany, and the Versailles Treaty," *Journal of Modern History* 85:3 (September 2013), 632–59.

19. Many historians have written on the complicated bargaining that took place during the course of the conference. Among them, see MacMillan, *Paris 1919: The Peace That Changed the World*, chap. 30–31; and Marks, "Mistakes and Myths: The Allies, Germany, and the Versailles Treaty."

CHAPTER TWO

1. Robert Lekachman, *The Age of Keynes* (New York: Random House, 1966).

2. John Maynard Keynes, "The End of Laissez-Faire," in *Essays in*

Persuasion (New York: Harcourt, Brace & Co., 1932), 337.

3. Ibid., 314–15. This was an early statement by Keynes of a theme later developed by Adolf Berle and Gardiner Means in *The Modern Corporation and Private Property* (1932), where the authors worked out the legal and financial implications of the growing separation between ownership and management in business corporations.

4. R. F. Harrod, *The Life of John Maynard Keynes* (New York: Harcourt, Brace & Co., 1951), 193.

5. J. M. Keynes, "The Great Slump of 1930," in *Essays in Persuasion*, 140.

6. J. M. Keynes, "Economic Possibilities for Our Grandchildren," in *Essays in Persuasion*, 358.

7. Quoted in Robert Skidelsky, *John Maynard Keynes*, vol. 2, *The Economist as Savior, 1920–1937* (New York: Penguin Books, 1992), 548.

8. J. M. Keynes, "Am I a Liberal?" (1925), in *Essays in Persuasion*, 335.

9. John Maynard Keynes, *The General Theory of Employment, Interest, and Money* (1936; New York: Harcourt, Brace & Co., 1965), 79.

10. Ibid., 377–79. Of this claim, Schumpeter wrote, "It has been said that 'the state can take the longer view.' But excepting certain matters outside of party politics…it hardly ever does." See Schumpeter, *Capitalism, Socialism, and Democracy* (New York: Harper & Brothers, 1942), 161.

11. Robert Lekachman, *The Age of Keynes* (New York: Random House, 1966), 285. On this general point, see also Herbert Stein, *The Fiscal Revolution in America* (Chicago: University of Chicago Press, 1969), chap. 15.

12. On the diffusion of Keynes's ideas in various countries in the postwar era, see Peter A. Hall, ed., *The Political Power of Economic Ideas: Keynesianism across Nations* (Princeton, N.J.: Princeton University Press, 1989).

13. It may be an overstatement to say that there is a consensus any longer in the economics profession around Keynesian theories and Keynesian remedies for slumps. Macroeconomists are now divided among Keynesian, neo-Keynesian, and neoclassical schools of thought. Some economists have gone so far as to say that Keynes is a "dead letter" in their profession, surely an exaggeration but at the same time an expression of a movement away from or beyond Keynes. Nevertheless, Keynes continues to have a popular following among pundits, politicians, and many economists, as witness the continuing debate over the causes of the recent slump and the effectiveness of stimulus packages. For a statement of where economists

now stand in relation to Keynes, see Oliver J. Blanchard, "The State of Macro," National Bureau of Economic Research Working Paper, 2008; and also Edward C. Prescott's 2004 Nobel lecture, "The Transformation of Macroeconomic Policy and Research."

14. Mancur Olson, *The Rise and Decline of Nations: Economic Growth, Stagflation, and Social Rigidities* (New Haven: Yale University Press, 1982).

15. Ibid., 44.

16. Ibid.

17. Ibid., 216.

CHAPTER SIX

1. Richard Hofstadter, *The Age of Reform* (New York: Vintage Books, 1955), 14.

2. Summaries of the Progressive point of view (especially the dual emphasis on democracy and expertise) may be gleaned from several works of the period, especially: Walter Weyl, *The New Democracy* (New York: Macmillan, 1912); Herbert Croly, *The Promise of American Life* (1909; New York: Capricorn Books, 1964); Walter Lippmann, *Drift and Mastery* (1913; Madison: University of Wisconsin Press, 1986).

3. Hofstadter, *The Age of Reform*, 18.

4. On the differences between Progressive and New Deal reform, see Hofstadter, *The Age of Reform*, chap. 7; and Arthur Schlesinger Jr., *The Vital Center* (Boston: Houghton Mifflin, 1948), chap. 8.

5. For an insightful critique of postwar liberalism, see Christopher Lasch, *The New Radicalism in America, 1889–1963: The Intellectual as a Social Type* (1965; New York: W. W. Norton & Co., 1986), chap. 9.

6. Schlesinger, *The Vital Center*, 182.

7. Ibid., chap. 6.

8. Senator Joseph McCarthy, "Enemies from Within," speech at Wheeling, West Virginia, February 9, 1950, reproduced at http://historymatters.gmu.edu/d/6456/.

9. Quotation from Daniel Bell, "Interpretations of American Politics, 1955," in *The Radical Right*, ed. Daniel Bell (1955; New York: Doubleday & Co., 1963), 58.

10. Quoted in Clinton Rossiter, *Conservatism in America: The Thankless*

Persuasion, rev. ed. (1955; New York: Vintage Books, 1962), 93.

11. Louis Hartz, *The Liberal Tradition in America* (New York: Harcourt, Brace & World, 1955).

12. On these points, see ibid., chap. 11.

13. *The Radical Right*, ed. Bell (1963) was an expanded and updated version of *The New American Right* (Criterion Books, 1955).

14. Richard Hofstadter, "The Pseudo-Conservative Revolt" (1955), in *The Radical Right*, ed. Bell, 76.

15. Ibid., 85.

16. Ibid., 83.

17. Daniel Bell, "The Dispossessed," in *The Radical Right*, ed. Bell, 3–8.

18. On the subject of status and its link to radicalism, see Bell, "The Dispossessed," and Hofstadter, "The Pseudo-Conservative Revolt."

19. Bell, "The Dispossessed," 10.

20. Richard Hofstadter, "The Paranoid Style in American Politics," in *The Paranoid Style in American Politics and Other Essays* (Cambridge, Mass.: Harvard University Press, 1965). The article, which originally appeared in *Harper's*, October 1964, was based on a lecture delivered at Oxford University in November 1963. For a more general discussion of Hofstadter's thought, see David S. Brown, *Richard Hofstadter: An Intellectual Biography* (Chicago: University of Chicago Press, 2006).

21. See Hofstadter, "The Paranoid Style in American Politics," 37.

22. On Goldwater and the Republicans, see ibid., 3.

23. Richard Hofstadter, *Anti-Intellectualism in American Life* (New York: Random House, 1964).

24. Daniel Bell, *The End of Ideology: On the Exhaustion of Political Ideas in the 1950s* (New York: Free Press, 1962), pp. 402–3. Bell's argument drew heavily from a suggestive essay by Edward Shils, "The End of Ideology," *Encounter*, November 1955, 52–58. The theme was also taken up by Seymour Martin Lipset in "The End of Ideology?" chap. 13 of *Political Man* (Garden City, N.Y.: Anchor Books, 1963).

25. Herbert Butterfield, *The Whig Interpretation of History* (London, 1931; New York: W. W. Norton & Co., 1965), preface, v.

26. George Orwell, "Looking Back on the Spanish War," in *The Collected Essays, Journalism, and Letters of George Orwell*, vol. 2, *My Country Right or Left, 1940–43*, ed. Sonia Orwell and Ian Angus (Boston: David R. Godine, 2004), 259.

27. Richard Hofstadter, *The Progressive Historians: Turner, Beard, Parrington* (1968; New York: Vintage Books, 1970), 42–43.

28. Arthur Schlesinger Jr., *The Age of Jackson* (Boston: Little, Brown & Co., 1945). For a critique of Schlesinger's interpretation of Jackson, see Lee Benson, *The Concept of Jacksonian Democracy* (Princeton, N.J.: Princeton University Press, 1961).

29. See Peter Viereck, "The Revolt Against the Elite," in *The Radical Right*, ed. Bell, 169.

30. See Lasch, *The New Radicalism in America*.

31. Ibid., 90.

32. Lionel Trilling, *The Liberal Imagination* (New York: Anchor Books, 1950). Quotations cited are from the preface, xi–xii. On Trilling, see also Gertrude Himmelfarb, *The Moral Imagination: From Edmund Burke to Lionel Trilling* (Chicago: Ivan R. Dee, 2006), 219–29.

33. Trilling, *The Liberal Imagination*, xii.

CHAPTER SEVEN

1. Clinton Rossiter, *Conservatism in America: The Thankless Persuasion*, rev. ed. (1955; New York: Vintage Books, 1962), 269.

2. Raymond English, "Conservatism: The Forbidden Faith," *American Scholar* 21:4 (Autumn 1952).

3. See John Micklethwait and Adrian Wooldridge, *The Right Nation: Conservative Power in America* (New York: Penguin Press, 2004).

CHAPTER ELEVEN

1. Victor Lasky, *J.F.K.: The Man and the Myth* (New York: Macmillan, 1963). Lasky's was the first comprehensive and critical study of Kennedy's career, and it laid the foundation for subsequent Kennedy biographies. Kennedy was killed before he and his aides could mount a campaign against the book. After the assassination, Lasky's publisher withdrew the book from circulation. However, subsequent biographies by members of Kennedy's inner circle, particularly Arthur Schlesinger's *A Thousand Days*, can be read as official answers to the main points made in Lasky's book.

2. For example, Mark Gillespie, "JFK Ranked as Greatest U.S. President,"

Gallup News Service, February 21, 2000.

3. "JFK Remembered for More Than Just His Death," YouGov, November 22, 2013.

4. Quoted in Arthur Schlesinger Jr., *A Thousand Days: John F. Kennedy in the White House* (1965; Boston: Houghton Mifflin, 2002), xi.

5. See Theodore C. Sorensen, *Kennedy* (New York: Bantam Books, 1966), 751, 758; and Schlesinger, *A Thousand Days*, 1031.

6. Paul Healy, "The Senate's Gay Young Bachelor," *Saturday Evening Post*, June 13, 1953.

7. Many sources document Kennedy's efforts to position himself as a moderate during his congressional career. See Thomas C. Reeves, *A Question of Character: A Life of John F. Kennedy* (New York: Free Press, 1991), chap. 8–9. Also, Schlesinger, *A Thousand Days*, 9–14; John P. Avlon, *Independent Nation: How Centrists Can Change American Politics* (New York: Three Rivers Press, 2004), 137–61; and Robert Dallek, *An Unfinished Life: John F. Kennedy, 1917–1963* (New York: Little, Brown & Co., 2003), chap. 6. References to *Time* and *Newsweek* articles are in Reeves, *A Question of Character*, 141–51.

8. On Kennedy's record in the Senate, see (for example) Dallek, who wrote, "His Senate career had produced no major legislation that contributed substantially to the national well-being." *An Unfinished Life*, chap. 6, quotation on 226.

9. Lasky, *J.F.K.: The Man and the Myth*, 212–13.

10. On the Kennedy family's association with McCarthy, see Michael O'Brien, *John F. Kennedy: A Biography* (New York: Thomas Dunne Books, 2005), 252–53; Lasky, *J.F.K.: The Man and the Myth*, 141–43; Reeves, *A Question of Character*, 87–88; Dallek, *An Unfinished Life*, 162–63, 191; Joan Blair and Clay Blair Jr., *The Search for JFK* (New York: G. P. Putnam's Sons, 1976), 522, 526.

11. Quotation cited in Lasky, *J.F.K.: The Man and the Myth*, 238.

12. Ibid., 27.

13. The elder Kennedy's business activities (especially his interests in liquor and film companies) are described in Richard J. Whalen, *The Founding Father: The Story of Joseph P. Kennedy* (New York: New American Library, 1964), chap. 4–7. See also Seymour M. Hersh, *The Dark Side of Camelot* (New York: Little, Brown & Co., 1997), chap. 4–6.

14. Joseph Kennedy's diplomatic and political career is discussed in

several places, including Barbara Leaming, *Jack Kennedy: The Education of a Statesman* (New York: W. W. Norton & Co., 2006), chap. 3–4. See also Dallek, *An Unfinished Life*, chap. 2; and Hersh, *The Dark Side of Camelot*, chap. 3.

15. On insinuations of anti-Semitism, see Dallek, *An Unfinished Life*, 175; and Hersh, *The Dark Side of Camelot*, 63–64.

16. On Kennedy's master's thesis, see Leaming, *Jack Kennedy: The Education of a Statesman*, chap. 4.

17. Dallek, *An Unfinished Life*, 63.

18. On the revisions to Kennedy's thesis, see Leaming, *Jack Kennedy: The Education of a Statesman*, 104–8; and Dallek, *An Unfinished Life*, 65. See also Arthur Schlesinger's discussion in *A Thousand Days*, 84–85.

19. Chamberlain went to Munich to secure "peace in our time," not to buy time to prepare for an unavoidable war. Churchill did acknowledge later that Britain was not ready to confront Hitler in 1938. See Winston Churchill, "Munich Winter," chap. 18 of *The Gathering Storm* (New York: Houghton Mifflin, 1948), 326–27.

20. On the publication and reviews of Kennedy's book, see Leaming, *Jack Kennedy: The Education of a Statesman*, 109; Dallek, *An Unfinished Life*, 65–66; Whalen, *The Founding Father*, 294–95; and Reeves, *A Question of Character*, 49–51.

21. On Churchill and Kennedy, see Schlesinger, *A Thousand Days*, 83–84. Also Leaming, *Jack Kennedy: The Education of a Statesman*, especially chap. 11. Kennedy's father did not give up his resentment of Churchill. When Churchill published *The Gathering Storm*, the first volume of his war memoirs, Kennedy wrote a long letter to the *New York Times* claiming that his treatment of the Prague and Munich crises was filled with errors. See David Reynolds, *In Command of History: Churchill Fighting and Writing the Second World War* (New York: Random House, 2005), 136–37.

22. The book diverged substantially in style from Kennedy's master's thesis. Arthur Krock contributed his editorial skills to the project. As the publisher's deadline closed in, the senior Kennedy gave the project to his personal speechwriter, who turned the manuscript into publishable form. Up to that point, it was (in the speechwriter's description) a "mishmash" of ungrammatical sentences and news clippings. See Reeves, *A Question of Character*, 49; also, Herbert Parmet, *Jack: The Struggles of John F. Kennedy* (New York: Doubleday Books, 1983), 77–78.

23. John F. Kennedy, *Profiles in Courage* (1956; New York: HarperCollins, 2003). Biographers who have examined Kennedy's notes for *Profiles in Courage* suggest that Theodore Sorensen actually wrote the bulk of the manuscript based on Kennedy's oral comments and rough notes, supplemented by Sorensen's own research. This judgment is based on the lack of correspondence between Kennedy's handwritten notes and the contents of the book. Sorensen drew on the assistance of several others, including historians Allan Nevins, Arthur Schlesinger Jr., and Jules Davids. See especially Herbert Parmet, *Jack: The Struggles of John F. Kennedy*, 320–33; and Reeves, *A Question of Character*, 126–28. Sorensen consistently maintained that, although he assisted in the drafting of the book, Kennedy was its true author. See Sorensen, *Kennedy*, 68–70.

24. Kennedy, *Profiles in Courage*, 5.

25. Quoted in Lasky, *J.F.K.: The Man and the Myth*, 144.

26. Parmet, *Jack: The Struggles of John F. Kennedy*, 240–41; Lasky, *J.F.K.: The Man and the Myth*, 144–45.

27. Dallek, *An Unfinished Life*, 288–89; Leaming, *Jack Kennedy: The Education of a Statesman*, chap. 11.

28. Leaming, *Jack Kennedy: The Education of a Statesman*, chap. 11, quotation on 244.

29. Lasky, *J.F.K.: The Man and the Myth*, 510–13; Reeves, *A Question of Character*, 249, 365; Dallek, *An Unfinished Life*, 289.

30. Richard Rovere, "Letter from Washington," *New Yorker*, November 30, 1963.

31. On plans to assassinate Castro, see Hersh, *The Dark Side of Camelot*, chap. 13–14; Reeves, *A Question of Character*, chap. 12; and Dallek, *An Unfinished Life*, 439–40.

32. On Kennedy's rhetorical debt to Churchill, see Leaming, *Jack Kennedy: The Education of a Statesman*, chap. 11–12. With respect to his inaugural address, see especially 258–60.

33. Dallek, *An Unfinished Life*, 583.

34. Schlesinger, *A Thousand Days* (2002), 725–29; Robert Frost, "For John F. Kennedy, His Inauguration," in *The Poetry of Robert Frost*, ed. Edward Connery Lathem (New York: Holt, Rinehart & Winston, 1969), 422–25.

35. Daniel J. Boorstin, *The Image: A Guide to Pseudo-Events in America* (New York: Atheneum, 1978), 61.

36. Norman Mailer, "Superman Comes to the Supermarket," *Esquire*, November 1960, reprinted in *Smiling Through the Apocalypse: Esquire's History of the Sixties*, ed. Harold Hayes (New York: McCall Publishing Co., 1970), 3–30.

37. Sorensen, *Kennedy*, 244–45.

38. Schlesinger, *A Thousand Days* (2002), 115–16.

39. Mailer, "Superman Comes to the Supermarket," 17.

40. Garry Wills, *The Kennedy Imprisonment* (New York: Houghton Mifflin, 1981).

Chapter Thirteen

1. For an exhaustive factual refutation of all the prominent conspiracy theories in the JFK assassination, readers should consult Vincent Bugliosi, *Reclaiming History: The Assassination of President John F. Kennedy* (New York: W. W. Norton & Co., 2007).

2. Taylor Branch, *Parting the Waters: America in the King Years, 1955–1963* (New York: Simon & Schuster, 1988), 917.

3. Robert A. Caro, *The Years of Lyndon Johnson: The Passage of Power* (New York: Alfred A. Knopf, 2012), chap. 26.

Epilogue

1. Geoffrey Kabaservice, *Rule and Ruin: The Downfall of Moderation and the Destruction of the Republican Party* (New York: Oxford University Press, 2012), xvi.

2. Thomas E. Mann and Norman J. Ornstein, *It's Even Worse Than It Looks: How the American Constitutional System Collided with the New Politics of Extremism* (New York: Basic Books, 2012), xiv.

3. Walter Russell Mead, "The Once and Future Liberalism," *American Interest* 7:4 (March–April 2012).

Index